January 31, 1968. SEAL Team No. 2, 8th Platoon, discovered fourteen hundred enemy troops near the river by Chau Doc. Enormously outnumbered, they linked up with a handful of U.S. Army advisers in the town. They found two jeeps and mounted a .50-caliber machine gun on one of them. Several American civilians were missing. The Viet Cong attacked about an hour later, seizing the city piece by piece. At the house of a missing American nurse, the SEAL team found that the Viet Cong had gotten there first and were ransacking the place while the nurse hid in a wardrobe in the living room.

As the Viet Cong came near her hiding place, she panicked and bolted for the back door. As she swung the door open, she was met by Viet Cong in the backyard.

They were as startled as she, and just stared at her. The SEALs kicked in the front door, and the nurse turned to run to them. She opened a clear field of fire for the SEALs and they began shooting, but as their bullets hit the back door, they knocked it shut. The SEALs grabbed the nurse and sprinted for the jeep with the Viet Cong racing after them. . . .

THE DELL WAR SERIES

The Dell War Series takes you onto the battlefield, into the jungles and beneath the oceans with unforgettable stories that offer a new look at the terrors and triumphs of America's war experience. Many of these books are eyewitness accounts of the duty-bound fighting man. From the intrepid foot soldiers, sailors, pilots, and commanders, to the elite warriors of the Special Forces, here are stories of men who fight because their lives depend on it.

☆ ☆ ☆ ☆ ☆ ☆ ☆

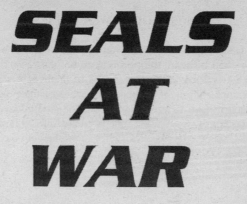

SEALS AT WAR

The Story of
U.S. Navy
Special Warfare
from
The Frogmen to the Seals

EDWIN P. HOYT

A DELL BOOK

Published by
Dell Publishing
a division of
Bantam Doubleday Dell Publishing Group, Inc.
666 Fifth Avenue
New York, New York 10103

Interior design by Jeremiah B. Lighter

The trademark Dell® is registered in the U.S. Patent and Trademark
Office.

ISBN: 0-440-21497-1

Printed in the United States of America

Published simultaneously in Canada

February 1993

10 9 8 7 6 5 4 3 2

OPM

INTRODUCTION

The Making of a SEAL

SSSS
SSSS Over the past quarter century the art of
warfare has changed as it has become
apparent that most operations in which
the military is involved (Operation Desert Storm ex-
cepted) do not require the deployment of large numbers
of ships, aircraft, and land armies but of small, efficient
forces that can move swiftly and strike precisely. Such
affairs as Israel's Entebbe raid showed how quickly a
small force could strike, and such as the failed American
raid to rescue hostages in Iran showed why the striking
force should be homogeneous and self-contained. To
meet this challenge the United States has now developed
the Special Warfare Command, representing all three services. The Navy arm is the Naval Special Warfare Command, and its backbone is the fighting team called the
Navy SEALs, who can operate on land, sea, and from the
air. Two of these attributes they exhibited in Operation
Desert Storm. In one operation, with only a handful of
swimmers, they gulled the Iraqis into believing that an
amphibious action was imminent in the beginning of that
war. Their efforts and a few explosions caused the Iraqis
to move troops into the beach area, troops who otherwise
would have been pitted against the Marines inland. The
SEALs also staged a lightning raid into Baghdad during
the war, indicative of their land-operating potential.

These successes did not come about by accident.
They were the result of what is now fifty years of effort by
the Navy to improve its combat capability in special ways,
based on experience. This increased capability is developing constantly, as the SEALs hone the sharp edge of their

training programs and make use of every new development in warfare, from improved landing craft to improved computers and sophisticated computer programs. As one veteran SEAL at the Special Warfare headquarters in Coronado, California, said, "The new breed of SEALs is smarter and more experienced and all the way around more capable than we were."

That statement is a proud reminder of the strong bond that exists between these underwater warriors of two generations. SEALs tend to work together and play together, further cementing ties woven during their initial and subsequent training. The older generation, now lieutenant commanders and warrant officers and chief petty officers, are the instructors of the young, retaining the traditions of this very special service and working to improve the standards of performance. It is all very real and all very deadly, for the SEALs are a combat unit, and in every clandestine operation every man's life is on the line.

The roots of the Navy SEALs lie in the development of amphibious warfare by the U.S. Navy, beginning in 1942. Before that time the Navy did not have any underwater capability except for the helmeted Navy diver, whose tasks were primarily salvage and repair. The Europeans were far ahead in this field, particularly the Italians, whose frogmen accomplished some remarkable feats in the war, crippling several elements of the British fleet with limpet mines at Alexandria and in similar operations elsewhere.

The American amphibious program was designed to meet needs in the Aleutians and at Guadalcanal, but it was so hurriedly constructed that no thought was given to the conditions and problems an amphibious landing force might encounter in the shallow waters just offshore. The Guadalcanal landing was misleading. It was too easy, except on the Tulagi side of the channel; the Marines did not encounter any combat troops at the beginning. The ships came right up to the land, with no reefs or obstructions to bar their way, and began to unload supplies without difficulty. But that was not the pattern that would develop, as the Navy discovered in their next major operation, halfway across the world, in North Africa. There the Navy did find obstructions and did learn that it needed information and the capability of creating suitable conditions for the landing of small craft on an enemy shore.

One of the first, and most famous, of the underwater men was Phillip H. Bucklew. He was a college football player who turned professional before World War II. During the war he became an instructor in the Navy/Marine Corps Scout-Raider School in Florida. Before the North Africa landings, the commanders of the invasion force became concerned about the conditions of the beaches. What kind of beaches were they? What conditions would the landing troops face? Bucklew went into the beach alone, to gather intelligence about landing beaches, and returned with the information and a bucket of sand for the officers to study.

In July 1943 Bucklew led a team of the eleven new frogmen from a submarine onto the Sicilian beach. The team was discovered and attacked by the Germans, but Bucklew led them to the completion of their mission and guided the first waves of troops ashore. He did the same two months later, in the invasion of Italy. For these exploits he won the Navy Cross and a Silver Star. Early in 1944 Bucklew carried out a single-handed reconnaissance of the Normandy beaches. On that mission he was discovered by German soldiers, who surrounded him. He fled into a swamp and lay silent, concealed, until the Germans gave up searching and went away.

When the invasion came, Bucklew went in with the troops and won a second Navy Cross for valor under fire. Toward the end of World War II, Bucklew carried out a long reconnaissance mission of the South China coast, north of Hong Kong, to find the answers to questions about the Japanese defenses and the beaches. At this point Adm. Ernest J. King was proposing an invasion of China before the invasion of Japan. Bucklew, disguised as a coolie, traveled four hundred miles with a band of Chinese guerrillas. At one point he evaded a Japanese Army patrol by hiding in a haystack. He was the epitome of the underwater hero and was so recognized within that special group of men to which he belonged. In 1987, when the Naval Special Warfare Command was established at the amphibious base in Coronado, it was dedicated to him, and his shadow still hovers above the training schools located there.

Training of SEALs is a compendium of all that has been learned in the past, from the days of Draper Kauffman and the original demolition training program at Fort Pierce, Florida, where many of the concepts were born. The most spectacular of these is Hell Week, the culmination of the basic training of a SEAL or Underwater Demolition Team (UDT) man. The program called BUD/S means Basic Underwater Demolition/SEAL. It goes back to those early days, when Draper Kauffman conceived of the idea that a man could put forth ten times as much physical effort as he thought he could if he had the proper training, indoctrination, and spirit. Spirit is one of the aspects of SEAL training not talked about much, but it is the essence of the whole organization. Most of the men who drop out of the program (and this has been as much as 90 percent of a class) leave because they change their minds about their aspirations, or lose heart to face the challenges of the training program. This change can occur at any point along the way in the program, but most often during Hell Week, that week of applied torture testing the physical strength of the SEAL candidates, but above all, their spirit.

BUD/S has evolved to be the most difficult course offered within the U.S. military forces, and the SEALs and the UDT men are proud of that fact. The BUD/S class number is an important matter to all of them, and endless hours are spent in scuttlebutt about the rigors of the training program and the personal characteristics of the instructors.

The BUD/S training center is built around a courtyard in the center and on the ocean side of the Naval Amphibious Base at Coronado. On the outside, fronting on Highway 75, is the headquarters of Naval Special Warfare, or the quarterdeck, as the SEALs call it. This is the Phillip H. Bucklew Building. Above the door to the training quadrangle hangs a plaque embellished with two carved wooden seals, one diving and one standing, with the legend "The more you sweat in peace, the less you bleed in war." This is one of the mementos—each class has given at least one—that the classes have left the school since the SEALs were established. They include a statue of a creature that is part frog and part man, and a wheel of misfortune, which is divided into sections showing the various hardships a SEAL aspirant must undergo. One sign on the building says, "The only easy day was yesterday." All these are symbolic of the intention of SEALs training, which is to stretch each man's capabilities to the limit, relax the pressure for a little, then to stretch them again.

Much of that stretching goes on in the courtyard here, which is known as "The Grinder." At one corner of The Grinder stands the post that holds the brass "quitting bell." Any SEAL candidate who feels that he has reached the limit of his endurance and cannot take any more is free at any time to ring the bell. Lying on the ground next to the bell is a line of helmets from the trainees of the particular class in progress who have quit in midstream. In Hell Week, the line of helmets grows longer and longer.

The high rate of dropout is a matter of concern to the SEALs and the Navy, but it is one of the built-in hazards of the program. A man has to be highly motivated to want to become a SEAL, and his motivation must be stern and lasting. As the old SEALs say, the emphasis in BUD/S training is 90 percent mental and 10 percent physical. They say that any man could get through one day of training. But twenty-six weeks of it, day after day, is another matter, and the weak of heart drop out. Those who survive know that they are the ones who can be counted on in moments of crisis and that every other survivor of their class has those same attributes. That is one of the psychological factors of becoming and being a SEAL.

The nature of the training changes them, and they are never the same again.

The training does not avoid any physical challenge to which the SEALs might someday have to respond.

Overlooking the training complex is the dive tower, which contains a fifty-foot-deep tank of water in which SEALs learn free ascent and the techniques of working with submarines. West of the tower are the beach and the Pacific Ocean. South of the headquarters buildings is the obstacle course, which the SEALs say is the most demanding of its kind. Extending far to the south is a long beach, where the water remains at an almost constant 55 degrees Fahrenheit year-round.

Near the beach is a rack that holds a dozen innocent-looking big rubber boats known as IBSs (inflatable boats, small). On the beach near the boat rack is the fifty-foot stand that holds six climbing ropes. Here the trainees learn to build the strength of their shoulders and upper bodies, a part of the obstacle course. Over the twenty-six-week training course the men will become completely familiar with every aspect of this course, going over it time and again. It has been perfected by experts, men who went through the training and stayed or returned to consider how to make it more demanding.

Despite the apparent emphasis on individual effort, the whole focus of the training program is on teamwork.

From the outset the trainee is taught that his life is going to depend on other people and that in the SEALs program there is no room for emphasis on the individual.

Only 5 percent of those who start with a class will finish with that class. But for many reasons men are "rolled over"—they begin with one class and finish with another. They might have suffered some injury that caused them to be forced out of the one class. But when the Navy spends eighty thousand dollars on making a SEAL, then anything that can be done without lowering standards to promote retention of candidates is done. The result is that the average actual dropout rate is about 60 percent, although occasionally a class almost disappears; one class, No. 78, did disappear altogether. Not a man finished the course.

For a SEAL trainee, the beginning is what they call the "fourth phase," a four- to seven-week period of indoctrination during which the candidate gets his equipment, begins to break it in, and learns what will be expected of him in the future. He learns what the requirements are. In the "first phase" of training, which includes the Hell Week testing, here are the requirements, with their time in minutes:

1/2-mile pool swim without fins, 30
3/4-mile pool swim without fins, 45
1-mile pool swim without fins, 60
1-mile bay swim without fins, 70
1-mile pool swim with fins, 50
1-mile bay swim with fins, 50
11/2-mile ocean swim with fins, 75
2-mile ocean swim with fins, 95
Obstacle course, 15
2-mile timed run, 16
4-mile timed run, 32

For the first weeks of training, while they do calisthenics and concentrate on body-building, the candidates can study these requirements and estimate what they must do to meet these standards. They learn the requirements of distance running and the proper way to swim the strokes they must use to pass the required tests. After this period of the "fourth phase," the candidates start their BUD/S training, which is the basic seven-week conditioning program. The fourth week of this phase is Hell Week, where the aim of the instructor is to push the students beyond what they believe to be their physical limitations. Those who complete Hell Week then have an additional three weeks in hydrographic reconnaissance, beach surveying, and underwater mapping, all skills that go back to the original UDT training days.

Besides the physical testing, the candidates must pass written tests in various subjects, with a grade level of 70 percent for enlisted men and 80 percent for officers.

Before they come to grips with Hell Week, the candidates have had some new experiences. One set of experiences is with the Physical Training Log. These are a group of wooden telephone poles, each weighing several hundred pounds, that are piled up on the beach like so much driftwood until they are wanted. They will be wanted early in the training phases, when the men have been ordered into boat teams. The logs and the IBS boats are two of the important aspects of training to instill a sense of teamwork in the men.

The logs are brought out and presented to a boat crew, and they are told to do sit-ups while lying with the log on their collective chests, seven men and one three-hundred-pound log. It is an experience in teamwork because if every man does not heave his own weight, the log will not move, and the sit-up exercise will fail.

The men also do push-ups with their toes on top of the log. This increases the tension of the arms to raise the upper body. They do bench presses, with the log lying on their chests. They raise it up while lying down, to the full length of their arms. They do press-ups, which involve raising the log above their heads from a standing position.

They run races carrying their logs on their shoulders —up to fourteen miles. Or they race with the log over the sand dunes into the surf, drop the log into the surf, flop down in the surf, get up, and pick up their log and race back across the beach to the start. There are other exercises with the log, all involving the teamwork of seven men to build strength and cooperative spirit.

The log and the IBS become part of the lives of these teams. The boat weighs 289 pounds and is 12 feet long and 6 feet wide, built to carry seven men with 1,000 pounds of equipment.

The boat crew carry their boat everywhere with them, and are responsible that it is always kept inflated and in good condition. The instructors like nothing better than to find an unattended boat and deflate it. So one man of the boat crew is always on duty. When the crew goes to chow, one man stays with the boat and then the first man finished eating takes over and the guard goes in to eat.

Boat drills consist of manning the boat in the water and much more. The men carry the boat on their heads or at arm's length to the water, and sometimes their instructor jumps onto the boat to give it more authority.

Thus the candidates train for four weeks doing boat drills, log drills, swimming, running, and calisthenics in addition to studying academic subjects such as hydrography and learning first aid and life saving. Then comes Hell Week (or Motivation Week, as it is less sophomorically known).

The purpose of this rigorous week is to instill in the candidate a memory of the incidents and a strong feeling of association with the system. The candidate goes through the ordeal hating the whole of it, yet knowing that by surviving he has conquered his environment and triumphed over the system that has tested him. These are impressions he never loses, as can be vouchsafed by the almost constant harkening back of the successful to their BUD/S experience for years afterward. They draw strength and confidence from it, and it serves them well in difficult times, besides instilling in them a sense of confidence that they share only with men who have undergone the same ordeals.

Hell Week begins at one minute past midnight on a Monday morning and lasts for six days. During that period the brass bell that means relief and quitting is with the candidates at all times. All they have to do is ring the bell three times on one occasion, and almost immediately they will be back in an environment of clean sheets, hot and cold water, and plenty of sleep.

The whole experience is designed, and has been redesigned, to test a man's resilience and resolve. He has the "right stuff" or he does not, and this is the acid test. What becomes important during these days is his ability to hang on, to continue to perform after his body says that it can take no more punishment. That is the extra mile that a man must go for success in this environment.

Hell Week begins when the candidates are awakened by instructors turning on the lights in the barracks, by the sound of grenades going off nearby and automatic weapons being fired. From that point on, for six days each man is faced with moving to his own point of exhaustion, and through it, if he is to survive the program. The primary motivation is to bring the men to the point of exhaustion and its concomitant confusion and see if they can pass through that to continue, like automatons, to make physical exertions they never believed possible. During this week the men get only a total of four to six hours of sleep.

The exercises they are forced to undergo are based on combat experiences of UDT men and SEALs in the past. For example, there is one exercise that involves a race of seven-man teams in their rubber boats, planned to occur at just about the time of a tide shift, so when the men come paddling in, they find that as they approach the shore after a grueling run, the going gets harder rather than easier, and the last few hundred yards may take them hours to negotiate.

During the exercises, the men must work closely together, compensating for physical differences if the team is to survive. There are tall men and short men in a boat team. The tall men must bend their elbows when performing press-ups with the boat, so the short men can lift their end to the same height. Sometimes the short men must put a tin or another object on their heads so they can carry their share of the load without tipping.

Besides the grueling physical exertion, runs, swims, boat drills, calisthenics, and more runs, swims, and boat drills interspersed with log exercises, the men must perform academically. They are tested on what they were supposed to have learned in classes, no matter that they have had next to no sleep. If a man fails to answer the questions correctly he is ordered to drop and begin a thousand push-ups. That number is the number of push-ups for the team. And so other men who have answered the questions drop and begin doing the push-ups, too. Ultimately every man is involved, and the one thousand push-ups are done, not by individuals, but by the team.

In the last days of Hell Week at Coronado the men are sent to the mud pits south of the community. They spend many hours in the mud, doing physical exercises under the most trying and debilitating of circumstances, filthy with mud, slippery and stinking, and above all exhausted almost to the point of being unable to perform. They then go to the best performance the instructors can orchestrate of an actual beach landing against enemy positions on an unfriendly shore, with explosions all around them, the noise and confusion of battle everywhere, and working in the mud all this time. They are given almost impossible exercises, such as the caterpillar race, in which the whole team links arms and legs and sits in a line. Then they are told to move backward—as a unit. The result is squirming, slow movement with no apparent purpose until the instructor orders a halt.

Some of the men come through all this ordeal, and at the end of the sixth day are released from the hellishness of the torture. It is an experience none of them forgets. It remains so high in their consciousness that the tendency is for them later to recall it with the same relish and embroidery of difficulties that men attach to their sea stories and war experience stories.

The survivors of Hell Week are like the survivors of a landing on an enemy beach under intense fire. They have made it, and that is all that counts. Once they have made it, they have twenty-four hours off for cleanup and celebration, and then they move to the next phase of their training. And then after three more weeks of basic training, they go to "phase two." During this period they can contemplate with a little more consciousness some of the things they have undergone during this week and understand the reasons for them.

They also will learn now many things they have not been told. Some exercises during this week seem strange and meaningless. One such involves a command to the men to run, and then subsidiary commands to fall down every thirty yards, to cover their ears, open their mouths, and cross their legs, and then to get up; and start running again, only to be stopped thirty yards later with the same orders. Only at the end do the men learn that this is the best way to protect oneself from a nearby explosion. After Hell Week this exercise makes much sense. Before it might have seemed to be just another form of the instructor's torture.

Having survived the rigors of Hell Week, the remaining SEAL candidates finish off the last three weeks of their "first phase" of training and then move into a phase devoted to land warfare, something new for the SEALs as compared to the UDT. The class learns the tactics of conducting raids from the sea and how to conduct ambushes. They also learn patrolling and various means of moving from one place to another. (In SEAL talk this is called insertion.) They learn to slide down ropes from helicopters (rappelling), and they learn about explosives and demolitions. At the end of this phase of training they repair to San Clemente Island for a twenty-one-day exercise that tests their skills in all these departments. By the end of this phase, the men must meet these new requirements (with time in minutes):

Obstacle course, 12
4-mile run, 31
2-mile ocean swim with fins, 75
5.5-mile ocean swim with fins until completion

The next phase of SEAL training involves advanced swimming techniques, the use of scuba gear, and specialized warfare techniques. The men practice long-distance underwater compass swims, swimming in pairs in the bay on set courses, and towing a red buoy with their number on it. They practice attacks on ships and work with submarines. Their physical endurance is increased, and they run until they can do a fourteen-mile distance run. They have academic work in physics and medicine. At this stage the attrition rate may be 50 to 80 percent of the class. At the end of this phase they must meet new requirements (with time in minutes):

Obstacle course, 10
4-mile run, 30
2-mile ocean swim with fins, 70

This phase marks the end of BUD/S training, and after graduation the class is shipped off to Fort Benning, Georgia, where they learn parachuting. At the end of this training the young men, now almost SEALs, are assigned to SEAL teams or UDT teams for a six-month probationary period. If they survive this test, they go before a board that judges if they have qualified as SEALs, and if so, after more than a year of training, they will be able to wear the Trident, the Naval Special Warfare Command insignia, and claim proudly that they belong to the most exclusive society in the U.S. Navy.

November 20, 1943

Tarawa Atoll, Betio Island

The lone amphibious tractor swam slowly in toward the sandy beach, carrying marines of a scout-sniper platoon and of a flamethrower platoon. Their mission was to neutralize an L-shaped pier that stretched out into the water, but to be sure it was not destroyed so the marines could use it to land medical supplies, ammunition, and food and to evacuate wounded men.

This amtrac hit the pier fifteen minutes ahead of the first wave of landing craft. Then the boats and amphibious tractors of this first wave of marines started coming in to the beach. The naval barrage lifted, and when it did, "all hell broke loose." Along the beach ran a seawall constructed by the Japanese, who poured fire from field guns, machine guns, mortars, and rifles onto the beach. They fired antiboat guns along the long axis of the marines. Many of the 125 amtracs were destroyed, and the survivors were slowed as they waded in toward the beach in water sometimes shoulder-deep. Many men were killed or wounded, so many that the water at the shore began to run red.

The wooden landing craft drew too much water to cross the reef. They had to unload on the edge of the lagoon. Some of the amtracs began to run a shuttle service to the beach, but most marines had to wade in, running the gauntlet of enemy fire.

The tank lighters came in. They had to drop their ramps at the edge of the lagoon. The tanks wallowed in across the shallow water. Some of them fell into holes in the coral, blasted by shells or by the Japanese as tank traps. Tanks drowned out. Some were knocked out by direct hits from the Japanese guns, whose gunners had carefully worked out the ranges and the fields of fire.

Landing craft found channels through the reef, only to discover that these channels had been created by the Japanese to draw the landing craft under their guns and into their mined tetrahedron defenses.

The second wave came in and the third. The slaughter continued. Many of the troops never reached the beach, cut down in the water. A third of the five thousand marines in the assault force that day were killed or wounded. Once the survivors reached the seawall, they were pinned down behind it, and the assault gained no momentum.

That day the issue was in doubt—the amphibious command was not sure the men could gain and hold the beach.

The problem was the tide. They had hit a tide that was unusually low and the water unusually shallow. At last the tide rose normally; ramped landing craft could bring in men over the reef. The fight was still hard. The Japanese were dug in securely, and their defenses were well planned and often linked. Pillboxes of concrete, steel, and logs covered the islands. Underwater obstacles were many and unexpected. American casualties were very high, more than 3,000 dead and wounded of 16,800 Marines in the operation. It took four days to win the battle, and when it was won all but a handful of the Japanese were dead. The cost of the victory was too high. When the admirals and generals returned to Pearl Harbor they realized that something had to be done to prevent such losses in the future. Thus were born the Underwater Demolition Teams of the U.S. Navy, from which would develop the Navy SEALs.

SONG OF THE DEMOLITIONEERS

The men of the Underwater Demolition Teams never got a nickname like Navy SEALS. They were almost always known as the UDTs or UDT men, virtually never as frogmen, although a figure of a frogman stands in the courtyard of the Naval Special Warfare headquarters in Coronado, California, as a reminder of the past. But the UDT men did have their own ways, and a song, which was sung to the tune of the Georgia Tech football fight song. ("I'm a rambling wreck from Georgia Tech and a helluvan engineer. . . .")

> *When the Navy gets into a jam*
> *They always call on me,*
> *To pack a case of dynamite*
> *And put right out to sea.*
>
> *Like every honest sailor*
> *I drink my whiskey clear.*
> *I'm a shootin', fightin', dynamitin'*
> *Demolitioneer.*
>
> *Out in front of the Navy*
> *Where you really get the heat*
> *There's a bunch of crazy bastards*
> *Pulling off some crazy feat.*
>
> *With their pockets full of powder*
> *And caps stuck in their ears*
> *They're shootin', fightin', dynamitin'*
> *Demolitioneers.*
>
> *They sent me off to Italy*
> *To clean the fascist up.*
> *I put a case of TNT*
> *Beneath the dirty pup.*

And now they're rushing madly
Straight up into the air.
I'm a shootin', fightin', dynamitin'
Demolitioneer.

Some day we'll see the coast of France
Put Jerry on the run.
We'll wrap a roll of primacord
'Round every Goddam Hun.

Goebbels and Herr Goering
Can blow it out their rears.
We're the shootin', fightin', dynamitin'
Demolitioneers.

When our marines reach Tokyo
And the rising sun is done
They'll head right for some Geisha house
To have a little fun.

But they'll find the gates are guarded
And the girls are in the care
Of the shootin', fightin', dynamitin'
Demolitioneers.

When the war is over
And the Wacs and Waves are home
We'll swim back to the USA
And never more shall roam.

All the local maidens
Will get the best of care
And we'll raise a bunch of squallin', bawlin'
Demolitioneers.

From Fane's *The Naked Warriors.*

1 The Virtue of Necessity

The U.S. Navy entered World War II with virtually no knowledge of amphibious operations, to say nothing of underwater operations. In the early 1940s the Italians exceeded all others at the latter, and the Germans, British, and Japanese were all far ahead of the Americans in amphibious landing techniques.

The first American amphibious assault was staged at Guadalcanal on August 7, 1942. It turned out to be relatively easy, because the Marines on Guadalcanal Island were at first unopposed. Although the fighting by the few hundred Japanese troops on little Tulagi and Gavutu islands was fierce, the Japanese did not have the power to offer sustained resistance, and they had no basic defense plan. The Japanese had not expected opposition after their string of quick conquests in Southeast Asia and the Pacific.

But when the American invasion forces got ready to move into French North Africa, it was a different story.

The Allied North Africa landings were divided into three task forces. In the planning for the western task force operation the Allies decided that the force would land at the mouth of the Wadi Sefou River, near Casablanca in French Morocco. The planners soon learned that the Vichy French had constructed a massive boom and net arrangement across the river just inside the jetties that flanked the river mouth. This structure was overlooked by a large stone fortress. The fortress was a formidable place, with 155mm guns, 75mm guns, and many smaller field pieces.

Army intelligence suggested that the fortress was manned by the Vichy French and that they might give only token resistance. But the Germans were also in the area, and it had to be presupposed that they might take over the defenses.

Maj. Gen. George S. Patton, Jr.'s, task force target was Port Lyautey and the airfield that lay behind it, which, if captured, would give the Allied troops air cover as soon as the invasion began.

What was needed were demolition experts to destroy the boom and underwater defenses in the river. In 1942 such men were hard to find in the U.S. Navy, but there were a few, particularly operating around Pearl Harbor, where a number of unexploded Japanese bombs from the December 7 attack had to be dealt with, and the ships sunk in the attack had to be salvaged. One of those involved in these operations was Lt. Mark Starkweather. When the need was seen for the North Africa operations, Starkweather and a team of sixteen men were recruited for the job. They were given a rush course in cable cutting, underwater demolition, and commando fighting tactics. Their official name was Combat Demolition Unit. They began training in September, and two months later they were on their way into action.

Early on the morning of November 8 the demolition team was put over the side of its transport into a landing craft a few miles outside the river mouth. The sea was rough, a strong wind was blowing, and heavy overcast hung low on the water, then gave way to rain. As the landing craft neared the mouth of the river, it was struck by a rain squall. Moments later it was caught at the top of a thirty-foot ground swell and literally rammed through the channel between the jetties on the banks of the river mouth. There was serious danger of being pooped and swamped by the swell, but the boat's coxswain applied full power and kept just ahead of the wave. Then the swell receded and the coxswain was in full control again.

A red flare went up, an indication that the enemy was not surprised. The coxswain took the boat close along the south bank of the river toward the boom. Then the Higgins boat began to draw fire, but at that time the fire was erratic and not damaging. But moments later a searchlight came on and began playing down from the high walls of the fortress. Another joined in, and they swept the river, caught the boat, and moved on, then came back and held the boat in their glare. The coxswain put on full power and began to take evasive action to escape the tracing searchlights.

One of the Allied destroyers just outside the river mouth began firing on the fortress. The fortress's big guns started firing back. Whatever chance there had been that the attack could be pursued with the element of surprise was now completely gone. The searchlights clung tenaciously to the landing craft, and Lieutenant Starkweather saw that he could not escape them. He ordered the coxswain to head back for the mouth of the river. In a few minutes they were out of the protective cover of the shore of the river and back in the Atlantic, first plunging through the surf at the river's mouth. The boat began to pitch and toss. Lieutenant Starkweather was thrown head first into the cockpit coaming and injured his face. A sailor had both ankles broken when he was thrown across the bottom of the boat.

By the time the boat got into the vicinity of its transport, the main assault landings were under way.

So the Combat Demolition Unit had failed in its mission that day. But the whole invasion was ragged. Because of the weather, it took two days to get Patton's troops ashore. He still wanted the airfield and the blowing of the river boom, so orders were given to Starkweather's unit to make another attempt. If they were successful, a force of highly trained men were waiting on board a destroyer to make the landing assault on the airfield.

Just after midnight on the morning of November 11, Lieutenant Starkweather and his men were back in the

Higgins boat, heading for the shore again. This time they had some extra equipment: two .30-caliber machine guns, two inflatable rubber boats, and a massive underwater demolition bomb that one member of the team had constructed while they waited for this second attempt. No one knew quite how they were going to use the bomb.

This time the seas were rougher than they had been on the first attempt, but their coxswain got them through and into the mouth of the river. This time there was no red flare and there were no searchlights. Perhaps the French were persuaded by the very viciousness of the weather that no attempt could possibly succeed on this night.

The coxswain throttled back as they slid along the shore. They found the boom cable and its net. The cable was buoyed along its length by a number of small boats. Above the cable was strung another wire. Suspecting it might be an alarm or a booby trap, Lieutenant Starkweather warned his men not to touch that wire.

The members of the team attached explosives to the main boom cables. They were to employ a heavy-explosive boom cutter, but in training they had found that it did not always work very well, so this night they had also brought extra explosives as a hedge against failure. As the cable cutter was installed, so were hundreds of backup explosive charges. Finally the job was done and the explosives were all installed. The men got out of the water and back into their Higgins boat. The charges were blown, and they worked. The cable broke, and the two heavy sections dragged down the supporting boats. The way was now clear for the invasion of the airfield.

The explosion of the cable had attracted the attention of the fortress—the searchlights came on, and the guns began firing. One of the machine gunners in the Higgins boat managed to knock out one of the searchlights, but the fortress began firing flares, and the Higgins boat was caught in the light. The fortress guns began hitting closer and closer, so the coxswain zigged and zagged to throw the enemy gunners off. The team was firing the two machine guns, and their gun flashes seemed to be drawing enemy fire, because the Higgins boat began to take some hits. Lieutenant Starkweather ordered his men to cease firing, and soon the enemy gunners could not find them, and the shells stopped coming in. But now the problem was going to be the sea. Lieutenant Starkweather ordered all the leftover explosives jettisoned. The two rubber boats were heaved over the side, and the big incendiary bomb went, too, unwanted and unneeded. One of the machine guns was also dumped to save weight for the ordeal into the surf and the crashing waves beyond.

As the Higgins boat emerged from the mouth of the river, the station destroyers began to deliver covering fire against the fortress. The boat sped on through the rough sea and back to the transport, where the men scrambled up the nets, and the boat was hoisted aboard. They counted thirteen major holes and a number of smaller ones in the boat, but nobody was killed, or even badly hurt, although many of the team suffered from the long immersion in the water and some had been knocked about in the boat on the way in.

The mission was a success—the troops were delivered to the shore and soon had the airfield under control. So the first action involving underwater demolition men had proved their value to the Navy and to amphibious commanders. The Americans had been slow to start, but they were learning.

2 The Beginning— Underwater Demolition Teams

◈◈◈◈
◈◈◈◈ Early in 1943, when Adm. Ernest J. King suggested to the Pacific Fleet that it would be a good idea to seize the Ellice and Gilbert Islands, Adm. Chester W. Nimitz discovered that his staff knew virtually nothing about the Gilberts. Their attention was turned to the Marshall Islands, which seemed to be the next target for invasion to begin the Central Pacific campaign.

A little had been learned about the Gilberts in the summer of 1942, when Lt. Col. Evans Carlson's 2d Marine Raider Battalion had made a raid on Makin Island. But at that time there were scarcely a hundred Japanese on Makin, and the information gathered by Carlson's men was very meager.

A series of carrier raids and submarine reconnaissance missions to the Gilberts was staged in the spring and summer of 1943, partially to get information about Japanese defenses, and the Seventh Army Air Force moved some B-24s up to Canton Island and stayed at Funafuti, an island captured by the Americans.

On January 26, 1943, three B-24s made a combined bombing and photographic mission on Tarawa. They discovered that the Japanese had built an airstrip on Betio Island. On February 17 bombers flew over Butaritari Island in the Makin atoll, which Carlson had raided, and discovered that one result of the Carlson raid was the heavy fortification of that island by the Japanese. It now had a seaplane base.

This news was bothersome. Maj. Gen. Howland M. Smith, the Marine officer who had been supervising amphibious training on the West Coast and was now to be ground commander for Nimitz, said brusquely that all this was the result of the Carlson raid, which in his estimate had been a bad mistake.

These bombing and photo missions triggered Japanese response. Funafuti airfield was bombed and two B-24s were destroyed. After that Admiral Nimitz warned the Joint Chiefs of Staff that the Gilberts represented a serious threat to an invasion of the Marshalls and ought to be taken first.

All this was decided in the summer of 1943, and Vice Adm. Raymond Spruance, who would command the invasion force, flew to Canton, Upolu, and Funafuti islands to study the problems of getting troops across a coral reef, for in spite of the success of the Guadalcanal landings and other Solomons landings, the Americans were just learning the techniques of amphibious operations.

In September the submarine *Nautilus* went to Tarawa and spent eight days photographing the beaches. The special cameras rigged up to the periscope did not work, but the submarine's executive officer did the job with his own German-made camera. The bombers continued to take photos, but they came back to report that there were no signs of life on Tarawa nor any apparent fortifications. Fortunately the Marines had better information than that, and knew almost precisely how many defenders there were on the island, although they did not know how sophisticated the defenses were.

The big problem was the tides. An Australian naval officer on Nimitz's staff who had lived in the Gilberts warned about "dodging" tides that came at this time of year, and others warned against the uncertainty of the tides around November 20, but Adm. Richmond Kelly Turner, the amphibious commander, decided to take a chance. He guessed wrong, and the tide the Marines came in on was a "low dodging tide," which meant at the low point, during the landings, no landing craft could cross the reef.

When Admiral Turner returned to Pearl Harbor after the Gilberts operation, he and the others involved in the critique of operations concluded that more information had to be obtained in the future about what the invaders would face. Only swimmers could give accurate information about the depth of water and about underwater obstacles placed by the enemy.

The Navy was then already creating such units. In June 1943 Lt. Comdr. Draper L. Kauffman, a bomb disposal expert, was given the job of organizing the first Underwater Demolition Team, at Fort Pierce, Florida.

Late that summer the first Combat Demolition Unit —six men—was given the name CDU No. 1 and shipped to San Francisco under secret orders to pave the way for the reoccupation of the Aleutians. But in those days virtually no one in the Navy knew what a UDT was. Their orders got mislaid and they missed the ship that was to take them north, so Kiska Island, which, it was discovered, the Japanese had already abandoned, had to be captured without their participation. Later UDT No. 1 was shipped off to Hawaii to join other UDTs.

The next two teams were shipped to the Southwest Pacific to join MacArthur's Navy, the Seventh Fleet. By the time they arrived, MacArthur was so used to doing what he could with what he had that he was employing the Army engineer brigades to do the work the UDTs could do. So the UDTs were not used out front, but to clear boat channels on the beaches of New Guinea as MacArthur moved up toward Hollandia.

Two UDTs went to the Mediterranean, where they participated in the invasion of southern France. One unit went to England, two units went to Admiral Wilkinson at Guadalcanal, and three units were sent to Hawaii for Admiral Turner's operations. Lieutenant Commander Kauffman's unit was not far enough advanced in training to participate in the Gilberts invasion or that of the Marshalls.

Admiral Turner and Captain Hill, who had headed one amphibious unit, and others recommended the organization of Underwater Demolition Teams of a hundred men, each with four operating platoons.

Admiral Nimitz soon had approval from Washington. A school for UDT training was established in Hawaii, for the attacks on Kwajalein, Roi, and Namur. One month was allocated to find volunteers and organize and train the men. Comdr. Edward D. Brewster, a Seabee, was chosen to command UDT No. 1. Another Seabee, Lt. Tom Crist, was given temporary command of UDT No. 2. When the men arrived from Fort Pierce they came into these organizations, to join Marines with experience at Tarawa and Army demolitions experts. The training began at Waimanalo Amphibious Base, across Oahu Island from Honolulu.

The UDTs developed a secret weapon they called the "Stingray." It was a wooden landing craft filled with several tons of explosives. Steering and firing were radio-controlled. This "drone" could be radio-directed to a reef or an obstacle. Admiral Turner brought up drones that would be sent in to blow a gap through which other landing craft might move. After the craft were "perfected," rocket launchers were added to them. A demonstration was given for Captain Hill. The "Stingray" drone was started in toward its target, the rockets were fired, but their thrust flames set the dynamite in the boat afire, and the boat blew up in midpassage, killing several hundred pounds of tuna fish, which one of the Seabees loaded up and traded ashore for two cases of whiskey.

Just before Christmas, UDT No. 2 went to San Diego to report to Rear Adm. Richard Connolly, who would conduct the Roi and Namur operation. They picked up more Stingrays, inflatable boats, Bangalore torpedoes, and explosives. Admiral Connolly then put Lt.

Comdr. John T. Koehler in charge of UDT No. 2. Lieutenant Commander Koehler had been involved in the landings on Sicily.

That Sicily invasion had marked a point of departure. A special emergency team of demolition men had been created at the Dynamiting and Demolition School at Fort Perry, Virginia. Lt. Fred Wise of the Seabees was in charge of this thirteen-man team of volunteers. They were joined by others, trained as well and as quickly as possible, and shipped to the Mediterranean in time for the invasion of Sicily on July 10, 1943. The organization got a name: Naval Combat Demolition Unit (NCDU).

When the invasion began, the NCDU was ready to search out underwater obstacles, but there were none; however, a number of ships and landing craft sunk by German bombers were near the beach, so the NCDU was put to work blowing up a different sort of obstacle. Some of the men were also sent inland with the Army to blow up obstacles and enemy strongpoints. Lieutenant Koehler was executive officer of a unit at Gela on the southern coast of Sicily when the Hermann Goering Panzer Division broke through the American lines. His men and other naval people were thrown into the line to help rout the Germans with a counterattack. After a few days the NCDU was shipped back to the United States and the men scattered among various demolition organizations.

The other UDT men trained on Oahu and Maui in Hawaii, in December 1943. They learned hydrographic reconnaissance and mapping. Little by little more emphasis was put on distance swimming. By the time the Marshall expedition was being planned, Underwater Demolition Team No. 1 had also been organized.

But none of these men was a frogman. They were to operate out of small boats, and they wore combat fatigue uniforms with life belts. They were hooked to safety lines and were not expected to do any swimming. They wore combat boots to protect their feet from the coral reef.

The first step in the Marshalls invasion was the occupation of the Kwajalein atoll group, the largest atoll group. The Northern Invasion Force would attack Roi and Namur, two islands in the north connected by a causeway. The Southern Force would attack Kwajalein Island. One of the UDTs accompanied each expedition.

At dawn on January 31, 1944, the invasion forces reached the Kwajalein Island area. The battleships and aircraft had been pounding the reef island. Now it was time for the UDT men to test their secret weapons against the islet of Enubuj, west of Kwajalein. Admiral Turner wanted to test the Stingray drones.

Each drone was loaded with three tons of explosives. The UDT had to complete its mission on the reef and get out of the way before the troops left the line of departure and headed in to the beach.

Two drones, manned by a coxswain and a mechanic, started in to the beach. They set the controls, threw over a rubber boat and jumped in, and were picked up by the following control boat. Each control boat controlled two slave boats.

One of the two drones slowed down suddenly and dropped deeper in the choppy water, then went under while six hundred yards from the beach. Its pumps had failed.

The second drone sputtered, the motor stopped, and it drifted to a stop. A third drone was started toward shore, but after the crew left, the motor quit. The crew paddled back and tried to restart the motors of both drones. Now the invading troop waves were starting toward shore. So the Stingray operation was abandoned as a failure.

(Later Admiral Turner discovered that his officers in charge of dispensing equipment had not wanted to waste good boats, so had given the UDTs old, worn-out boats and motors. The admiral was not pleased.)

UDT No. 1 had other missions at Kwajalein. One

was a midnight reconnaissance of the reef that ran from
Enubuj to the western end of Kwajalein. Air photos
showed that the Japanese had been working on a seawall
similar to the one that had run along the beach at Tarawa,
a wall of rocks set in concrete with hardwood posts sticking seaward to impede amtracs and assault boats. Were
there mines or underwater obstacles? Nobody knew.

So Admiral Turner sent the UDT men in on two
daylight reconnaissance missions, one at high tide and
one at low tide. They would be covered by the guns of the
fleet.

At ten o'clock on the morning of January 31 the
battleships *Pennsylvania* and *Mississippi* began bombarding Kwajalein. Four ramped landing craft loaded
with UDT men, photographers, leadsmen, radio men,
and machine gunners approached the island on the
morning high tide. Ahead of them was the long reef and
the stone wall, behind which the Japanese crouched for
protection from the shelling. There was very little fire
from the beach.

Two of the UDT men in the leading boat stepped
outside regulations. Ens. Lewis F. Luehrs and Seabee
Chief Bill Acheson were wearing swim trunks under their
combat fatigues. When the boat's coxswain began to get
nervous seeing so many coral heads around him, they
took off their clothes, slipped over the side, and swam.
They spent forty-five minutes in the water, got up near
the beach, waded in to measure the depth of the water
and found gun emplacements and a large log barricade
on the entire tip of the island. There were many coral
heads, which would prevent effective use of landing craft
but no mines.

When they got back to the ship they were taken immediately, still in their trunks, to Admiral Turner's flagship *Monrovia* to retell their findings. The admiral was
impressed, and when they advised the use of amtracs in

stead of boats, he listened. The landing took place in amtracs.

That afternoon at four o'clock the low-tide reconnaissance men went in in amtracs. The landing went fine, even though there was heavy rain.

And from the UDT reports about the wall, Admiral Turner decided to devote more bombardment to the area. So on D+1 Admiral Turner ordered a new bombardment of the wall, and on the morning of D+1, February 1, the two Army regimental combat teams that assaulted Kwajalein went in to the island in armor-plated amtracs, with three machine guns each and led by a wave of amphibian tanks. They swept through the broken wall and drove inland, where the infantry dismounted. Later, at high tide, the landing craft came in over the reef and landed safely.

The next day UDT No. 1 was landed on the west end of Kwajalein Island to blast channels through the reef inside the lagoon for LSTs and supply ships. They also blew up a number of Japanese barges on the shore. During the march up the island the UDT men also helped out with some pillboxes, packing haversacks of tetrytol against the concrete and tying it together with primacord fuse and then moving back to take cover from the explosion. The pillboxes crumbled, and the Army troops shot down the Japanese as they poured out.

It took the Army four days to take Kwajalein. The UDT men then moved to Ebeye Island, which was the site of a seaplane base, again to make channels through the reef.

As this was going on to the south, Admiral Connolly's Northern Attack Force was moving on Roi and Namur. It, too, would take the small adjoining islands on January 31 and strike the main target on D+1.

The two islands were named Jacob and Ivan. Lt. Tom Crist in a landing craft scouted the Jacob passage and reported to Commander Koehler that the island would make a good base for the team. By noon their ship was putting their drone boats and explosives over the side, and the men took over the island as the bombardment force pounded Roi and Namur and as minesweepers cleared the passage into the lagoon.

The UDT men unloaded more drone boats and loaded them up with explosives. At an hour before midnight the fire support ships speeded up their bombardment of Roi and Namur to cover the UDT night survey of the landing beaches along with Marine scouts. The reconnaissance crews went in rubber boats with outboard motors, all in full combat uniform with life belts. If a swimmer went over the side, he was supposed to use a lifeline. The boats cruised along the beach and came back to report that all the beach seemed good enough for landing.

At dawn on D+1, UDT No. 2 launched its drone boats into the lagoon, followed by amtracs, which controlled them. This was the test of the drones against the reefs, just before the troops landed, as in the south.

The sea was so rough that Admiral Connolly sent the LSTs into the lagoon to unload the Marines into the assault craft, and they milled around, trying to get into formation for the assault waves. Lieutenant Commander Koehler had been given good landing craft for his drone boats, unlike the other team. The amtrac control vessel was manned by Lt. William Gordon Carberry and Crist and Lt. William Lambert Hawks was at the controls.

They aimed the first drone at the pier in the center of the enemy beach. The drone was loaded with five tons of dynamite. It vanished into the smoke of the bombardment. Crist told Hawks to push the arming switch as the boat headed into the chop; a few minutes later, Crist gave the order to fire. Hawks pushed the firing switch on the radio. Nothing happened. Then, out of the haze, the drone boat appeared, traveling in a tight circle. Somebody guessed that the radio signals were being jammed by the Japanese. Hawks hailed a standby craft and boarded it with two other UDT men. They had to get that drone with its ten thousand pounds of explosives, out of the way of the troops. They ran up to the drone, under Japanese machine-gun fire from the beach, and boarded. They cut out four fuses. The drone was armed and ready to fire and could have been set off by machine-gun fire. They brought the drone back under manual control.

Crist and Carberry tried another. This one started out straight, then circled and came back and rammed their amtrac. Luckily the dynamite did not go off, but one man was knocked overboard. So the drones had failed again. They were steered back out of the way, and the invasion went on without them.

On Roi and Namur the UDT men went ashore to help the Marines blast blockhouses, then cut out parts of the coral reef to let the LSTs come up over the reef to drop their ramps.

After Kwajalein and Roi and Namur were secure, Adm. Harry Hill went on to Eniwetok. UDT No. 1 went with him, in an infantry landing craft, as part of the reconnaissance party.

Using captured Japanese charts, the minesweepers went in first and moved to the lagoon. At five o'clock in the afternoon, the UDT scouting parties boarded amtracs and headed into Engebi Island. They were under gunfire. Lieutenant Luehrs led one of the UDT groups. By this time it seemed quite acceptable that they were in swimming trunks. A lot of ideas had changed. Admiral Turner, who had been so high on the Stingrays, now realized that they were a "gimmick," and when he got back to Pearl Harbor he would tell Admiral Nimitz that the only way to deal with coral and underwater obstacles was to send in individual swimmers.

This day, as Luehrs and his men went in to the beach, they were under fire from Japanese mortars and machine guns. The amtracs fired back and called for spot fire from the bombardment force. The UDT men spotted coral heads, then stripped down to their trunks, put on their goggles, strapped on their sheath knives, and dove over to check the depths. They marked the dangerous heads with yellow buoys. For two hours they cruised fifty yards off the beach, under fire, and then pulled back to mark the boundaries of the four-hundred-yard-wide lanes they had explored. While they worked they watched, and when they got back to the fleet they reported on pillboxes that were still standing ashore after the barrage. Those targets got special attention that night and the next morning.

On the next morning three UDT men went in with the first landing craft to guide the landing waves to the beach. Commander Brewster, Lieutenant Luehrs, and Chief Acheson rode the amtracs. The first wave began slanting off to the left, out of the landing lane. Luehrs, under fire from the Japanese, sped over to herd them back. The wave barely missed grounding on many coral heads in the danger zone. For his work that day Luehrs won the Silver Star. Commander Brewster was wounded.

The Marines took Engebi that day but discovered that the Japanese had strong forces on Eniwetok and Parry islands nearby. So the following day they hit Eniwetok without naval preparation. It took them four days to dig out the Japanese and another day to take Parry, but the beaches offered no problems. The UDT men were occupied clearing up the lagoon channels and anchorages and making ramps ashore for the LSTs. By the time UDT No. 1 left Eniwetok, Lt. Comdr. John Koehler was back in Hawaii establishing a training program for UDTs. Admiral Turner was completely sold on the concept but recognized that they had to be swimmers, not just demolition men, so the concept began to change. In the next operation westward, Admiral Turner intended to use five different UDT groups.

In the meantime, Lieutenant Commander Kauffman had begun an extensive program at Fort Pierce designed first of all to toughen the men for this demanding duty.

His theory, based on the operation and training of the Navy and Marine scouts and raiders, was that a man should be capable of ten times the physical effort he thought he had. To that end a rigorous program was developed. Because the demand for trained men was so immediate, the program was accelerated.

3   Breaking the Atlantic Wall

〰〰〰〰 In November 1943 Lieutenant (jg) Hei-
〰〰〰〰 demann brought a six-man Naval Combat Demolition Unit from the first class
of the Fort Pierce school to England to report to the
commander of American naval forces in Europe, at Plym-
outh. There the command had absolutely no idea of what
to do with them nor any concept of what the UDT men
were to do because the whole matter was still under such
secrecy wraps.

During the next month nine more units from the
second Fort Pierce class were shipped to England and
chivvied from one end of the country to the other without
finding a home until Lt. Robert C. Smith, who had participated in the Sicily landings, was put in charge, and a base
for all Naval Combat Demolition Units was secured at
Falmouth. For the next few months the demolitions men
wandered about the English countryside searching for
roadblocks and other barriers put together by the British
back in 1940, when a German invasion of England
seemed imminent, under a plan that had long since been
discarded. Lieutenant Heidemann had wriggled himself
into a course in British explosives techniques, and the
Americans then practiced those along with their own on
the salvaged counterinvasion barriers.

In the spring of 1944 Allied intelligence officers began studying the German beach defenses of Normandy
and were soon appalled at the knowledge reflected in the
complete job that had been done under the supervision
of Fld. Mar. Erwin Rommel. As commander of the defense of that Atlantic wall, Rommel wanted to stop the
invasion on the beaches, and he invented many obstacles

that he designed himself. The most formidable object was the Belgian gate, named because of its resemblance to the steel gates found on virtually every Belgian farm. These were ten-foot-square frames bolted and welded together and held erect in the water by a large framework of steel. Once in place they were virtually immobile.

When the underwater demolition teams began studying the Belgian gates, at first they seemed too formidable to tackle. Explosives placed around the gate and blown up in the usual fashion produced a tangle of steel that was just as formidable an obstacle as the original. The only method seemed to be to use so much explosive that it would blow the whole gate into tiny pieces, but this plan was very dangerous to the UDT men and also to the soldiers who would be on the beach when the gates were blown.

The solution was found by Lt. Carl Hagensen. He devised an explosive pack of canvas that could be easily handled by one man. This forty-pound pack limited the zone of the explosive. The UDT men could thus control the area. The pack was loaded with a new plastic explosive compound called C2, which was detonated by the new waterproof explosive detonating fuse known as primacord. The pack had a metal hook on one end and a short length of rope on the other end. The pack could be fastened to a gate, and the primacord tied by an ordinary knot to the main fuse line. Sixteen of the Hagensen packs placed around a gate could blow the supporting structure to pieces, and then the gate would collapse on the sea bottom, harmless to the landing craft. It was March 1944 before the Allied high command really became cognizant of the state of the German shore defenses and the UDT men were consulted on the problems. As far as intelligence was concerned, there were no differences among any of the beaches. All five landing beaches would be formidably defended by Belgian gates, concrete and steel tetrahedrons, jagged hedgehogs, and wooden beams placed facing seaward to impale the bottom of a landing craft. The American high command began calling on the U.S. Navy for more demolition experts, but not enough were available. Thus the teams were reorganized into forty-five-man units. Added to these underwater team members were another three Navy men recruited from bases in Scotland and England, and five U.S. Army engineers. These sixteen-man Gap Assault Units were each assigned a platoon of twenty-six Army engineers under an Army officer.

In the second week of April all the underwater demolition teams were assembled at Appledore on the Devon coast, and there they learned something about what they would be up against: minefields on the beaches as well as the underwater obstacles, and now intelligence had discovered that Rommel was furthering the defenses by mining the underwater obstacles as well. By mid-May the training phase was over, and the UDTs moved to Salcombe, where the men were employed making Hagensen packs, ten thousand in all, for the coming operations.

At this point the UDTs numbered 550 men. They were split into two groups for the American beach landings, one for Omaha Beach and one for Utah Beach. Capt. Thomas Wellings took command of the Omaha group, and Lt. Comdr. Herbert Peterson took command of the Utah group.

The invasion was scheduled to take place on June 5 but was postponed for twenty-four hours because of the weather. Even so, the weather was very rough on invasion day.

At Utah Beach, a navigational error caused the first assault wave to land a mile farther southeast than had been planned. In fact, this turned out to be fortuitous, because the Utah landings were thus virtually unopposed in the first few hours. Nevertheless, the underwater demolition teams had their work cut out for them because the Rommel beach defense obstacles were many and well planned. The thirteen teams on Utah Beach suffered 30 percent casualties.

But there was no question about it, the big show on D-day in the American sector was on Omaha Beach, where everything went about as badly as it could go from the outset. Omaha Beach stood before a line of French hills five miles long, marked at the ends by cliffs and segmented by five narrow ravines that gave access through marshy ground to a central slope. The beach was a shingle of bare round rock eight or ten feet deep, banked against dunes and a seawall, a real barrier to tanks and vehicles. It extended out at ebb tide three hundred yards, wide open to gunfire from the hills above, where the Germans had sited their field guns, machine guns, and mortars, in protected positions, with fields of fire carefully laid out and even diagramed on the sides of the gun positions. The beaches were alive with traps, some of them four and five rows deep and a hundred yards from front to rear, running parallel to the shoreline, out to where they were covered by high tide.

For hours before H-hour the guns of the ships had been booming, laying down a barrage that was supposed to destroy the German field guns and protective positions. Planes had been bombing, but the bombing and the bombardment had been too far inland, and the defenses remained. Shortly before the landings, British rocket ships came in and fired thousands of rockets into the beach positions.

Meanwhile, the first wave waited, and with the first wave, the UDT men waited, too. The initial landing was to be made by dual-drive tanks equipped with propellers as well as tank treads and encased in waterproof canvas sheaths that would protect them while swimming through the water. When they reached shore they would shed the sheaths as a snake sheds its skin and proceed as ordinary tanks. The tanks would each protect a company of combat infantry who would deal with snipers on the beach, to protect the Army combat infantrymen and the UDT men who would come in at that point to clear the beaches of underwater obstacles and mines.

The five exit points from the beach, up those ravines, were guarded by twelve German strongpoints, around which the Germans had sited their heavy weapons. The Navy assured everyone that those strongpoints would be knocked out, but in fact they were not, because the shooting had been over the mark. And no one knew that just recently a German combat infantry division of the first rank had replaced the garrison division that was supposed to be here.

There were many false starts and accidents on the crossing of the channel in very heavy weather. Landing craft broke down, tows broke, and men were seasick all the way across. But finally the men were loaded into fifty-foot landing craft at the line of departure. The demolition crews were wearing gas-impregnated coveralls over khaki shirts and trousers and long underwear, and field boots. Each man had a web belt, wire cutters, mine horn crimper, cartridges, gas mask, life belt, canteen, first-aid pack, helmet, fur-lined coat, and a forty-pound load of explosive packs. Some carried carbines, some carried signal reels wound with primacord. Some carried bags of waterproof two-minute delayed-action-fuse assemblies that could be exploded by bullet to fire the primacord.

As they came in toward the beach after six o'clock that morning, the tanks on the left were unloaded by the TLCs three miles from the shore. As they came those three miles, wind and the heavy waves ripped off the canvas sheaths and buckled the frameworks, filling the tanks with water and drowning most of the tanks before they got to the line of departure.

The demolition men's landing craft had to pass by and continue to head in. On the right, the tank landing craft came in so close they almost touched bottom, and the tanks and the regular tanks that followed mostly made the shore to offer cover for the men. But the tanks had no cover, and many of them hit mines as they maneuvered on the shallow beach. The German artillery that was supposed to have been knocked out accounted for some more of the hits. For by this time the barrage from the ships was moving inland on schedule, but the German barrage was just beginning. As the first wave came in, and was half a mile from shore, the German 88's began to score hits on landing craft.

H-hour was six-thirty. The first wave dropped ramps, and the troops went over into waist-deep water under very heavy enemy fire. Beyond the surf they had that three-hundred-yard dash across the wet sand to the dubious safety of the seawall. Intermixed with the infantry and sometimes ahead of it came the demolition teams, strung along three miles of beach, with most of them drifting in the strong tide to points left of their intended destinations.

The right-hand gap assault team in the first boat was supposed to land on the beach farther west. It drifted a whole beach to the east. The effect was like an accordion, each boat farther to the east.

This right flank of demolitions on Omaha was supervised by William Freeman. The wave of boats came in three hundred yards apart, under fire while still half a mile out. Freeman's landing craft scraped bottom at six thirty-three; three minutes later, with their forty-pound packs and laden down with all their personal gear, the men leaped into waist-deep water, splashing toward the line of Belgian gates on the sand ahead of them.

Army engineers and Navy men worked together on the gates while covered by some tanks on the beach but also under fire from German 88's, rifles, and machine guns.

Two seamen brought their rubber boat in to work on gates. The boat was sunk by enemy fire and their reserve explosives were lost. Then the seamen were hit; an Army aid man tried to help them but was killed by a sniper.

Men were falling between obstacles. A gunner's mate . . . his buddy . . . an Army private with them. . . .

The survivors worked on, loading the obstacles with explosives. The surf was rising on the obstacles at the rate of a foot every eight minutes.

When the one team finished loading its obstacles, it lit the purple smoke signal to warn of coming demolition. Everybody dropped. The blast sent a rocket of flame, smoke, debris, and shrapnel into the sky. The engineers started to work toward the Navy men then; the Navy men were now onto rows of ramps and hedgehogs, and Belgian gates. There were lines of ramps and posts, each post a heavy timber, its seaward end buried deep in the sand and sloping toward the shore, so that a boat would ride up the ramp and capsize, or hit a teller mine at the end. The posts were braced on stout vertical or V-shaped supports, each topped by a teller mine. Nearest the enemy beach was a line of hedgehogs.

These hedgehogs were made of steel angle irons connected so that they offered some protection against snipers. Three irons joined and crossed in the middle like an X and were footed in a steel and concrete base. All points were tipped with mines. The demolition men had to pack explosives around the mines as well as the structure because to blow the hedgehog alone could leave a floating mine to kill men and sink boats.

After five minutes Gunner's Mate Bass began to race from one obstacle to another, rolling out primacord and tying the main fuse to each of those on the obstacles. Then he attached the waterproof detonating assembly that would fire all the charges. When the time came to fire, he looked at Chief William Freeman. There was no word. He looked around.

There was another obstacle: human, American. A

platoon of the riflemen who were supposed to hit the beach to protect the UDT men had been blown off course and had drifted down here. Now they hit the beach, under fire, and began to huddle among the obstacles for what shelter they would give. Chief Freeman yelled at them and then began dragging them away and kicking them. They had to be gotten out of there, fast.

The riflemen got out, and Freeman gave the signal. Bass pulled the fuse. "Hit the deck!" shouted Freeman. The explosives went up; a huge geyser of sand, metal, water, wood, and shrapnel rained debris on the men. The gap was blown—fifty beautiful yards of unimpeded water and beach from sea to shore.

Freeman put a green can buoy on one side, and the Army lieutenant put one on the other. Then they headed inshore, carrying several wounded men. An 88mm shell tore open Bass's shoulder, but he survived and would get the Navy Cross for the day's exploits.

One UDT man was killed by a sniper as he was going ashore. The others made it to the rocks below the seawall and dug a trench there. The men, wounded among them, crouched in the trench, and they all waited.

Two landing craft were hit by 88's on the way in through the gap and very nearly blocked it. Nearly, but not quite.

The troops came in, but the going was very tough against strong opposition. All morning and afternoon the UDT men stayed in their trench. At low tide in the afternoon Freeman took the men who were on their feet and salvaged explosives from wreckage and from engineer units and commandeered a bulldozer and two double-drive tanks. His men went back to the sand to double the width of the gap they had cleared that morning.

The wounded were not evacuated until seven o'clock that night. The Freeman unit suffered 67 percent casualties—four killed or dead of wounds and four wounded.

Freeman's was an extremely successful mission. But

of the sixteen channels that were scheduled to be blown through the obstacles, a total of only five were cleared along all of Omaha Beach that morning.

Four units were supposed to land just east of Freeman's. One had its LST sunk underneath it on the channel crossing and did not arrive until the obstacles were covered by the tide at 8:00 A.M. They had to wade all the way in under fire.

The second boat dropped its ramp as a salvo of 88mm shells hit the LCT and blew the explosives, killing all but one of the crew.

The third boat crew was shot up while trying to load obstacles with explosives. All but one UDT man were either wounded or killed.

The fourth boat went in straight, and all the men hit the beach ahead of the supporting tanks and infantry. But by the time they got the obstacles loaded, the beach was full of Americans—too many of them to drive out of the area.

The demolition men had to wait while the infantrymen slowly made their way to the beach, driven by the advancing tide. By the time they were able to fire their explosives, all were flooded, and only half the gap blew open.

The next boat managed to blow a wide gap in Easy Green Beach, where the Germans had not put in steel gates, but only two lines of ramps and a line of hedgehogs.

Here the problem was to get the troops off the working beach. Lt. (jg) William M. Jenkins had a scheme, and he and a chief went among the troops, pulling out fuse igniters and yelling at the men that they would be blown up in two minutes if they did not get out. They moved.

The firing on the beach was heavier, and it grew heavier as the Germans unleashed rockets of their own. In that attack a chief and a seaman were killed, but the other men kept working and finally blew a gap almost a hundred yards wide. However, one had to be careful to get through the gap. Later, two LCTs came in, missed the markers, and both of them then missed the gap and hit mines. They sank, closing half the gap.

There were many other difficulties as the crews and troops arrived late and got into trouble. Many of the units were badly shot up trying to place their demolitions.

One of the toughest beaches on Omaha was Easy Red, named by some optimistic staff officer. This was the first beach on the left flank of this invasion sector. Three of the four groups assigned to this beach got in and blew their gaps successfully. The first boat, however, struck disaster in the form of German shells, which killed one man of the crew and wounded another. Still the demolition men got ashore and worked with the Army engineers to blow their assigned obstacles.

Ens. Lawrence S. Karnowski's team pushed their boats offshore and worked the line of obstacles in the surf while the Army engineers worked inshore. The troops began to come in and cluttered up the gap, so the Navy team moved out to load a hundred-yard gap. The troops moved and they blew the hundred-yard gap, then turned to working on the pilings. All this time they were under converging fire from two of the twelve German strongpoints. Soldiers and sailors were falling. When the Navy chief was killed, machinist Lester Meyers took command. The tide was already rising among the obstacles when they were ready to fire. They fired, a huge geyser shot up, and they dropped again as the engineers next to them fired. Then engineers and Navy men scrabbled to the cover of the seawall with their wounded, Karnowski carrying one man. First aid was given to the wounded. Then Karnowski and his opposite number, Lieutenant Gregory of the Army engineers, grabbed explosive packs and went into the surf to destroy some obstacles that had not gone up. They cleared almost all of them and returned, but Gregory was killed on the beach. Five of the seven Navy men were also casualties.

Of the boats farther to the east, only one managed to blow a gap on the left side of Easy Red Beach. Chief Aviation Ordnanceman Loran Barbour was leading this boat. He and his men packed the obstacles with explosives, and a gunner's mate ran the primacord between two groups. He was shot down by a sniper and killed, but another UDT man grabbed the reel and finished the task. Barbour had been about to light the purple smoke signal when a German shell struck the pack and exploded it. Five of the Navy men were killed, and Barbour and all but two others were wounded. The Army engineers' unit suffered fifteen casualties. Barbour continued to direct marking and evacuating wounded until he collapsed. John Line, a gunner's mate, who was also wounded, stayed on with two other Navy men and the Army survivors to get the job done.

One boat support team ran into a tetrahedron, which drove through the bottom of the boat, impaled it, and held it fast five hundred yards from the beach. The ensign in charge ordered the men to inflate their life belts (lest they drown from the weight they were carrying) and swim for the beach. Only a few of his men made it.

The German fire was ferocious. A mortar round set off one team's boatload of explosives, killing the officer and three men and wounding several others. Chief Markham assembled the survivors and blew a partial gap in the barrier, then led the wounded to the beach. The men made a shallow trench and stayed there until an 88mm shell buried them. Markham dug them all out alive.

The next two boats were hit by 88mm shells, and Boat 13's entire crew but one were killed. The next boat was hit by a shell that left more dead and wounded.

Boat 15 faced a line of Belgian gates, with Germans shooting at it very accurately with their artillery. Their demolitions were drowned out by the incoming tide before they could be fired.

Boat 16 then came to its position on the left flank beach. The officer in charge had been given an intelligence chart that showed the locations of the German strongpoints and had been told that these would all be disabled by the time the UDT men hit the beach. So the men of Boat 16 were relaxed, enjoying the sound of gunfire and the sight of the British rocket vessels swooping in to plaster the beaches with rockets. They counted a thousand rockets that hit in the area where they would land. It looked very promising.

But twelve hundred yards from the high-water mark, an army sergeant on the boat pointed out a German pillbox on the hill above that was sending heavy machine-gun fire at the boats. The men hit the deck, and then could hear the drumming of the bullets as they ricocheted off the sides of the landing craft.

Then the boat grounded on a sandbar. The boat crew dropped the ramp. Immediately the soldiers in the bow were spattered with machine-gun fire. The army lieutenant was killed and most of the Army men were wounded. The men were getting the rubber boats full of explosives off when an 88mm shell hit in the engine room and the boat began to burn. The UDT men grabbed all the explosives they could carry and left the craft before the other explosives went up.

The ensign in charge of the UDT group was hit through the shoulder and then in the leg. Chief Alfred Sears inflated his life vest and towed the ensign to the beach. Behind them they heard the landing ship blow up.

They were pinned down on the beach for hours by machine-gun and mortar fire. Their situation would have been desperate had they not been protected by the bed of a narrow-gauge railroad that the Germans had set up to move obstacles down to the beach. They huddled in the declivity on the beach side.

Everything that landed seemed to get shot up. Two tanks came by and were put out of action. The crews joined the UDT men along the little railroad. As darkness came they could move around enough to dig foxholes on the side of the hill a little up from the beach. When they woke next morning they discovered they had bivouacked in a German minefield.

The control boats for this sector fared little better. Three control boats managed the eight-boat support wave, carrying Lieutenant Commander Gibbons and Lts. Larry Heidemann and Walter Cooper. Each rode with an Army officer: Lieutenant Colonel O'Neill, Major Isley, and Major Jewett.

On the way in, Lieutenant Commander Gibbons's boat hit a mined stake, but the teller mine did not explode. The boat grounded in waist-deep water, and Gibbons ordered the troops ashore and began to wade. He stepped in a hole and went underwater. He inflated his life vest and popped up into a hail of bullets. He threw off the life belt and swam, keeping underwater as much as he could.

On the beach he found two men who reported that they were all who survived of one crew. He sent them to join another boat crew.

Six of the sixteen bulldozers and tankdozers in that first wave got ashore. Three of them were knocked out in short order. More were landed on the high tide. The Navy men then remained on the beach, with some Army combat engineers, following the receding tide out, destroying obstacles including some new obstacles, the wrecked landing craft, and tanks that cluttered the shore.

The men worked into the evening, using all the explosives they could find, and even converting German teller mines. When the tide came in again that evening, thirteen clearly buoyed gaps had been blown, some of them 150 yards wide.

The result was that the next day the troops came in

on a clean beach and moved up past the wreckage. The cost: More than half the Army and demolition men had been casualties.

Many medals were awarded to survivors of Army and Navy units, and the entire Navy Combat Demolition Unit of the Omaha invasion force received a Presidential Unit Citation, for extreme bravery under fire, initially blasting five gaps in the enemy obstacles and within two days destroying 85 percent of the German obstacles. They had done their job.

4   Saipan

〰〰〰〰 〰〰〰〰 Since the early employment of the Underwater Demolition Teams of the U.S. Navy was in response to need, the program developed separately in the European and Pacific theaters, although many of the men were trained at the amphibious training base established under Lieutenant Commander Kauffman at Fort Pierce, Florida. Some, who predated the school, were trained at Solomons Island, Maryland. But in spite of the North African, Normandy, and southern France invasions, in all of which UDT men were employed, the real impetus for the Underwater Demolition Teams came from the Pacific, and the driving force was Adm. Richmond Kelly Turner.

Thus had been born Underwater Demolition Teams No. 1 and No. 2 at Waimanalo, Hawaii, when it was discovered by Turner that the only men in the fleet who knew much about blasting coral reefs were the Seabees. A modest training program was begun there just before the Tarawa invasion, too soon before to have any outcome on that campaign. The results of Tarawa were stated by the command thus: "It was obvious that since some future amphibious operations were to be directed against coral atolls, passage to the beaches involved might have to be secured by demolition personnel in marine-blasting in coral-choked areas.

"Although it was known that the Japanese had never used mines or barricades either as profusely or as cleverly as the Germans, it was not known in what manner, with what obstacles, or to what extent the enemy might employ such devices to prevent or impede future landings."

The results of Tarawa proved to Admiral Turner and Gen. Holland Smith that troops should not be sent against enemy beaches until thorough offshore reconnaissance had been made. UDT personnel would have to search for obstacles and mines, and blast and mark channels. So the Fort Pierce school, which was basically oriented to such operations as the cross-channel attack, and the Waimanalo training program both received an enormous impetus from Tarawa.

Thus as of December 1, 1943, about 30 officers and 150 men were in training at Waimanalo, and Underwater Demolition Teams No. 1 and No. 2 were established. There was no service homogeneity—because of the need for men who knew something about the matters at hand, men were recruited from the Seabees, the Army engineers, the Marines, and several units that had undergone training at Fort Pierce. As noted, Team No. 2 was given to Lt. Comdr. John T. Koehler, and the team was sent to San Diego to join Rear Admiral Connolly's invasion unit scheduled for the Roi and Namur phases of the Marshalls campaign. Team No. 1 remained at Waimanalo under Comdr. E. D. Brewster and then became part of Admiral Turner's Task Force 52 for the attack on Kwajalein.

After the Marshalls campaign, the two UDTs returned to Hawaii. In the critiques that followed, a number of changes were made in the type of explosives and the techniques to be used. The drone boats, which had failed, were sent "back to the drawing board" for rethinking and readjustment. The most important change for future operations was the coming of age of the UDTs when it was established that each unit would have its own ship in the future.

When Lieutenant Commander Koehler returned to Hawaii, he was assigned to prepare a plan for future team organization and the establishment of a training base. The Koehler plan was taken through the Pacific Fleet chain of command, and the resulting revised plan was adopted by the fleet. A major change was the reduction in number of officers employed in a team from sixteen to thirteen and the increase in the number of enlisted men from eighty to eighty-five. The new training base was established on the island of Maui.

Koehler realized that the future of UDT operations lay with swimmers, not trick boat gadgets. He began the study of the use of fins and dive masks, compasses, and mine-detecting devices. A few of the men were familiar with these items, but mostly because they had been scuba divers, and there were few of these in 1943. Only a few face masks could be found in Hawaii shops, but one of the officers spotted an advertisement in a magazine, and a rush order was sent by radio to appropriate the whole stock of the sporting goods store involved. The face masks were flown out to Hawaii on a top secret basis.

Under Koehler as acting commanding officer, the whole UDT swimmer program was begun on Maui.

After the formation of the new hundred-man teams, No. 1 and No. 2, Team No. 3 was formed under Lt. Thomas C. Crist and Team No. 4 under Lt. William Gordon Carberry. They were soon sent to the Solomons Islands to train with the Marine V Amphibious Corps for coming operations.

The UDT men trained and helped build the base around them as they trained. The existence was Spartan, with six men or three officers to a tent. The quarters had neither hot water nor lights. The recreation areas were a bare ball field, and a bare hall where nobody wanted to go because the base commander prohibited smoking. In May 1944 the mess hall burned down, and after that they ate outside with the flies. But there was always the ocean, which became their recreation ground as well as their workplace.

When Lieutenant Commander Kauffman saw what was going on in the Pacific, he began a campaign to get himself assigned to the Pacific Theater and to an action unit. Although he ran into opposition from the Navy system, by April, when a number of his classes had been shipped wholesale to Hawaii, Kauffman managed to get appointed commander of the new Underwater Demolition Team No. 5. Lt. (jg) J. K. deBold was his executive officer.

Kauffman set up his organization of Team No. 5 with one headquarters division and four operations divisions, each consisting of three officers and sixteen men. This became the pattern for the UDTs.

In April Lieutenant Commander Kauffman learned what role the UDT men would play in the Saipan invasion, scheduled for June 1944.

The Marine 2d Division and the Marine 4th Division would land on the west coast of Saipan on the morning of June 15. Before they landed they had to know about the area, and this was the task assigned the UDT: to find out the lay of the water, the beaches, and any enemy obstructions. They knew that from nine hundred to eighteen hundred yards off the invasion beaches lay the barrier reef, with its lagoon inside. The Marine 2d Division was assigned to four beaches, each seven hundred yards long. The Marine 4th Division's beaches started about seven hundred yards south of the 2d's. One entirely new element entered the plan: The UDT men were to make their reconnaissance in broad daylight, and not by boats, as in the previous system, but by swimming.

This word was given to Lieutenant Commander Kauffman by Admiral Turner. Kauffman blanched visibly and predicted 50 percent casualties, but Turner's mind was made up. He knew from the Kwajalein experience that reconnaissance at night was a failure, so it had to be in daylight. This involved a whole new approach to UDT training. It was to employ swimmers, and some of the UDT men did not know how to swim. In the next few weeks they would have to learn and would have to pass a one-mile swimming test to qualify for team operations.

From the meetings of Admiral Turner's planning staff came more responsibility for the UDT. It would be entrusted to make a detailed hydrographic survey of the area. For this, Kauffman came up with a "string system," using fishline with knots at 25-yard intervals, where soundings would be taken.

So the training and the planning went on. The UDT men were assigned to work with destroyers. To train the men, ships were used in simulated operations, including the battleship *California*. Thus the UDT men became used to having a ship's guns firing over their heads as they worked in the water. The training was so intense that it led to an equally intense pride in unit by the UDT men. The first loyalty was in the two-man swimming teams, each man to his buddy, on whose skills his life might depend. Second was to the boat crews and the platoons. The rivalry became so intense between teams that when two UDTs were in port together, liberty was not usually granted to both teams at the same time, after a series of fights had brought out the shore patrols on Maui and in Honolulu.

On May 29, UDT No. 5 got its ship, the old four-stack World War I destroyer *Gilmer,* which had been converted for transport work and was now known as an APD. It was anything but palatial: The quarters were cramped, and the men were jammed in this ship and its sister ship, the USS *Humphreys.* Room for passengers had been created by taking off two of the four stacks and eliminating one fire room of the old destroyers. The result was that eighty bunks were crammed into the new space, four-deep. Their explosives were stowed in special magazines but some of the tetrytol was packed between the deck and the bottom tier of UDT bunks. Everyone said tetrytol was a very stable explosive, but it would burn, and so the smoking lamp was doused in the men's quarters.

The destroyer then set sail for the Marshalls, which would be the jumping-off point of the invasion forces. On the trip across the central Pacific, Lieutenant Commander Kauffman and his staff made plans for all eventualities they could imagine in the forthcoming operations. When they arrived at the Roi and Namur atoll they had two days of practice with amphibious tractors in techniques of blasting their way through coral to establish rampways on the edge of a reef for landing craft, specifically LCMs.

Team No. 5 was assigned to the Marine 2d Division beaches, Red 2, Red 3, Green 1, and Green 2. The line of the coast along the northern three beaches was absolutely straight, but on the fourth beach, Green 2, the coastline jutted out to form the point called Afetna or Susupe. The defenses all along consisted of fire trenches, located just behind the beaches, about ten yards from the waterline, and machine-gun positions forty to fifty yards back. Afetna Point was heavily defended, and so were the hills immediately behind the beaches. Off the beaches the barrier reef, about a hundred to two hundred yards across, came to within eight hundred yards of the waterline at the bottom of Green Beach 2, but was eighteen hundred yards off the Red beaches. Neither the depth of the water over the reef nor the depth of the lagoon were known.

Maj. Gen. Thomas Watson, commander of the Marine 2d Division, had twenty-five questions about the Saipan reef and lagoon, and told Kauffman he did not expect the UDT men to be able to answer 5 percent of them. Kauffman disagreed. He would get the information, he promised.

The team would have fire support from the battleship *California* and the cruiser *Indianapolis.* It would have air support from one of the escort carriers in the area.

The team would have two and a half hours to make its reconnaissance mission on the morning of June 14, which was D-1 day. The mission would begin at nine o'clock in the morning.

Within that time frame they would leave the ship; go in to the beach, four thousand yards away; carry out their tasks; and return.

The missions for the Red beaches and the Green beaches were quite different. Lieutenant Commander Kauffman did not think there would be enough time for the men assigned to the Red beaches to swim in and do a thorough job of reconnaissance. So six advance recon men on the Red beaches were assigned to go in on flying mattresses, to a position three hundred yards offshore and two hundred yards apart. Then they would anchor their flying mattresses—rubber boats with quiet electric motors attached—and start reconnaissance.

Kauffman still expected 50 percent casualties, and made his men memorize the chain of command so they would know who succeeded whom as the officers and noncoms began to fall.

The swimmers would go to the same point, three hundred yards off the beach, and then turn around and return. There were seven pairs of swimmers per platoon, with twelve hundred yards between them. The two men of each pair would remain about twenty-five yards apart, for safety's sake, so that one shell would not kill or injure more than one man. One of the pair would go over the side with a reconnaissance reel, attach the bitter end to the buoy, and anchor at a position. Then he was to start swimming in a straight line perpendicular to the beach, writing down the depth of the water every twenty-five yards and watching for changes in depth, particularly potholes. The second man would come along in zigzag fashion, his principal job being to look for mines and other obstacles. When they reached the three-hundred-yard line, the lineman was to anchor his reel on the bottom, and both men would then swim back, zigzagging.

Since the Green beaches did not seem to warrant so much pains, there would be no advance reconnaissance party, but the swimmers would do it all, going in three hundred yards from the beach. At that point the odd-numbered unit would take all the slates from the even-numbered units, giving the water depths, and swim out with them. The even-numbered unit would then swim in to the beach for reconnaissance. If they were killed by enemy fire, the basic depth information would still thus be safe.

The whole concept of UDT operations had been revolutionized since the Marshalls operation. Swimming was the service. Each man had swim fins, and knew how to use them; swim shoes; swim trunks; a dive mask; gloves and kneepads, a knife and life belt; a first-aid packet; two pencils; and four Plexiglas slates, three inches wide and ten inches long.

Lieutenant Commander Kauffman would oversee all the operations from one of the flying mattresses, and all of the mattress teams had 536 radios, 630 binoculars, and helmets. The executive officer remained on the command ship, and all orders to the team were issued by him or by the CO through him.

Every man of the team participated in some way in this operation. Each landing craft had a boat officer, a UDT coxswain, a coxswain from the destroyer, a machinist from the destroyer, two destroyermen as gunners, and a UDT radioman. The reef edge would be buoyed and marked so that men who would be doing night demolition work on the reef could locate any position along the reef. To help pick up stragglers, a rubber boat was to be sent in to each beach to cruise off the reef. The one-man crew had an outboard motor.

While the UDT was going in, the ships offshore would be firing in support, getting as close to the water on the landward side as they could but not putting any shells into the water.

The swimmers were not to go into the shore, no closer than a hundred yards from the waterline, until sixty minutes after the start. Then they had to be back outside the hundred-yard line by ten-thirty. While they were moving inland, the fire support ships would move their fire inland and make it more intensive. The air support planes were to come in and make strafing runs on the beaches, to keep the Japanese from firing on the UDT men. At eleven-thirty, when all the landing craft returned to the ship, the division officers would bring the information together and make charts, and all the officers were to meet on the *Gilmer* and prepare a joint report for the task force command.

That was the plan.

Here was what happened.

Late in May the three teams (one in reserve) that would go to Saipan loaded up for the voyage. The UDT men had requisitioned all the available waterproof watches and binoculars in Hawaii, and they were being loaded for the voyage when the landing craft carrying them to the *Gilmer* smashed against the dock and sent them to the bottom. Using an Aqua-Lung, Lt. John deBold dove down after them and found the waterproof watches in one package. Most of the binoculars were also recovered.

The advance group arrived off the western coast of Saipan on the morning of June 14. Day dawned, a beautiful day. By eight in the morning they were about five thousand yards off the beach in bright sunlight, under a clear sky, and in a calm sea that made about a two-foot surf at the edge of the reef.

The *Gilmer* was off the northern end of the beach, out about four thousand yards. Suddenly, at about eight forty-five, the Japanese changed the plan. They began firing on the *Gilmer*, straddling her fore and aft, and straddling her port and starboard a moment later. The shell that nearly missed her wounded two of the crew.

At the same time the *California*, the main fire-support ship, took a direct hit in the control tower. This damage diverted captain and crew, and they pulled out to five thousand yards from the beach. The ship's fire efficiency in support of the team thus suffered.

The four landing craft left the *Gilmer* a little before

eight-thirty and fanned out to head for the points where they would begin dropping swimmers. The Japanese mortars began searching for them, but the boats zigzagged and stayed afloat. One landing craft was trailed by twenty-six rounds of mortar fire, all of them close but not too close.

The swimmers were crouched in the open cockpits, wearing cork gloves to protect their hands from the coral, and with face masks and helmets. Each man was flagged with blue paint and was painted from toes to chin and down each arm with stripes of black paint a foot apart. When the boats came within five hundred yards of the reef, they came under Japanese fire. The boats zigzagged wildly, but the officers did not lose their heads, and they all reached the control point.

A buoy was dropped with the first swimmers to mark the point of departure. The first team flopped into the water here. The buoys were spaced a hundred yards apart and dropped over to mark the point where each set of swimmers was released. The boats completed their runs into the beach and then headed out to sea, five hundred to a thousand yards off the reef. There they cruised back and forth along their beaches while the boat officers watched the swimmers, looking for wounded men and returning swimmers. From time to time a landing craft would move in too close for Japanese comfort and the Japanese gunners would fire mortars at it, but the mortars missed.

One or two swimmers came back early, but most of them began to return to the landing craft at about ten forty-five. The boat crews were watching, and as soon as a swimmer was spotted on the reef, the landing craft would zigzag in to pick him up. The pickup was accomplished by throwing a Jacob's ladder over the side of the craft, one on either side, and stopping the landing craft beside the swimmer, who climbed and then was pulled up.

As the swimmers went in toward the beach, the platoon leaders cruised back and forth on their flying mattresses. Immediately it was obvious that these were prime targets for the Japanese.

As Commander Kauffman wrote about the incident:

"The mattresses were the main targets. I got no mortar burst nearer than fifteen yards, but four other mattresses were sunk without scratching the men on them. . . . anchored my mattress three hundred yards from the beach and started in . . . , expecting heavy air support as promised during the half hour while we were attempting to get into the waterline. Not one plane appeared. I got to about a hundred yards from the beach and even with my bad eye I could see Japanese moving around, manning their bloody machine guns. I set up my radio and called for the damned aviators, but quickly closed it up after that one transmission as it secured too much fire."

In rapid succession four of the mattresses were hit by enemy fire. On three of the flying mattresses the crewmen were unhurt, but the mattress ridden by Ens. Bill Running took a shell, which killed S1C Robert Christiansen.

On the way inshore, several of the reconnaissance reels jammed up and some had to be abandoned. Others were patched up on the scene. So, in total, the reel men performed successfully, and this method became the basis for charting.

At ten o'clock the planes from the escort carrier were to deliver an air strike. It never came. The *California*'s fire support was very badly done. Her gunners were so afraid of hitting the UDT men with shells in the water that they put them about five hundred yards inland, way over the heads of the Japanese on the beaches, who could be seen standing firing their rifles and machine guns at the UDT crews.

When Lieutenant Commander Kauffman saw that the fire support was not effective, he tried to stop his men from getting close to the beach, but in spite of his signals, some of the men got in as close as thirty yards from the waterline. One of the dangers to the swimmers was mortar fire, and many mortar rounds went off underwater near swimmers. Six of the team suffered internal injuries from the concussions of near-misses. One man, Harold Hall, was thrown completely out of the water by a mortar shell that exploded beneath him.

As the mission ended, Lieutenant Commander Kauffman looked for missing men. Christiansen was dead, swimmers Root and Heil were missing. They were from Ens. Jack Adams's boat, and he stayed out looking for them until he was recalled by Kauffman.

At twelve-thirty the cruiser reported what might be two men clinging to a buoy about a mile and a half south of where they had swum in. Kauffman headed there with a landing craft. He saw what looked like a man's head and dove off the landing craft and swam along the reef until he saw that it was just a coral outcropping. While he was searching, the crew of the boat found the missing men. Heil's leg had been hurt going in; his buddy had bandaged him and then made his survey as ordered. He picked up Heil on his return and towed him to a buoy several hundred yards at sea, to get him out of the line of Japanese fire.

From the information collected the UDT officers decided they would not have to send men to blast ramps on the beach for the landing craft, because the slope was so gradual that an LCM could ride up on it. Their tanks could get off easily enough.

So that was the initial experience of Team No. 5. UDT No. 7 also participated in this operation at Saipan. Team No. 7 was commanded by Lt. Richard F. Burke. By the time of the operation Lt. Bruce Onderdonk had been made executive officer. The team was aboard the USS *Brooks,* another APD of the World War I four-stack class.

This team was assigned to beaches Blue 1, Blue 2, Yellow 1 and Yellow 2, and Yellow 3.

Team No. 7 had the same negative experience with fire support from the ships that was reported by Team No. 5. Team No. 7 also ran into some barges moored alongside a pier at Blue 1 Beach, which bothered them with heavy mortar and machine-gun fire. As with Team No. 5 there was virtually no support from the carrier planes that were supposed to strafe and bomb the beaches. They simply did not show up.

Team No. 7's executive officer, Bruce Onderdonk, had to survey the channel at Charan Kanoa, where a sugar refinery stood. One of its smokestacks, which survived the bombardment, stood as a landmark for the channel that cut through the reef. A dozen Japanese barges were anchored on the lagoon just south of the channel, and to the rear of the beaches the woods were full of Japanese snipers. Lieutenant Onderdonk ordered mortar fire as his boat went in, dropping buoys as he went. The crew thought that the fire they came under was bad shooting by the American ships, until they learned that no ships were dropping shells in the water. Then they realized that they were under Japanese fire.

The six reconnaissance swimmers, wearing inflatable life belts around their necks and dangling slates, headed into Charan Kanoa, into the heart of the gunfire from the barges and the land beyond. Two of the six men were wounded while in the water, but all of them kept swimming to within fifty or a hundred yards of the beach. Lieutenant Burke called for smoke shells on the beaches and the ships responded, giving the men a protective smoke screen that undoubtedly saved them from further casualties.

Burke's boat was hit while zigzagging away after dropping its swimmers. A Japanese mortar round burst on the craft, blowing the UDT coxswain away from the wheel and killing the ship's gunner and wounding another man. Burke took the boat back to the *Indianapolis* to deliver his casualties and then returned to pick up his swimmers.

One of Team No. 7's boats was so badly shot up by the Japanese that no attempt was made to drop the swimmers. The coxswain was hit in the spine before they reached the reef.

The last Team No. 7 boat, which was Lieutenant Robbins's, dropped his swimmers in spite of fire so heavy that one of the crewmen of the landing craft was hit twice in fifteen minutes. But the swimmers got away safely and did their job.

Because the landing craft were bothered by Japanese fire as they tried to pick up their swimmers, the men of Team No. 7 changed the procedure, and their landing craft did not stop to become a dead-in-the-water target for the Japanese, but trailed a life ring behind them that the swimmer caught as they passed him; he was then dragged into the landing craft.

While the men of Team No. 7 were making their reconnaissance, they saw many Japanese moving along the beaches. Their landing craft opened up on the Japanese with .30-caliber machine guns, and decreased the Japanese fire by doing so. Some of the landing craft were hit on the way in, and some of the men were wounded.

After the operation had ended for the day, at 2:00 P.M. Lieutenant Burke reported to the *Gilmer* to confer with Lieutenant Commander Kauffman and their division officers. They assessed the casualties: one man killed from each team and one from the APD *Brooks*. They drew up a joint dispatch for the brass and took it to Admiral Oldendorf aboard the cruiser *Louisville*. After it was approved, the two commanding officers of the teams spent the whole night making charts for the task force commanders. They had to get their findings in shape for presentation, because the UDT men had discovered several changes that should be made in the invasion plan.

The principal change was to the route the tanks should follow onto the beaches. The route selected before the reconnaissances, Lieutenant Commander Kauffman had found, would have been disastrous, and many tanks would have been lost. But the UDT men had discovered a narrow diagonal path across the reef starting in the middle of Green Beach 2 and ending in the center of Green Beach 1.

On the morning of D-day Lieutenant Commander Kauffman went aboard the *Cambria,* the flagship of Rear Adm. Harry Hill, second in command to Admiral Turner. Ensign Marshall reported to Admiral Turner personally. Ensign Adams reported to Lt. Gen. Howland Smith, the marine commander. Ensign Suhrland reported to the commander of the amphibious tractor force. The big news was that the route chosen by the Marines to cross the reef would lead them into water two feet too deep for the tanks, and they would drown out. When General Watson learned this, and the recommendation that the tank route be changed, he blew up at Lieutenant Commander Kauffman.

"Are you the man who's been ordering my tanks around? Whose tanks do you think they are?" He finally agreed to the changed landing plan, which put the tanks on his right instead of his left, as he had wanted them to be. But he warned that if every tank wasn't ashore by noon or that if any tank drowned out on the new UDT route, Kauffman would either be court-martialed or shot by the Marines.

At H-hour, as the Marines began to move, the UDT men were right there with them. They rode in the control landing craft to give advice and to worry lest somehow they had been wrong.

The landings began. The barrage pounded the shore and then began moving up toward the hill and steep slopes. The tanks moved in toward Susupe Point, and Team No. 7's officers guided the fifty-foot tank landing craft onto the shelving reef the UDT men had found. The landing craft dropped their ramps. The tanks rolled out and splashed through shallow water to move rapidly toward the Japanese trenchline.

Farther north, Ensign Adams led the way for the tanks across the disputed new route in an open amtrac, followed by Lieutenant Commander Kauffman in another, with marking buoys and anchors they installed to show the route. The first coxswain of a tank landing craft was skeptical about the whole operation, but he was ordered by the Marine liaison officer to ram the landing craft full speed ahead; he did so, landing high and dry on the reef. The ramp dropped, the tanks crawled out, and the first one followed the two amtracs across the slanting path that moved across the lagoon bottom. Japanese mortars began firing. They did not hit the tank, but they did hit Adams's amtrac several times. Kauffman's amtrac, which stopped several times to drop buoys, took a direct hit, but the shell did not hurt anybody.

Aboard that stranded LCT on the reef, the crew clung to their vessel, although it was immobile and under Japanese fire. Finally a UDT man swam to the stranded LCT, tied ropes around the crewmen, and pulled them off through the surf to be rescued in spite of themselves.

The other LCTs began to land and discharge their lumbering cargoes. They moved slowly across the reef to support the Marine infantry, who were having hard going in some places.

Lieutenant Commander Kauffman was called by the beachmaster to come for a consultation on the beachhead, and he and Lieutenant Leslie, the Marine liaison officer, hailed a passing amtrac, which took them in. They were dressed in swimming trunks, light blue canvas shoes, and still had the stripes around torsos, arms, and legs that were used to measure water depths. As they came up, a Marine looked out of his foxhole.

"By God, I've seen everything. We ain't even got the beach yet and the tourists are here already."

But in a moment the "tourists" were in foxholes, too, diving in as they became aware of the Japanese rifle fire aimed at them. They came up for air, then slunk along the beach, keeping as low a profile as possible, until they found the beach commander.

The beachmaster wanted Kauffman to begin blasting a channel through the reef for his deeper water vessels to bring in supplies. But D-day was not the time for it. The amtracs were keeping up a shuttle service, bringing men and supplies to the beachhead. There was no time for blasting.

The unloading went on until dark and later. That night Lieutenant Burke and seven of his men installed flashing buoys at the entrance to the Charan Kanoa boat channel, and the amtracs continued to come in.

That night of D-day, the *Gilmer* was inadvertently listed as a defending destroyer and put on the outer screen of ships of the force. She was attacked by five Japanese assault craft. She was hit eight times by shells from the Japanese boats, but sank four of them; a destroyer sank the other one. This engagement, for which Comdr. Jack Horner of the *Gilmer* received the Silver Star, was called the Battle of Marpi Point.

At dawn of D+1 the lookout of the *Gilmer* spotted Japanese survivors of the boats still in the water and set out to rescue the enemy sailors. The first Japanese fought against being rescued but was hit on the head with a boat hook, rendered unconscious, and rescued in defiance of *bushido*. The others then followed meekly into captivity.

That day the UDTs were turned over to Capt. Carl Anderson, the beach commander. Anderson was just over five feet tall, and was privately called Mr. Five-by-Five. On the beach he was a tiger, his high-pitched voice never running out of invectives, and completely visible to the Japanese, with his dirty baseball cap and chest barely hid den by a Marine shirt; the pant legs of his combat trousers he had torn off at the knee, and he wore shined black shoes, black socks, and garters. He had gotten into the beachmaster trade in the Aleutians and had stayed with Adm. Harry Hill ever since, using his Alaska sourdough's savvy to run the beaches as he had run fish canneries in Alaska before the war.

In his squeaky voice he outlined the job he wanted the UDT men to do for him: Blow channels through the barrier reef, as many channels as possible. So they began with their explosive packs, blowing the coral to smithereens and making the way for the speedup of the trucks and tanks and infantry that were needed to subdue the island.

The need was real. The Marines ran into serious trouble on Saipan, and soon—too soon—they were calling for their reserves, and the Army 27th Division came ashore to join the fighting. Because of the difficulties the scheduled invasions of Tinian and Guam were postponed, and thus UDT No. 6 also became available for the beachwork at Saipan. By June 20 (D+5) the southern beaches of Saipan were sufficiently cleared of Japanese to permit building ramps. Beachmaster Anderson wanted these for the LSTs, and Team No. 6 was assigned the job, which took four days to complete. Part of the time they were under sniper fire from the Japanese.

On the beaches the Navy found antipersonnel and antiboat mines all piled up and ready for installation. The Japanese had just not had time to perfect their defenses, but here was a warning for the future—for at Magicinne Bay on the eastern coast, where the Japanese apparently assumed the Americans would land, the offshore defenses, mines, and obstacles were in place.

Four men from Team No. 5 disappeared during the next few days and were put down as missing in action. But sometime later they were returned by a chagrined Marine officer, who said they had been up front with his troops fighting and doing their demolition work against pillboxes and other hiding places.

Kauffman then had to resolve the problem of discipline. Many of his men had wanted to do the same, but had obeyed orders to stay put, and these men had not. He gave them their choice: They could be dropped from the team for misconduct, or they could go on the burial detail. They chose the unpleasant latter, as a relief from real punishment. For to a UDT man of the time, the demolition team was everything, as the SEAL organization was to become to a later generation. After three days of handling stinking, rotten bodies they were ready to change their minds, but Kauffman decided they had been punished enough, and took them back onto the team. He needed them for the coming invasion of Tinian.

The beachmaster's chores were completed on D+12. They had included a detailed hydrographic chart of the area and the charting of a boat pool off Beach Green 3. The following day they made some experiments with the Japanese mines they had found and decided on the best method of exploding the next ones they saw underwater with a half-pound block of explosive. On D+14 Lieutenant Commander Kauffman was ordered to make an aerial survey of the beaches of Tinian for Admiral Turner, for that was to be the next job for the UDT and the fleet: the invasion of Tinian.

5   Marianas, Round Two: Tinian

〽〽〽〽 The fighting on Saipan had been so
〽〽〽〽 much more demanding than expected
that once the island was secure, the Ma-
rines looked anxiously over at Tinian, just two miles away
across a channel that separates the islands. The island
itself is fifteen miles long and two miles across. On the
northwestern side lie two small beaches, called by the
Americans Beach White 1 and Beach White 2, separated
by about twelve hundred yards. The best beaches were
the Red, Green, and Blue beaches, on the southern end
of the island, near Tinian Town. But the problem here
was that the beaches were so close to the town, the Marines would be involved in street fighting almost immediately after landing, with no time to consolidate. Further,
there was high ground on both sides of the beaches,
which offered the Japanese excellent defensive positions.

The plus side of landing at Tinian Town was the
prospect of securing swiftly the good harbor available
there. But the minus side, which the Marines found more
impressive, involved the high losses they could expect on
this terrain, based on their experience on Saipan. So the
tilt was toward the northwestern beaches. The terrain
there was not nearly so hilly, not so advantageous for the
defenders. In addition, the American artillery sited on
Saipan could cover the northwestern landings.

But the northwestern beaches also had their minus
side. They were very small. White 1 was only sixty yards
wide, and White 2 was only twice as wide as that. From
the aerial reconnaissance photos the beach conditions
seemed less than ideal—the reef seemed to drop sharply,
to make it impossible to use the beaches for landing craft.

Immediately behind the beach the land was covered with trees and bushes, so it was impossible to tell if the exits from the beaches were wet or dry or even usable.

As the commanders of the invasion forces, Admirals Spruance, Turner, Hill, and General Smith—conferred over these matters, Lieutenant Commander Kauffman sat in on most of the meetings. As the meetings continued, Kauffman suspected that Team No. 5 would be asked to make a night reconnaissance of the Tinian situation, so he told his executive officer and others to start drawing up plans for a night mission.

It happened on July 7. On that day the command ordered Team No. 5 to conduct a night mission on July 14 in connection with the Marine Reconnaissance Battalion. They were to check out Beach White 1 and Beach White 2. The UDT men would reconnoiter the approaches to the beaches, and the Marines would check the beach exits.

On July 9 Lieutenant Commander Kauffman went to see Capt. J. Jones, the commander of the Marine Reconnaissance Battalion. Realizing that they employed different methods, they decided to hold a rehearsal the next night in Magicienne Bay. It was arranged that Marine guards would simulate Japanese, and engineers laid mines on the beaches to see if the UDT men would locate them.

The idea was good.

The UDT men could not have asked for better weather conditions for the rehearsal than they had on the evening of July 10. The sky was clear and the water quiet. Four UDT officers and eight men, led by Lieutenant Commander Kauffman, participated in the UDT side of the practice.

The first problem occurred when the *Gilmer*'s radio and gyro went out of service. So the swimmers had to be guided by flashlight. Previous research had indicated that the men could expect a current of about a half knot, running south, just off the coast. But in fact the current ran north.

The men got into their rubber boats and proceeded according to the information they had to carry out the plan. The first group headed north, for its position five hundred yards off White Beach 1. The second group headed south, for its position off Beach White 2.

As they neared their positions, a light fog came in, and in the misleading light the boats went in too close. The first group never did find its beach, and when the second group got to Beach White 2 they thought they were in the wrong place. They did, however, make their beach reconnaissance, but when they started back, because of the current going the wrong way, many swimmers missed their boats. It was four-thirty in the morning before all the swimmers were rounded up and retrieved.

In the critique that followed it was discovered that the second group had indeed reconnoitered the wrong beach and the first group had gotten lost. Of course, Admiral Hill and Gen. Howland Smith learned about the disastrous rehearsal, and they decided that a reconnaissance should be made on Beach White 2 on Tinian, and that only. The APD *Stringham* was used for guidance into shore, using its radar. Two boatloads of men moved in and went into the water a hundred yards north of the Japanese beach. That night the Japanese were working on defenses down on the beach itself, setting mines just twenty yards from the water, and several of the swimmers had narrow escapes from disclosure. Still, by 3:30 A.M. all were safely back in their boats.

The high command decided, on the basis of what had been learned, that the landing would be made on the White beaches. On July 13, Admiral Hill requested Team No. 5 to go in with enough explosives on the night before the landings, blow up all the mines, and ramp the beaches.

Lieutenant Commander Kauffman did not like the

idea. Mines only twenty feet from the beach meant plenty of trouble, and he protested that the danger to the swimmers was too great. Admiral Hill was adamant: They must give it a try, he said.

So for the next week the UDT men considered their problems. The biggest problem was how to get the explosive to shore. They decided to lash a thousand pounds of explosive to a long tube and to load up a rubber boat with another thousand pounds. These conveyers were to be towed to shore by a swimmer.

Ensigns Suhrland and Adams worried about a method to deal with the mines. They would fix half-pound blocks of TNT to each mine and then hook them all together with primacord. Each circuit would be attached to the main ramping charge.

So when D–1 night came, the night before the invasion, on July 23, the men of the UDT felt they were ready for their difficult assignment. It was a rough night on the Tinian shore, with heavy seas lashing the surf and squalls whipping the water. The result was that the swimmers could not get in close before they had to go into the water. The going was slow, and it was not until 11:00 P.M. that the landing craft reached a point two thousand yards off the beach and the rubber boats were put in the water. A squall scattered the boats like matchsticks. Nothing went right, and at 2:30 A.M. Lieutenant Commander Kauffman ordered the explosives jettisoned. All they could do now was make a final reconnaissance of the beach.

Next day, when the marines went in, there were only five casualties on the beaches because the Japanese had not expected the landing there. So without really accomplishing the mission, the UDT men had lucked out. A few days later, the men of Team No. 5 were on their way back to Maui.

UDT No. 7 also participated in the Tinian invasion. The team was transferred to the APD *Stringham* on June

22 and on July 10 made a reconnaissance of the Yellow beaches along the northeastern coast of Tinian with the 5th Amphibious Reconnaissance Battalion of the Marines.

They went in with Captain Jones's battalion. Jones and Lieutenant Burke were warned not to alert the Japanese on the beaches with this maneuver lest they arouse them and make life more difficult for the early waves of invading troops. Burke gave orders to his swimmers that if any signs of alert were observed, they must clear out as quickly and as silently as possible. The rubber boats had reached a point only about five hundred yards from the beach when shots were fired, so they turned about, and all the swimmers in the water were recovered; they returned to their APD. The Marines, however, finished their mission on the beach and retired without seeing any enemy.

The invasion came off on schedule and proved much easier than the fighting on Saipan. UDT No. 7's main operation came on July 23. It was a diversionary daylight reconnaissance of a barrier reef off Red, Green, and Blue beaches. The distance involved in the work was twenty-five hundred yards of beach and reef just off Sunharin Town. The idea was to make the Japanese believe that this would be the site of the major landings scheduled for the following day.

Three landing craft were employed in the mission. Each of them dropped seven swimmers; a fourth, standby boat had seven more swimmers aboard to be used in case of trouble.

The preliminary gunfire was excellent and eliminated all but sniper fire against the swimmers, and there were only three shots by snipers in the whole operation.

The swimmers found that the barrier reef extended from the beach out five hundred to a thousand yards. Since it was only a feint, the swimmers were ordered to go no closer to shore than the edge of the reef. They had been shown aerial photos that indicated one natural channel through the reef and another possible small-boat channel, but when they got into the water, they found that the small-boat channel really did not exist and was a product of photo misinterpretation. The reef was flat, with a smooth top, and would offer no obstruction to the passage of LVTs and amtracs. The Japanese had done nothing about presenting underwater obstacles, and no mines were found in the forty-five minutes of observation. Nor were any casualties suffered.

On D-day, Team No. 7 was put to work searching for antiboat mines off the reefs fringing beaches White 1 and 2. No mines were found, but some unexploded rockets and bombs delivered by the American forces were removed from the area lest they go up in the faces of the troops. When the swimmers hit the shore they encountered machine-gun fire but suffered no casualties.

On D+1 and D+2 the UDT men placed pontoons on the beaches and carried out some necessary beach demolition.

After Tinian, Team No. 7 did not get sent back to the United States, as many of the men had hoped. A few men were transferred to Team No. 5 and sent to Maui, but the team itself was taken to Turner City on Florida Island in the Solomons, just across the sound from Guadalcanal. They arrived on August 24, 1944, and were scheduled to go into training for the Peleliu operation in the Palaus, but the climate in the Solomons did not lend itself to UDT operational work, and so on September 6 the *Stringham* picked up the team and took them to Manus Island, where the task force for Peleliu was assembling.

6 Guam

~~~~ Guam, which the Americans knew was
~~~~ going to be stoutly defended by the Japanese, was to be taken by Rear Adm.
Richard Connolly's Southern Attack Force. The troops
would be the men of the Marine 3d Division and the 1st
Provisional Brigade. One reason for the delay in taking
Guam was that the Army 27th Division had been committed to the battle at Saipan, and a new Army division had
to be brought to Guam, to be held in reserve for the
fighting there.

Admiral Connolly's task force arrived off Guam on
July 14, 1944, and with it came Underwater Demolition
Team No. 3, with Lt. Thomas Crist in command. For
three nights the men of the UDT reconnoitered the attack beaches and other areas that might possibly be sub-
stituted. They were operating from the APD *Dickerson,*
supported by the destroyers *Dewey* and *MacDonald.* On
the fourteenth the first mission was to reconnoiter two
thousand yards of Asan Beach and make a diversionary
reconnaissance of Agana Beach. That night the UDT
men swam into all four Asan beaches to the high-water
mark. At eleven o'clock that night one of the rubber
boats was fired upon several times by Japanese machine
gunners, and three of the swimmers were missing at the
end of the confrontation. Search was made, but at a few
minutes after midnight they were given up as lost and the
boats withdrew. But just after dawn on July 15 the *Mac-
Donald* picked up all three men, who were suffering
slightly from exposure. They told their story. They had
been going about the work when the firing began. The
Japanese fire and the return American fire both had
menaced them, and they had been forced to leave the

edge of the reef. They swam out to sea, and kept swimming for five hours until picked up only slightly the worse for their long swim.

Later on July 15 the UDT men made a daylight reconnaissance of Dadi Beach. Their LCI came under heavy fire from the Japanese on Orote Peninsula, and the battleship *Pennsylvania* came in and silenced the enemy artillery that had been firing on the boat, but not before the LCI was hit, causing five casualties.

The team also made a reconnaissance of the Agat beaches and a beach between Facpi Point and Bangi Point. On this mission CWO R. A. Blowers was killed by enemy fire when his landing craft grounded on a coral head.

On that night of July 15 Team No. 3 made a night reconnaissance of the Agat beaches—or tried to, but heavy rain and extreme darkness that night prevented the landing craft control from getting on station, and the men in the rubber boats could not find their beaches, so after three hours the operation was canceled.

On July 16 Team No. 3 made a diversionary reconnaissance of Tumon Bay. On the night of the seventeenth they began to remove the underwater obstacles the Japanese had been building. The Japanese had just started this program recently, putting together coral obstacles, most of them made with wire nets and piled-up coral. The obstacles ran out as far as three hundred yards from the high-water mark along the reef and were completely exposed at low tide. They were three to five feet in diameter, three to four feet high, and about eight feet apart. While the UDT men were working, one of the LCIs that had just joined the operation went aground, and the divers had to spend several hours removing the men from the vessel. Still, they managed to take out 120 obstacles on the Asan beaches with twenty-four hundred pounds of tetrytol.

On July 17 UDT No. 4 also began working in the Guam Beach area. These men had quite a time getting to Guam. For a time at the height of the Saipan battle, the members of the team thought they would never get there. Their ship took them to Eniwetok, then toward the Marianas with the task force. But their ship, the APD *Talbot*, collided with the battleship *Pennsylvania* at sea and had to go back to the Marshalls for repairs. Then after bombarding Guam, the bombardment vessels moved to Saipan, and there the men of Team No. 4 waited. They waited so long they were sent back to the Marshalls for practice, based on what had been learned in the early days of the Saipan operation. Still, the Japanese stubbornly resisted on Saipan, so it was July 16 before Team No. 4 arrived off Guam.

Underwater Demolition Team No. 4 had been formed in Maui in March 1944 from men trained at Fort Pierce and men from Team Nos. 1 and 2. Lt. W. G. Carberry was commanding officer; his executive officer was Lt. (jg) W. F. Downes. In mid-April the team was sent to Guadalcanal and then to Florida Island, where it trained in advanced maneuvers for seventeen days aboard the *Talbot*. They had more advanced training and practice than any other team yet.

At three o'clock on July 17 two platoons of the team carried out a reconnaissance mission on Beach Yellow 2, and here the team found various obstacles devised by the Japanese. Most of them were either coral-filled cribs built with palm logs and filled with coral debris, or barbed-wire entanglements. On the basis of the reconnaissance, a demolition mission was scheduled for that night, and the platoons went back into the water at 9:00 P.M. and swam to the area near the beach. They could hear the Japanese on the beach talking as they went about their work, but no contact was made, and by 2:30 A.M. all the men were back aboard the *Talbot* and all was secure.

On July 18 Team No. 4 looked over the White Beach area, while Team No. 3 removed obstacles on the Asan beaches, using three thousand pounds of tetrytol to remove 150 obstacles. Team No. 4 spent that day and the next blasting obstacles and coral heads on its beaches to make channels for the landing craft and buoying them for the landing craft coxswains. Six LCIs and a destroyer, cruiser, and battleship stood by to fire on the beaches. The men looked for mines but found none. As a joke they put up a sign, "Welcome Marines," which the Marines encountered as they landed in the first combat wave on July 21. The photograph, when it appeared in American newspapers, created a happy sensation.

The team made charts of the channels, beaches, water depths, buoys, and improvements, and sent the charts to the command ship, where they were photographed; copies were sent around to the transports for the edification of the Marines.

During the four days just before the invasion, the men of Team No. 3 removed 620 obstacles. It was demanding and dangerous work. A platoon of two or three officers and fifteen men would leave the APD in an LCPR, towing two rubber boats loaded with thirty packs of tetrytol. As the landing craft approached the reef, the boats would be cast off, with five or six men in each boat. They paddled or dragged the boats as close to the obstacles as possible and ran a primacord line along the length of the obstacles to be removed, tying in one pack of tetrytol to each obstacle. When all obstacles had been loaded, the men got back into the boats, the firing signal was given, and the fuse was pulled.

Sometimes the underwater obstacles were less than 50 yards from the shore and the reef was dry, which meant the men had to run across the exposed reef for as much as 150 yards, carrying the forty-pound powder packs, to get at the obstacles. They were very efficient in the work, taking an average of sixteen minutes to pack and prepare thirty obstacles and fire the shot.

When D-day came on July 21, the men of UDT No. 3 were on the edge of their reef to guide in the eighth wave, which was made up of LCMs carrying tanks. The UDT men then reported to the beachmaster and were available all day, but there was no call for demolition work.

On their beaches, the men of Team No. 4 led the landing waves ashore, acting as pilots for LCTs and LSTs. Ens. T. D. Nixon was killed by a sniper while doing this work. He was the only UDT casualty of the day. The team blew a channel that day off Yellow Beach in front of Ogat Village, a large enough channel to accommodate LSTs. Later in the day the men also cleared a section of the beach near Ogat Village.

UDT No. 3 worked under the beachmaster on the Green and Red beaches, marking places for LSTs, removing a handful of antiboat mines, and marking channels. They found eight sunken barges and sampans blocking Piti Channel and blew them away.

On the invasion day, members of both teams were occupied marking the beaching places and enlarging facilities. Team No. 3 blasted a two-hundred-foot unloading slot in the reef at Dadi Beach. The work done, UDT No. 3 was then released and sent back to Manus.

On July 23 UDT No. 4 left Guam as well, then went to Saipan and then to Eniwetok and prepared for the landings in the Palaus.

There was nothing more for the UDT men to do on Guam, but plenty for the Marines, for the Japanese resistance was stubborn and long. The island was declared secure on August 10, but at least nine thousand Japanese troops were still loose in the jungle, and sporadic raids and fighting continued until the end of the war. After the emperor's broadcast of surrender on August 15, Japanese began to give themselves up, and on September 4, a lieutenant colonel and 113 officers and men were induced to surrender, but many more lingered in the jungle, many of them to die of starvation and a few to give themselves up later.

7   Stingrays in the South of France

After the disastrous experience with the Stingrays, or drone boats, in the Marshall invasion, their use might have ended except that Admiral Turner learned afterward that the basic reason (he thought) for the failure of the drones was the allocation of old, tired, and leaky landing craft to the task by an overzealous supply officer who did not want to risk any of his good boats on such a "damn-fool" experiment. That officer got a royal chewing out from the admiral personally for his usurpation of authority, and Turner kept the Stingray concept in the back of his mind.

But where the Stingrays got their next baptism of fire was in the invasion of southern France on August 15, 1944. Meanwhile, in Europe and the Pacific, UDTs were experimenting with other devices. One was the Reddy Fox, a giant tube filled with explosives for reef work. It was actually an elongated warhead attached to a torpedo. When it hit the reef, it was explained, it would explode. The charge was so large it would blow a large gap in the reef.

The one problem was that the giant torpedo was uncontrollable insofar as depth was concerned in anything but the calmest of water. It might porpoise and then dive back in, going straight to the bottom, where it would explode with an enormous geyser. Or it might hit a rock on the way to the reef and explode prematurely.

The Reddy Foxes that did manage to make the reef would sometimes be deflected upward, leaping over the reef and exploding on the other side; sticking on the reef and causing another obstruction in themselves and a very dangerous one; or stranding themselves on the beach, where again they were an obstruction to the troops. And finally, when the Reddy Fox was modified and worked over and developed to the point that it would hit the reef and explode properly, it was discovered that the size of the hole it blew was disappointing.

So Reddy Fox was dropped from the list of UDT weapons.

Another invention of the UDT men was the "woofus boat," a landing craft loaded with rockets that were aimed down at the reefs. It was spectacular in operation, one rocket after another going off with an enormous whoosh, but the results were not worthwhile. So the "woofus boat" also was discarded.

But the Stingray got a new chance. The operation began at Salerno on the Italian coast, where the UDT men were training for the invasion of southern France. The new version of the Stingray was called the Apex boat. A number of them were assembled at Salerno, and crews to maintain and operate them were flown in from the United States.

The Apex boats had to be an improvement of the old Stingray because the defenses on the French coasts were much more sophisticated than the coral reefs and coral traps of the Japanese. There were Belgian gates and concrete caissons and other steel and concrete structures. So two different sizes of drone boats were to be used in the assault. The smaller ones were called males, and each would carry a ton of high explosives sent in first to blow small gaps in the defenses.

Once these males had breached the defenses, the female drones, each filled with four tons of explosives, would be sent in to widen the gaps. The landings were scheduled to take place between the cities of Cannes and Toulon. On the west flank or left were the most heavily protected beaches, where rows of large concrete tetrahedrons had been installed, and, as was the German fashion, each installation was studded with mines. Here the Americans planned to use the largest concentration of drone boats, six males and eighteen females. But now the bugaboo of extreme secrecy raised its head. The UDT men were told that they must practice with six male drones and eighteen females but were not told where they were to be used, or anything about the water in the area or the beaches. The team was given a beach area outside Salerno and practiced running the drones right up onto the beach. All this was in plain sight, but when the UDT men asked questions, they were told that everything was secret and that they must observe security. Apparently, what everybody could see was not important. Nor was it important that the men have some correlation between their weapons and the target they were going to use them against. It was all ridiculous because security was so lax that the Germans knew the Allied landing plans down to the dates and the precise beaches on which they would land.

So the UDT men trained and also made preparations to use traditional swimmer control of the beach obstacles if the drones failed.

Early in August the drones were packed up, filled with explosives, and moved to the ships that would take them to the invasion beaches. The UDT men boarded their vessels and by August 14 were nearly in place. At 2:00 A.M. on August 15 the invasion fleet was in position off the coast of France. The aerial bombing and naval shelling began, and the paratroops who would lead the way were in the air. When the naval and aerial bombardment began, the drones were sent into the beaches in waves two hours before the landings would begin.

On the left, in front of Cavalaire Bay, six male drones were sent in, followed by eighteen female drones. The six male drones appeared to detonate in their assigned positions. Of the females, which were then released, fifteen exploded at least close to their assigned areas, and from the debris and excitement in the water it appeared that they had opened up the beaches. Two of the female drones refused to explode, and a submarine chaser was sent to chase them and detonate them.

The last female drone malfunctioned completely. It went into full throttle and began moving in one direction, then shifting to another. In the attempts to blow it up, the gunners on the control craft were firing in all directions, and on their fellows. Finally the drone charged in the direction of the subchaser and exploded so close to it that the subchaser was put out of action for the rest of the invasion.

The UDT men moved in for an examination of the landing area. The drones had not done what they were supposed to, they discovered. So the UDT men went in then and began placing their charges by hand and blasting the obstacles to the landings out of the way.

On the left flank a large antisubmarine net blocked the entrance to Agay Cove. Lt. Edward Clayton led in two small groups of men in high-speed boats. They got into the water and placed hand charges along the net, all the while under fire from the Germans, but the groups finished the job and blew the net apart.

In front of the town of St. Raphael the beach was blockaded by concrete and steel tetrahedrons, all of them mined. Rear Adm. Spencer Lewis, who was in charge of this sector of the assault, ordered in the drones to blow them up, so four male drones and twelve female drones went in toward the beach. But as they got to the point where control of the drones would be remote, the German 88's began opening up in a pattern that indicated they would soon blow the whole flotilla out of the water, so the effort was abandoned.

The invasion in this sector was in trouble. The men milling about in the boats behind the starting line could not head into the beaches until the obstacles had been removed. The drone plan had failed, and the landing craft were still milling about, while the bombardment vess sels carried out their bombardment of the beaches. With the softening of the 88mm fire, the drones were turned back toward their mission, but the 88mm shelling began again. At one thousand yards out the drones were set to operate on remote control by the command vessels. This time the fire from the German guns did not stop them.

At the eight-hundred-yard mark the men aboard the command vessels found that their drones were not responding to signals. The drones began to weave around. One female did a 180-degree turn and headed back toward the assault craft. The command landing craft raced after the drone; two men leaped aboard and disconnected the firing devices and put the drone under manual control.

No one could control the drones electronically; the system had gone haywire. Three drones arrived in the vicinity of the target areas and were blown up, but they did not clear a path. Two drones ended up on the landing beach with their propellers still turning. All attempts to detonate them failed. Another female drone turned about and headed for the ships and had to be boarded and controlled. One drone exploded on the beach, but the rest raced crazily around the landing area.

The whole invasion had to be put on hold while the drones were dealt with. No one could bring a landing force in through such confusion. In the end the St. Raphael landing was canceled altogether, and Admiral Lewis took his landing force to the east, where a beach had been opened without the use of demolition. So the force withdrew and the admiral told the UDT men that they should also withdraw and leave the circling drones to the enemy gunners.

So the UDT men withdrew, and the landings came off on the other beaches. But the drones had had their second chance and failed. From this point on, east and west, they were not wanted anymore.

〰〰〰〰
〰〰〰〰 The summer of 1944 marked several turning points for the Underwater Demolition Teams. One of these was the result of a conference between Admiral Nimitz and Maj. Gen. William Donovan, the director of the supersecret Office of Strategic Services, a combination of intelligence and direct-action operations that predated the CIA. When the two met in the middle of 1944, Donovan offered Nimitz his OSS Maritime Unit, under the command of Lt. Arthur Choate.

The training of these men had been far superior in many ways to that of the Underwater Demolition Teams. The former had been made skilled in raiding techniques as well as underwater work and land and sea sabotage. Their familiarity with weapons was superior, they had been to parachute school, they knew unarmed combat. They were much more like the Navy SEALs would be than the UDT men were then.

One of the OSS unit's skills, at the time unmatched by the UDT men, was in the use of swim fins and scuba equipment. The UDT men had tried swim fins, but not really successfully, since no one seemed to know how to use them properly until the OSS came along. In the summer of 1944, twenty-one enlisted men and five officers from the OSS joined the UDT school at Maui, and they were amalgamated into UDT No. 10 with the graduates of the Fort Pierce Class 6A. In June, when the two units arrived at Maui, Lieutenant Choate became the commanding officer of Team No. 10.

The OSS first contribution to underwater work was to change the attitude of the teams toward swim fins and to teach the UDT men how to use them, not only for swimming but also for scrambling about on coral and the beaches. All this was new to the UDTs, which at that time were still either swimming barefoot or with sneakers. Soon Commander Koehler, the CO of the Maui school, had an order out for every pair of swim fins in Hawaii and on the mainland as well. There weren't nearly enough available, and manufacturers had to be contacted and secret orders given for fins. But they started coming in, and eventually all of the UDTs would be equipped with the fins and would know how to use them.

The success of the Underwater Demolition Teams in the Marianas campaign opened a new era in amphibious warfare. When Admirals Turner and Spruance and General Smith returned from the Marianas, they recognized the continuing need for underwater reconnaissance and removal of barriers, and they recommended establishment of a centralized command. This recommendation was accepted by Admirals Nimitz and King, and in November 1944 Capt. B. Hall Hanlon was appointed first commander of Underwater Demolition Teams under the Amphibious Command, with a staff of fourteen officers and twenty-one men. The *Gilmer* became their flagship. But before the UDT command began functioning, two more major amphibious assaults were carried out, both with the use of Underwater Demolition Teams.

The first of these involved the Palau Islands. The Pacific Fleet and the Joint Chiefs of Staff had agreed that the Palau invasion would be necessary as a stage in the return to the Philippines. When Adm. William F. Halsey came out in September to these waters with the Third Fleet, he soon discovered that the Japanese air strength in the southern Philippines had been highly overestimated and that his carrier planes had almost finished the job of whittling it down in a few days. He recommended cancellation of the Palau invasion and the invasion of Yap. The Yap operation was canceled, but by the time Admiral Nimitz had digested Admiral Halsey's recommendation about the islands of Angaur and Peleliu in the Palaus, it was late, and the invasion fleet was already at sea. Nimitz decided to let the invasion go ahead, although it was not really necessary.

One of the problems with the Palaus was the paucity of American information about these islands. In March 1944 the fast carrier force had made some attacks on the Palaus, mainly to get photographic information. And in the summer it was seen that more details were needed, and the Pacific Fleet decided to send a mission to investigate. The findings were emphasized by aerial photographs that seemed to indicate that the Japanese were building underwater defenses on Yap and in the Palaus. So Team No. 10 was chosen for a mission to the area. Five members of the team, along with CPO Howard Reeder and five specialists from the Amphibious Operating Base at Waipio, Hawaii, were assigned to the task. The senior officer was Lt. Comdr. C. E. Kirkpatrick, and the other officer in the five-man group was Lt. M. R. Massey. The reconnaissance mission would be led by Chief Reeder, and he was thoroughly briefed on it by Navy intelligence.

This intelligence mission was regarded as so "spooky" that special pains were taken to brief the men involved about what to do if captured by the Japanese. If that happened, they were told they would be made to talk. They were to save themselves by telling the Japanese that they were UDT men and that the tactics had just been changed and that all UDT missions hereafter would be conducted by submarine. That should pull the enemy teeth and not give away the extreme importance attached to this particular mission by ONI.

They all went aboard the submarine *Burrfish,* and on July 9, 1944, that submarine slipped out of Pearl Harbor and went to sea. For three days and nights the *Burrfish* moved through the safe waters of the American Pacific at seventeen knots, on the surface. But on the morning of the fourth day she submerged. They traveled underwater then by day, surfacing at night to charge batteries. Early in August the submarine reached the operating area around the Palaus and Yap. At about this time the submarine's air conditioning went out, and conditions in the boat became almost intolerable. One of the OSS men knew a lot about submarines and suggested that the problem was on the outside of the boat, in one of the sea valves. He offered to dive down with mask and fins and make the repairs, and the skipper took him up on the offer. The next night at midnight, the *Burrfish* surfaced and the diver went down on the outside and soon had the trouble fixed. But then contact was made, and everyone on deck scurried below. The submarine dived and soon was being depth-charged by a Japanese subchaser. For the rest of the night the submarine worked to elude the Japanese sonar, but the Japanese were very persistent and in the morning sent air patrols with depth bombs that continued to harry the *Burrfish*. She did not escape the danger until the second night.

After a day of rest for the crew following that experience, the *Burrfish* headed for Peleliu.

The submarine reached the island late in the afternoon and settled on the bottom to wait for darkness. The first reconnaissance would be conducted that night, when they were sure there was no enemy on top of them. Chief Reeder and three of his men would swim in, and Chief Ball of the Amphibious Operations Base would man the inflatable boat, which he had much experience in doing.

The UDT men covered themselves with a silver-blue grease, and Chief Ball and his men got the inflatable boat ready on the deck of the submarine. The UDT men went on deck, and on a signal from Chief Ball, the skipper of the submarine took it down, and the inflatable boat and the men were left on the surface. The men paddled the boat away, and the submarine stayed underwater to conduct periscope survey at intervals for the boat's return.

Chief Ball took the boat to within two hundred yards of the shore, and the four swimmers went into the water. They swam along the beach for two hours, in a grid pattern. When they had covered the assigned area, they returned to the boat and Chief Ball. Ball, then, by dead reckoning, took the boat out to sea again and to the position where the *Burrfish* was waiting. In a few minutes the periscope sweep revealed the boat; the submarine surfaced and took the boat and men aboard. The skipper took the submarine down again and moved away from the island as Chief Reeder gave his report to Lieutenant Commander Kirkpatrick. The area was alive with underwater obstacles, he said. The Japanese obviously expected visitors and were preparing for them. He reported on wire entanglements and cribs full of coral linked together with steel cables and coconut logs. The submarine surfaced again before dawn, and the radio report went to Pearl Harbor.

The next night the *Burrfish* started again for the island, but a contact forced her to abandon the attempt and seek the safety of deep water. Next morning the *Burrfish* came up and took periscope pictures of the shoreline, but not for long. A pesky subchaser appeared again. It was obvious that the air and sea searches were correlated, and their signals picked up the *Burrfish*.

For two weeks the *Burrfish* remained in the area, trying to complete the surveillance job but frustrated day after day by Japanese vigilance. When it appeared that the Japanese would not stop trying, the skipper of the *Burrfish* set course for Yap, the other part of their mission. The Japanese vigilance that frustrated the mission on Peleliu would be very costly. At Pearl Harbor they seemed satisfied with the information they had, but what they did not have was any concept of the lay of the land on the island. It appeared to be flat and covered with vegetation. Actually it was rock, and the Japanese had built tunnels and cave defenses that would be almost im-

penetrable when the Marine 1st Division landed; this
would cost the Marines five thousand casualties before
the job was done.

The *Burrfish* moved close to Yap's southern shore on
the first night of this mission. Lieutenant Massey took the
swimmers in this time, in the inflatable boat. He took
four men from the OSS team into the island, and they
made the survey. They had scarcely returned to the submarine and been recovered and gone below when a contact was made, and again the submarine was playing cat
and mouse with the Japanese surface defenses.

For two days the *Burrfish* dodged in and around the
island to make its next approach on the eastern coast.
Finally on August 18 a respite from chase came and the
work could begin again.

The *Burrfish* came in to within two miles of the
beach. Intelligence reports indicated that Yap was heavily
fortified and garrisoned.

Chief Reeder was leading the team again on this
mission. And Chief Ball was the coxswain of the rubber
boat. The swimmers would be one of the amphibious operations base men and UDT men John McMahon and
Robert Black.

That night they surfaced in a choppy sea, which
ought to be an advantage and help prevent discovery by
the Japanese. Chief Ball took the boat in to within four
hundred yards of the beach when he came across the
barrier reef. He anchored the boat on the edge of the
reef, and the swimmers slipped over the side.

Fifteen minutes later Chief Ball saw two swimmers
coming back. One of the men was being helped by the
other. Something had gone wrong. They came to the boat
and Robert Black, who was helping the amphibious operations man, got him into the boat. The strong surf had
been too much for the man and he was fortunate to be
intelligent enough to know when to quit. Black headed
back to the beach to join McMahon and Reeder.

Ball and his assistant waited—and waited. When the swimmers did not come back at the prescribed hour, he waited for another half hour. Still no one came. He was concerned, and he hauled up the anchor and began to move along the reef in the direction the swimmers had taken. Still he found nothing. Finally the time ran out and the safety margin was exhausted. The two men in the boat began to paddle; it took them a long time to reach the place of rendezvous with the submarine. The skipper of the *Burrfish* was also concerned, and after the boat was pulled aboard and the submarine dived, he brought it up to periscope depth and hung around as close to the edge of the reef as he dared for the whole night, some of it on the surface. But as dawn was breaking he had to dive again and move away from the island without seeing a sign of the missing men. In the morning, search planes began appearing overhead, and the skipper of the *Burrfish* decided it was time to be getting out of the area. The UDT men pleaded with him to stay one more night. The swimmers would come back to the beach, they were sure. But the skipper refused. He had already lost three men, and to stay would be to endanger all the others. The surprise element had slipped away from them. So he made the decision to give up the men as lost. The *Burrfish* headed back for Pearl Harbor.

In fact, as Japanese documents showed, the swimmers did come back to the beach that following night, apparently having remained hidden from the Japanese all day. They were captured on August 20, the second day. The captured men were then placed aboard a subchaser and sent to the Philippines to go into a prison camp, but something happened either to the subchaser or to them, because they were never seen again, and no more was ever heard of them.

Had they survived, the Americans might have learned something more about the large number of Japanese troops stationed on Yap. But it would have made no particular difference, because in the end Yap was by-passed.

As for Peleliu, it remained a mystery to the Americans even after this mission because the UDT men reported on the characteristics of the beaches. They paid no attention to the topography of the island, because this was not within their purview. As it turned out, the realities of Peleliu geography—thick jungle and hilly terrain—were completely unknown to the American invaders at the time they arrived, and they had some shocks in store that could have been far less had the UDT men been used, as the Navy SEALs would be later, for varied sorts of reconnaissance, not concerned only with the bottom of the sea.

When the invasion fleet arrived at Peleliu on the night of September 14, the underwater demolition men of Team No. 7 made a beach reconnaissance and discovered a smooth, flat reef with steel tripods and rows of wooden posts put up to impede the landing craft about seventy-five yards from the beach. They also found log barriers and concrete cribs for coral about thirty yards above the high-water mark.

On that night of September 14 the UDT men went in to remove the obstacles from the beach but the effort was not successful, blamed by the UDT men themselves on poor planning and the inevitable confusion of night work.

On the morning of D-day the officers of the team went to the flagship with charts showing the beaches. But the *Stringham,* their APD, put them into their boats so far away from the flagship that by the time they got there the operation was already under way and the information's value was lost. It was a lesson for the UDT men of the future.

Although the first part of their job had come to very little, the underwater men reported to the beachmaster for duty at ten-thirty on the morning of D-day. They laid anchorage buoys and did some demolition work. On D+3 they conducted a reconnaissance for antitank mines but found none. However, on the Scarlet beaches on the southwestern side of the island they did encounter some mines and many obstacles, some of them very sophisticated, imbedded steel and concert rails and steel tetrahedrons. The rails were twenty-pound rails planted about five feet high. The tetrahedrons were seven feet square and constructed of lightweight pipe or reinforced bars. For two days the team labored to destroy these obstacles on Scarlet Beach 3, then turned their attention to Scarlet Beach 1 and Scarlet Beach 2, where they found many other obstacles. They were placed about fifteen feet apart, with barbed wire and plain wire strung among them. Around every third or fourth rail were wood tetrahedrons filled with rocks and coral. Mines were also located and blown up.

On Purple Beach the UDT men found three parallel rows of obstacles, the first composed of logs; the second steel rails; and the third, reinforced concrete posts. So Peleliu's underwater defenses were the most numerous of any the Americans had yet faced in the Pacific, and they were a good warning about what the Marines would face on Peleliu. This turned out to be one of the hardest fights the Marines had made, and it yielded very heavy casualties. For an unnecessary operation Peleliu turned out to be very expensive.

The simultaneous landings on Angaur Island in the Palaus were much less of a problem all the way around. Team No. 8 was involved here, arriving in the area on September 12, 1944. The team's first assignment was to make a daylight reconnaissance of Green Beach, on the southeastern shore of Angaur, on the morning of September 14. The mission was supported by thirty minutes of bombardment by a battleship, two cruisers, and three destroyers. Fifteen hundred yards of beach were covered in thirty minutes by using all four platoons of the UDT men. They did not find any mines or serious obstacles to landing. They came under only sporadic fire from the Japanese and suffered no casualties.

This mission was a feint. On the morning of September 15 they made a reconnaissance of Red Beach on the northern shore of Angaur, which was to be the beach on which the Army 81st Division would land. Again the bombardment lasted half an hour, and then two platoons of the team went in to cover four hundred yards of beach. Once more they found nothing and suffered no casualties. The only hazards offered were some jetted rails along the high-water mark in a double row at ten-foot intervals on the left side of the beach. On the afternoon of August 19, after another thirty-minute bombardment, the team took out the obstacles with demolition charges. The invasion was on September 17, and for the next week the UDT men cleared mines and floating hazards to navigation. Along with Team No. 6 the team made a reconnaissance of the channel between Angaur and Peleliu and later of the channel between Peleliu and Ngesebus Island, where they encountered some attack from the air. This was a grueling mission, mostly because the water was only four feet deep and the swimmer had to swim three thousand yards to a Japanese-held causeway and back under heavy small-arms and machine-gun fire.

The next amphibious operation, at Leyte Gulf, was the most ambitious yet staged by the Americans and the Allies.

The task force left Manus Island on October 12, 1944, and reached Leyte Gulf on the morning of October 17. The force ran into a typhoon, which delayed the minesweeping. The presence of the Americans was soon known to the Japanese, who then put into effect their celebrated A-Go (Victory) operation, in which they would employ all the remaining elements of their Navy and much of their Air Force to try to stop the Allies here in the Philippines. They would also unveil their most deadly weapon of the war, the kamikazes, or suicide pilots, whose chosen mission was to crash their planes into carriers and destroy them.

For the invasion, seven teams would be employed, four on the southern beaches around Dulag and San José and three teams in the northern area, around Tacloban.

Team No. 5 was one of those assigned to the south, and its first task was to survey the Orange 1 and Orange 2 beaches on October 18. One gunner was killed by sniper fire in the approach, and one pharmacist's mate was wounded by shrapnel. But the findings were all negative: No mines, no obstacles, good exit from the beach, little surf, and no demolition work needed.

So there was no work for Team No. 5 on invasion day, and very shortly the team left for Marcus.

Team No. 8 had a much tougher time on the beach. They had to reconnoiter Blue Beach 1 and Blue Beach 2, and the fire was so heavy that they suffered six casualties, one who later died of his wounds. The men saw their first Japanese planes and their first kamikazes and witnessed the attacks on the cruiser *Honolulu* and the Australian *Australia*. Their APD, the *Badger,* was one of the ships detailed to escort the crippled vessels away from the battle zone, and they were out of the Battle of Leyte before it really began.

The invasion of Leyte marked the end of the old ways and the beginning of the new. Captain Hanlon had been completing his organization of the Underwater Demolition Command, dividing it into operations, demolition communications, intelligence, and administrative departments. By the end of 1944 he was ready to move forward with operations and take tactical control of them. On December 25 he and two members of the staff left Pearl Harbor for the Lingayen Gulf operation in the Philippines. The flagship stayed in Hawaii. Captain Hanlon would observe operations from the flagship of Admiral Oldendorf, commander of the fire support force. In this operation Army liaison personnel were assigned to operating UDTs as observers, and much more information was passed around than in the past.

Lingayen brought another development: the realization that UDTs need not be limited to demolition of obstacles. Their training and their activity made them valuable for other sorts of reconnaissance, although most of them had not been trained in hydrographic reconnaissance.

During the preliminaries to the landings, Admiral Oldendorf's flagship, the *California,* was hit by a kamikaze, but none of the UDT staff was hurt. Lingayen marked a point of departure, and thereafter the UDTs would be an integral part of amphibious operations, not the afterthought they had been in the past.

SSSS
SSSS
     After Underwater Demolition Team No. 8 left the Leyte area and their ship escorted the two cripples, HMAS *Australia* and the *Honolulu,* to Manus, most of the members of the team went to Nouméa for rest and rehabilitation and the *Badger* for some needed repairs. They spent sixteen days in Nouméa and then left for Hollandia on November 26.

In the Hollandia operation the UDT was involved in what its historian termed "the most monotonous operation in the team's history." The major job was the clearing of a channel to a Seabee lumber camp at Bougainville Bay, twenty miles down the coast from Hollandia. The trip had to be made by small boat, carrying twenty-five tons of explosives. Two shots were fired, and the job was done. By ten o'clock that night the team members were back aboard the *Badger* and getting ready to celebrate Christmas, which was made bearable by the arrival of the mail. On December 27 the team left New Guinea, bound for Lingayen Gulf.

The *Badger* reached Leyte Gulf on January 3 and then headed for Mindoro. That's when the excitement began. On the evening of January 3, off Mindoro, one of the ships in their group, the escort carrier *Ommaney Bay,* was hit by a kamikaze and began to burn. She burned for three hours before she was sunk by American destroyers. And that attack was only the beginning. Over the next eight days the ship went to general quarters fifty-five times, some lasting as long as eighteen hours. On January 5 off Lingayen Gulf the group was attacked by a force of suicide planes, as many as three at a time diving at the

Badger. That day within a half hour thirty-five Japanese planes were shot down or crashed.

On January 7 the UDT men got their job. They would make a reconnaissance swim to the White beaches, comprising about two thousand yards. When the swimmers went in, they were covered by a pair of LCIs, which fired their 40mm guns steadily at the shore. The UDT men neither saw nor felt any opposition from the Japanese and did not find any mines or underwater obstacles. After that the *Badger* anchored in the gulf, and as it turned out, that was the end of the need for the UDT men. By January 19 the *Badger* was bound for Ulithi, where the team went ashore and stayed on the island of Asor for two weeks.

Team No. 5 also went into Lingayen in its ship, the *Humphreys*. The members of the team also watched with some consternation the many kamikaze attacks that cut the effectiveness of the task force by a figure that some put at 50 percent.

When Team No. 5 went in, there were many rumors of sandbars and mines, not obstacles. The swimmers went in during the middle of the afternoon, and two hours later every swimmer was back aboard the ship. The information was all positive: no mines, no obstacles, and a good exit from the beaches.

The work had been done. Lieutenant deBold took a composite chart of the findings of three teams to Captain Hanlon aboard the *California,* and from that point it went into the hands of the brass.

The landings came on January 9. The next day Team No. 5 was ordered to make a reconnaissance of beaches to the left and also of a river for use by landing craft. The men went in, but they found the undertow and surf so powerful that they did not all make it back, and some had to be picked up later. The findings were that the river could handle landing craft up to LCMs but that the new beach exits were inadequate.

That was nearly the end of Team No. 5. They then went back to Maui and home leave, and by the time the team reassembled it was down to skeleton size, many of the men either transferring out of UDT work or going to the Hanlon staff.

As the story of UDT No. 15 indicated, enormous change had come to the underwater warfare concept since those early days when Team No. 5 was organized and Lieutenant Commander Kauffman got his chance to go into action.

Team No. 15 men came primarily out of the Fort Pierce school in the summer of 1944. Orders came from Hawaii for seventeen crews, each consisting of five men and one officer, to the Maui school. They left Florida on August 31 by train; went through Nevada, where Ens. L. O. Smith managed to win a hundred dollars at a craps table in ten minutes during a train stop; and then to San Bruno, where they waited for shipment overseas.

The group had already acquired an entity of sorts because they had a mascot: a mongrel dog they called Esther Williams, because she was a beautiful swimmer. When they boarded the Dutch merchant ship MS *Tjisdane* at San Francisco's Pier 18, the first lieutenant of the ship declared the dog outlawed, so she had to be put into a crate in the hold and hidden from him. When they arrived at Honolulu she had to be smuggled off the ship over the fantail in her crate and put aboard the LCI that was taking the new men to Maui.

When the group arrived at the Maui Underwater Training Base, it was immediately given a name: Team No. 15. Six weeks of strenuous training followed, tough from the outset because someone in Florida had told someone on Maui that these men thought they were tough and could swim a mile with fifty pounds of tetrytol strapped to their backs. The first day after arrival they were put to this test, and most of them flunked it. So some Hawaiian pearl divers were given the job of teaching these *haoles* how to swim. For two weeks it was get up and do PT, go to breakfast and then swim until noon, have lunch, and swim in the afternoon. Late in the afternoon they made a reconnaissance swim and another at night. They had liberty on Fridays only.

After two weeks, swimming was almost automatic. For six weeks they trained—swimming, making reconnaissance swims, blasting coral during day and into the night. As one of them put it, the only one who really enjoyed all this was Esther. But they were dead serious in their approach, knowing that what they learned here at Maui from the veterans of Saipan, Guam, and Tinian might save their lives.

During the seventh week on Maui, Lt. Houston F. Brooks, former commander of Team No. 10, who had been replaced by the OSS commander and made head of the training program, was appointed to command Team No. 15. Lt. (jg) John G. Schantz, who had served with Team No. 5 and with Team No. 7, was made executive officer. Soon the supply NCO, Chief Carpenter Stoky Straight, was loading supplies aboard an LSM, and at the end of November they set sail for Pearl Harbor and then boarded their new home, the APD USS *Blessman*. On the afternoon of December 11, 1944, the *Blessman* sailed. The men of Team No. 15 were excited as Diamond Head disappeared over the horizon; they were "going off to war."

The ship reached Ulithi on December 24. On Christmas Day there was free beer at the recreation area of Nog Nog Beach, and the men got a look at Admirals Halsey and Nimitz, who were meeting here. The next day the *Blessman* sailed again, this time for the excitement of action. When they were at sea their secret orders were opened, sending them to Lingayen for the landings. On January 1 the *Blessman* joined Admiral Oldendorf's bombardment group with the other five teams scheduled for

Lingayen. Philippine guerrillas came aboard to brief the team on minefields and other Japanese defenses.

They saw their first Japanese airplane on January 3. It came overhead and then veered off as the antiaircraft guns of the ships began firing. They, too, saw the *Ommaney Bay* burning after she was hit by a suicide plane. On January 5 they also saw the cruiser *Louisville* hit by a suicide plane. Fifteen members of the team manned .30-caliber machine guns on the fantail of their ship, knowing that their fire was almost certainly futile but feeling the need to "do something."

On January 7 the team was scheduled to make its first reconnaissance for the landing that would be made two days later. On January 6 the bombardment ships moved into action, with the *California* leading the column and two other old battleships behind her; then came the three cruisers, all five hundred yards apart, with destroyers and APDs flanking the column. But quickly enough the distraction of attacks by the kamikazes began and they lasted all day. The *Blessman* saw the cruiser *Portland* hit and many men swept overboard. They passed the men in the water, but there was no way they could stop. The *Blessman*'s antiaircraft guns were working all day, and before dark the crew claimed one plane shot down.

Because of the delay in starting the bombardment, on January 7 the UDT was also delayed and did not begin its reconnaissance mission until two o'clock in the afternoon. They were comforted by the fire support, the big ships outside and landing craft giving support at fifteen hundred to five hundred yards.

Lieutenant Schantz, who was the boat officer, instructed the coxswain in getting in to the beach and supervised the dropping of buoys to mark areas for future work. Then they approached the reconnaissance zone.

"Now!" shouted Lieutenant Schantz, and Ens. H. W. Locke and his partner, R. J. Pfister, hit the water. The boat moved another hundred yards, and the command was repeated. Another pair of swimmers jumped in. The move was repeated until all five pairs of swimmers in the boat had been dropped, and then the boat moved out to sea to wait.

It was very quiet near the beach, virtually no enemy fire, and they swam to within three hundred yards of shore and finished their reconnaissance. The boat came back and began picking up swimmers, and soon all were aboard. It was just like the rehearsal at Ulithi.

Team No. 15's findings matched those of the other teams: no mines, no obstacles, almost ideal conditions for landing. On the day of the invasion the men were surprised by the quiet. There was no hustle and bustle and virtually nothing to see on shore as the waves moved in. There was some vicarious excitement on the second day, when swimmers of UDT No. 9 reported Japanese suicide swimmers among floating debris. Perhaps they were survivors of Japanese suicide boats that had tried to crash through the line of ships but with little success. On the afternoon of the second day Team No. 15 made a reconnaissance of those beaches on the left with the high surf and undertow and ended up leaving four men ashore. The *Blessman* pulled out that night, abandoning the four men, who had then to make their way as best they could. It was a sad moment for Team No. 15.

The *Blessman* returned to Leyte Gulf and anchored off Tacloban. The progress of the war on Leyte could be measured by the Filipinos. Their bumboats clustered around the *Blessman,* and the Filipinos offered native handicrafts, baskets, mats, and rice paddy hats for any articles of clothing. A few days at Leyte and they were off for Ulithi again. From there they would go to Iwo Jima, so there were rehearsals and more rehearsals and study of the operation plans. By early February 1945 the men of Team No. 15 were confident of their ability to do the job at hand and ready to go into action again. This time they would go in with Teams No. 12, No. 13, and No. 14.

The Underwater Demolition Team activities in the invasion of Iwo Jima were orchestrated by Captain Hanlon and his staff. The four advance teams arrived on February 16 off Iwo Jima and the transport destroyers circled the island, twenty-five hundred yards out, to make observations for their final operation planning.

Captain Hanlon had been assigned the job of making reconnaissance missions on the eastern beaches at 11:00 A.M. and the western beaches at 4:30 P.M. on February 17.

Team No. 12 did the reconnaissance on Red 1 and Red 2 beaches on the eastern side of the island and Brown 1 and Brown 2 beaches on the western side. During the mission on the eastern beaches the fire-support LCIs drew heavy machine-gun, mortar, and small-arms fire. Ens. Frank Jirka was assigned as an observer aboard *LCI-466*. The landing craft was hit by a Japanese mortar round on the bridge, and Jirka lost both feet. Also in the operation one of the swimmers did not return from the mission and was listed as missing in action.

On D-day several officers from Team No. 12 led the first waves into the Red beaches. After D-day the members of this team spent ten days clearing the eastern landing beaches of wrecked landing craft and vehicles. Then the team was detached and sent back to Ulithi.

Team No. 13 was selected to put up a navigation light on Higashi Iwa, an islet about four thousand yards offshore of Iwo Jima. Their transport destroyer, the *Barr,* came under heavy enemy fire, but this was soon silenced, and three officers and fifteen men installed the light successfully.

On February 17 the team did a reconnaissance on Green Beach 1 on the eastern side of Iwo Jima and of Purple Beach 1 on the western side, both in the shadow of Mount Suribachi. Japanese fire was intense during the whole operation, but the UDT men escaped without casualties. The light they had put up the night before, however, was shot out by the Japanese and had to be reestablished. The fire was so heavy that Captain Hanlon ordered the *Gilmer* to fire white phosphorous shells to make a smoke screen for the divers. Partly because of this, although many of the landing craft were hard hit, there were no casualties among the UDT men.

On D+5 some members of the team helped put a navigational light on Mount Suribachi. That was the team's last mission at Iwo Jima, and on the last day of February they left for Guam.

Team No. 8 was scheduled for the Iwo Jima mission as well, but when the men arrived on March 3, it seemed that their services were supernumerary. So they stayed only long enough to experience a Japanese air raid, pick up a battle star, and head for Guam, where they built their own camp. Almost as soon as they had completed the camp, they were ordered to move out, hopefully to go home to America, as some teams were doing. But instead they were assigned to take over the training program at Maui. But by July the team was sent to San Pedro, and then came leave.

The destroyer transport *Blessman* was a gloomy place after that morning operation. The men expected the afternoon to go harder, and their whole fleet of twelve LCI gunboats had already been battered and knocked out of action by the Japanese batteries on the eastern coast of the island. They would have no fire support in the afternoon when they went in. Although the morning had cost them only one casualty, the prospects for the afternoon mission looked anything but bright. But it had to be done. Ensign Phillips had been a fire-control spotter on an LCI that suffered 70 percent casualties. What would it be like without them there to keep the Japanese off?

Some changes in plan had to be made for the protection of the swimmers. The destroyers would close to the beach by another thousand yards to compensate for the absence of the LCIs.

The time approached. The men gathered on the fantail, bodies painted with silver camouflage, boat crews with heavy shrapnelproof vests and aprons. Platoons 1, 2, and 4 loaded over the sides in landing craft. Just as the second boat pulled away from the ship, a long spatter of 20mm Japanese fire traced a line that ended just short of the boat and near the ship.

The men's hearts sank. It was starting already, and they were still four thousand yards from the island.

But someone on a cruiser noticed that line of 20mm and traced it to the rocks. Barrages of eight-inch shells began to fall on those rocks, and soon all was quiet there.

It was Roger-hour + 10—time to go. The men headed for the island. They drew no fire at all. At five hundred yards they turned left, and still there was no fire. The swimmers began to go over the side, two men each hundred yards. The men began taking the bearings, heading in toward the shore.

Twice aircraft zoomed over, trailing thick smoke that hid the beach. Fighter planes came down to strafe and fire rockets, and the destroyers fired again and again. The result was that not one boat took a shell, not even Lieutenant Brooks's boat, which went in only a hundred yards from the beach and was nearly caught in the surf while they were looking for two evasive swimmers. But in spite of this there was only a ten-minute delay in getting all men back in the boats, given a shot of brandy, clothed in long underwear, and bound for the *Blessman*. Reconnaissance was over. There would be no need to go back.

Knowing that the task was over, the men of the

Blessman relaxed that night. It had been a hard day, with danger, rain, fog, and a cold damp that had spread throughout the ship. But that night the men gathered in the mess rooms, writing letters home or playing cards and gambling.

The *Blessman* was steaming at flank speed from Iwo Jima to the outer screen area, for the *Blessman* had opted to take the place of another ship that could not get into the screen that night because of engine trouble. She was moving at twenty-two knots, leaving a wake that could be seen for miles and was, by one of the snooping Japanese bombers that had come out that night. Suddenly a twin-engined Betty bomber came in along the ship's wake, swung left, made a 180-degree turn, came back on the ship's beam, and dropped one five-hundred-pound bomb.

The bomb struck on the port side, went through the deck, down through the starboard mess hall, and exploded when it hit the mess hall deck. A second bomb was a near-miss that first touched one of the boat davits and then went into the water, where it exploded.

The first bomb had done a great deal of damage. It had opened up the mess hall like a matchbox, and the middle of the ship was engulfed in flames. The smell of burning flesh was overpowering. The men who reached the stricken area began to run through the troop compartments, pulling injured men from their bunks and directing others to the fantail. Soon all the living had been brought out of the troop compartments. Ens. R. H. McCallum and Ens. E. F. Andrews went into the burning troop compartment and helped the wounded in spite of ammunition exploding around them.

In the officers' quarters of the underwater team, the lights were on and the executive officer was telling tall stories. They had a guest, Lt. David Pottorf of the Marine 4th Division, who was trying to listen although he was yawning and wanted to get to sleep.

Suddenly a loud noise came and something shook

the ship from stem to stern. All the lights went out. The officers realized that the ship had been hit. They grabbed their life belts and medical supplies and ran topside.

On deck the officers tried to make use of the fire-fighting equipment but discovered that it also was not in workable condition. They organized a bucket brigade, which checked the fires temporarily, but they broke out again and again. Two hours after the fires began, the *Gilmer* came alongside and used its fire-fighting equipment. Ens. E. B. Rybski led the fire-fighting party on the boat deck, jettisoning flaming material and working hoses supplied by the *Gilmer*. Soon the fire fighters managed to transform the blazing fires into a smoky cauldron. Next morning a repair ship came alongside and passed gasoline and pumps so that the crew of the *Blessman* could keep the ship afloat. That day Team No. 15 buried at sea eighteen of their friends and associates.

That night they had orders to transfer the team to the APD *Newberry,* and about a third of the men moved over, but two-thirds did not make it, and the LSM then retired. An LSM took the *Blessman* in tow, heading for Saipan. About halfway to Saipan they were met by an oceangoing tug that took over the tow.

When the team reached Saipan there was nothing to do. The enlisted men visited their buddies in the hospital; took trips around the island; and went on souvenir hunts, to the inevitable nightly movies, and to any beer parties. The officers got up late, censored mail, and played cards. At 1:00 P.M., when the officers' club opened, most of them retired there to see how quickly they could drink the club dry.

One night the team CO lived up to the reputation the UDT men were establishing for hard living and wild behavior ashore. He came back to his quarters drunk, and when he got into bed noticed that the lights were still on. He picked up his .38-caliber revolver and fired three shots. As the later report noted, "this officer at fifty yards did draw his revolver and fire at three light bulbs, hitting same," and turned them off. He was thinking about shooting out the rest of the lights in the BOQ when the officer of the day came into the quarters and placed the skipper on report. The next morning he was hailed before the island commander and was then directed to stay aboard a ship in the harbor.

So the Iwo Jima operation ended, and Team No. 15 made its way back to Maui and then to the United States mainland for thirty days' leave and then reorganization at Fort Pierce.

ʕʕʕʕ
ʕʕʕʕ On March 20, 1945, Underwater Demolition Team No. 13 arrived in the Ryukyu
Islands and was detailed to reconnoiter
Kerama Retto, a group of small islands west of Okinawa
that the Navy wanted to use as a supply and repair base
during the assault on the fortress island. Team No. 19 also
was to work the Kerama Retto group.

On the morning of March 25 the members of Team
No. 13 covered themselves with axle grease for protection
against the seventy degree water and swam to a beach on
the southern tip of Tokashika Shima and that afternoon
swam to the western side of the island. They were harried
by sporadic rifle fire. They found the island full of natural
channels, and no demolition work was necessary. They
then were assigned to blast a channel on Keiso Shima so
that LSMs could land heavy artillery for bombardment of
Okinawa. This task took them three days, until March 30,
but on April 3 the team was on its way back to Maui and
then to begin cold-water training in California for the
expected invasion of Japan.

Team No. 17 reached Kerama Retto on March 26
aboard the APD *Crosley* and was assigned to work the
northern Hagushi beaches, where the main Okinawa
landings would be made. At six-thirty on the morning of
March 28 the *Crosley* was attacked by a kamikaze, which
defied the ship's guns and kept boring in until a quick
maneuver by the captain at the last minute caused the
plane to miss the ship and plunge into the sea thirty feet
astern.

Team No. 12 also went to Okinawa and cleared the

way for occupation of three of the islands of the Kerama Retto group. Later the team staged a diversionary demolition of the reef on the southern coast of Okinawa to persuade the Japanese that the Americans were landing there, when the actual landings were farther north.

The next day Team No. 17 went to work as one of six teams of Demolition Group B, and that same afternoon a combined report was made by the commander of the Underwater Demolition Flotilla to the invasion high command. They found nothing more dangerous or troublesome than wooden posts imbedded on the ocean floor.

The most action the team had was in manning guns on the *Crosley* to fight off the constant stream of kamikazes. Others were part of the fire and rescue parties, and some passed ammunition. Twice the *Crosley* went to the aid of ships hit by kamikazes, and the fire and rescue parties went to work. Team No. 17 stayed with the invasion forces until April 20, undertaking various assigned tasks; then it was released.

Team No. 16 lost one man in the work on the Okinawa Blue beaches: Francis Joseph Lynch was killed by enemy fire on March 30.

Team No. 4 was brought in to work on Okinawa's beaches, and found rows of posts four deep imbedded in the bottom along the beaches. It took only two hours, however, to load the posts with explosives and fire the shots that destroyed them. Team No. 21 worked the Hagushi landing beaches and also found hundreds of yards of log obstacles imbedded in the reef and on the beaches. These obstacles had to be removed, and there was no cover for the demolition men. On March 29 they began work under cover of a bombardment so intense that the team historian noted "for every swimmer in the water there were well over a thousand men behind guns backing them up," and he named ten battleships and thirteen cruisers, not to mention dozens of destroyers and a large force of escort carriers.

On the night of April 2 the old converted four-stack destroyer *Dickerson* was hit by a kamikaze. The members of the team were sent into the water to rescue survivors; others helped put out the fires on the *Dickerson* after she was abandoned by the crew. At this point in the war, the Japanese were preparing for the assault on their homeland, and to them Okinawa was a very definite part of the homeland. So, in southern Kyushu the Japanese Army and Navy had massed hundreds of aircraft and suicide pilots to try to stop the Americans at Okinawa. They came in great waves, which the Japanese called *kikusui.* So great was the incidence of attack by kamikazes that it was decided at one point to protect the UDT men and make full use of the ships by transferring them off their destroyer transport to the *Bunch,* so that ship could be used in the screen for the fleet. That worked for twenty-four hours, and then Team No. 21 was back aboard its own ship.

On April 16, 1945, Team No. 21 had the responsibility of directing the landing of Army troops on the island of Ie Shima, near Okinawa. The commanders did not realize how heavily fortified Ie Shima was and that the UDT men would be under constant heavy fire as they worked the beaches. Only after newspaper correspondent Ernie Pyle was killed on this "safe" island by a sniper did the military men take notice. On April 21 the team was released and sent to Guam, but was recalled to Okinawa on May 16 and participated in the capture of Iheya Island, north of Okinawa, and Aguni Island in June. They did the underwater work for the invasion of Kume Shima, fifty miles west of Okinawa, on June 26. This was the last important Central Pacific invasion of Japanese territory until the end of the war.

Team No. 18 had a different sort of war experience. It was sent aboard the converted destroyer escort *Schmitt* to participate in the invasion of Balikpapan in Borneo. On June 21, 1945, the ship left Morotai and on June 23 arrived off Balikpapan. On June 25 the team made its first reconnaissance on the beach at Manggar Ketil, along with men of Team No. 11. The main obstacles were posts, and the problem was that about three feet of each post were exposed, and the men of the team were targets for sniper fire as they placed the top charges. But a combination of B-24s, B-25s, and gunboats from the fleet kept the Japanese from firing effectively on the underwater men, and on June 26 the obstacles were blown up.

On June 27 the team moved to the Klandasan Beach area of Balikpapan, one much more heavily mined along the shore and where sniper and mortar fire was much stronger. Several of the boats were hit by 37mm shells, but no men were wounded. The boats went in very close, but the gunboats closed to within a thousand yards and countered the enemy fire while the swimmers did their work and then led the first wave of Australian troops in for the landings. By July 3 the team's work was done at Balikpapan and the *Schmitt* was on its way to Guam and the men of the team were on their way home to the United States for leave before joining in the occupation of Japan.

〇〇〇〇
〇〇〇〇 Several of the Underwater Demolition Teams had been training for what the Navy considered to be their ultimate mission of World War II: the cracking of the Japanese beaches for the invasion of the Japanese homeland. They expected the Japanese to use every artifice possible to prevent and delay the Allied landings.

The new commander of the Underwater Demolition Teams was Capt. R. H. Rodgers, and in June 1945 he and his staff began planning for the invasion of Kyushu, Japan's southernmost island. They expected to send thirty teams in after they had spent a month in cold-water training at Oceanside, California. At that time the underwater command was made a flotilla, with two subordinate squadron commands.

On June 30, 1945, Captain Rodgers moved to Manila to prepare further for the invasion of Japan, in close consultation with Admiral Turner. After the Japanese surrender announcement by Emperor Hirohito, twenty of the UDTs were alerted for shipment to Japan. Captain Rodgers ordered his flagship, the APD *Hollis,* to sail for Tokyo Bay. From the flagship he supervised the activities of the underwater demolition teams in the Japanese occupation.

The UDTs accompanied every landing force, including some that did not land for combat, such as Team No. 8, which went to Chefoo and Taku Bar, China, but did not land there. Then they went to Qingdao, China, where they landed and had liberty but no work. And then they went home.

Team No. 21 went to Japan, arriving on August 29 in Tokyo Bay and putting up a sign, "Welcome Marines," for their friends who arrived the next day. They made a reconnaissance of Futtsu Saki, and Lieutenant Commander Clayton, commander of the team, accepted the surrender of the commanding officer of the fort that guarded Tokyo Harbor. The next day their ship, the USS *Begor,* was the first American vessel to enter Yokosuka Naval Base. The team spent the next few days demilitarizing Japanese naval vessels, stripping them of armament, and also carrying off seven tons of souvenirs, which were stashed aboard the *Begor.* They reconnoitered the beaches of Tatayama Wan, on the other side of Tokyo Bay. For a time they half expected resistance and violence, but there was none.

This team spent three weeks traveling along the coast of Honshu, from Tokyo to Sandai, along with the cruiser *Boston,* two destroyers, and a tug, searching for midget submarines, suicide boats, coastal defense guns, and other Japanese arms. They found 207 suicide boats and seven submarines, which they destroyed by demolition and sinking, chopping, and burning. They pressed Japanese soldiers and even civilians into helping with this work. Then there was liberty in Yokosuka, Yokohama, and Tokyo. On September 30 the team sailed for home.

UDT No. 3 had been scheduled to pave the way for the 33rd Infantry Division, which had been assigned to land on the beaches of Wakayama, in the southern part of the Japanese main island of Honshu, in the invasion. The team arrived offshore on September 23. They, too, half expected to meet resistance but did not, and they carried out their reconnaissance missions on the landing beaches and destroyed some hulks of vessels stranded there, as well as a sea mine just offshore of one beach. Soon they, too, were going home for leave and demobilization.

In September Commander Kauffman was reassigned to organize the permanent Underwater Demolition Team base at the Naval Amphibious Base in Coronado, California, and Team No. 25 was assigned to him to help with the task, which it continued until decommissioned in November.

At the end of 1945 the decommissioning of Underwater Demolition Teams was proceeding rapidly; the last of the wartime teams was decommissioned in February 1946 and the equipment put into storage or sold as surplus. Most of the thirty-five hundred men who had served with the underwater teams went back to civilian life, but a few hundred volunteers were retained in the service as four new teams were commissioned in 1946, Teams No. 1 and No. 3 remaining in Coronado and Teams No. 2 and No. 4 being transferred to the Atlantic fleet and stationed at Little Creek, Virginia.

The UDTs were almost immediately employed as arms of the new American peacetime fleet. Three months after commissioning, Team No. 3 took part in the atomic bomb tests at Bikini. In the summer of 1947 the team operated in the waters off Point Barrow, Alaska. In that same year part of the team went to the Antarctic. In 1948 the team operated for a time along the coast of China, and conducted experiments in endurance in winter operations in the Bering Sea. In 1949 the team was in Hawaii for Army-Navy war games, and in 1950 the team sent an expedition to Point Barrow again, practicing resupply of the Distant Early Warning Line. The UDT men experimented with the Aqua-Lung and other new devices and increased their expertise. They learned to operate from submarines while they were submerged, leaving and entering through the forward escape trunk. In one exercise the UDT men successfully "sank" a warship during maneuvers by attaching limpet mines to its hull. They also practiced diving for depth, and in one tank experiment a swimmer made the equivalent of a dive to more than 560 feet.

But the number of UDT personnel decreased steadily, until in 1948 each team consisted of seven officers and forty-five enlisted men.

Then came the Korean War. When the North Korean Army plunged across the thirty-eighth parallel in its lightning attack on South Korea on June 25, 1950, a detachment of ten men from UDT No. 3 were stationed in Japan, training with the Eighth Army. Immediately the unit was ordered to Rear Adm. James Doyle's flagship, the USS *Mount McKinley.* Since the inception of the demolition idea, significant changes had come in the training of the demolition teams, many of them the result of the belief of Comdr. John T. Koehler, the commander of the advanced training base at Maui, that UDTs should have far greater capabilities than simply working underwater for demolition of shore obstacles. He saw for the UDT men missions behind enemy lines, and he trained his teams to operate inland as well as on the shore. The head of this detachment had that type of training. He was Lt. (jg) George Atcheson. Thus the UDT men aboard Admiral Doyle's flagship were to have a mission quite removed from those of the past. They were to blow up a railroad bridge at Yosu, forty-five miles behind enemy lines, a plan proposed by Vice Adm. C. Turner Joy, commander of U.S. naval forces in the Far East. He and Admiral Doyle conferred with Lieutenant Atcheson, and Atcheson and his men got ready for the new sort of mission. Within a few hours they had been moved to the APD *Diachenko,* which would be their operating base.

But first they had a more mundane assignment: to discover if reinforcements could be landed in strength from the sea in South Korea, at the fishing village of Pohang. Reinforcements were needed in Korea, but the port of Pusan was badly overloaded. Atcheson and his men went to Pohang, checked the beaches and the water, and reported that it could be done, although the water was not as suitable as it should be. It would mean putting troops ashore in waist-deep water, and the larger landing craft would ground so far offshore that pontoon causeways would be needed.

Based on Lieutenant Atcheson's finding, Admiral Doyle ferried thousands of troops of the 1st Cavalry Division to Pohang, and in one day ten thousand men were taken across the sea from Japan.

The Yosu assignment was far more challenging. Yosu had three bridges and a tunnel only three hundred yards from the sea. Just after midnight on August 5, 1950, a rubber boatload of men from the *Diachenko* and their explosives were delivered to the shore. Atcheson and Boatswain's Mate Warren Foley swam ahead of the boat for the last two hundred yards, making sure there were not any enemy troops around. Atcheson carried a waterproof pistol and four hand grenades. They climbed the thirty-five-foot seawall from the rocky beach and moved toward the bridge at the north end of the tunnel. The moon was rising, which was going to make the mission dangerous. They could see the rubber boat, the landing craft that delivered it, and the *Diachenko* on the sea. Atcheson sent Foley back to guide the men with their explosives and to hurry them. Just about then a patrol of North Korean soldiers came out of the tunnel on a handcar and stopped. Atcheson crouched under the trestle ten feet below them. The North Koreans were suspicious, and they flashed lights onto the beach.

Foley got to the boat, grabbed a submachine gun, and hurried back to help Atcheson. He was followed by UDT men Austin and McCormick. Meanwhile, Atcheson had climbed the slope behind the enemy patrol. He lobbed one grenade at the patrol and another into the tunnel. The North Koreans started firing. Foley scrambled up the seawall and began running toward the bridge. Atcheson thought Foley was a North Korean and took a shot at him. But so did the North Koreans, and one of their shots hit Foley, who fell off the wall. Atcheson poked his head over the rails, and Austin shot his hat off.

Foley was wounded in the hand and leg. McCormick carried him to the boat, and Atcheson and the others came there, too. They paddled to the landing craft, which came to within seventy-five yards of the shore, under fire from the North Koreans.

So the raid was a failure, and it resulted in the first Underwater Demolition Team casualty of the Korea War. But the admirals were not dismayed and soon were organizing more raids by the UDTs. The commanding officer of Team No. 1, Lt. Comdr. D. F. Welch, came to Korea with the Marine 1st Provisional Brigade. He and Maj. Edward Dupras of the Marines joined forces in this enterprise. Atcheson and Lts. (jg) P. A. Wilson and Edwin P. Smith also joined. Altogether this group numbered twenty-five UDT men and sixteen Marines. Their modus operandi was simple: The Marines would establish a defense perimeter around the target, and the UDT men would blow it up.

This team now made a raid to Tanchon, 160 miles up the coast, inside North Korea. They were embarked in the APD *Horace A. Bass.* Their targets were a pair of tunnels and a railroad bridge close to the sea.

Lieutenant Commander Welch was in charge. On the night of August 12, seven rubber boatloads of Marines and UDT men moved into the beach. They had chosen a moonless night, but when they got to the shore there was so much activity and there were so many lights around the area that they scrubbed the mission as too perilous. The next day they moved farther north and found another tunnel, which had been an alternative selection. That night, their faces camouflaged black and green, they brought ashore the explosive packs, fuses, and weapons. This time all was quiet and no sentries could be seen until suddenly a North Korean popped out at them, so surprised and frightened that he dropped his weapon. They picked it up. It was a wooden rifle, with a bayonet fixed to the end. They moved up on the target. They had to stop and take cover when a freight train passed, an inviting target, but one they had to ignore, for their mission was to blow the tunnel, not just a train. Finally the tunnel was loaded with explosives and the cord set and the fuses ready, and the men, except for Atcheson, Wilson, Smith, and Major Dupras, were sent back to the beach. Wilson and Atcheson pulled the fuse, and all ran to the beach and waited for the delayed reaction. The boats got away, and as they were safely on the sea, an enormous explosion wrecked the tunnel.

A ton of TNT had been placed in that tunnel.

The next night the men returned to the scene of their first attempt, and this time they saw no sentries. But in a pillbox near the tunnel they found a family of four North Koreans who had sought shelter for the night. The raiders took the family quite a distance away and tied them up, but loosely enough that they could eventually work their way free. Then they loaded the tunnel, all hands got away, and the second tunnel went up, as did the railroad bridge adjacent to it.

The raiders then knocked out some more bridges and finally went to a point thirty miles from Chongjin to attack a rail bridge and highway bridge that stood side by side two hundred yards inland. During this raid the *Bass* assisted. The lookouts on the ship saw headlights moving north along the highway. The ship's radio reported the headlights to Major Dupras, and they plotted the movements of an approaching truck. When the truck was a quarter mile away from the bridges, Dupras ordered all the men to take cover. When the truck passed, they saw it was loaded with North Korean troops. After the truck was safely gone for a few minutes, the men completed the mission, set the fuses, and went back to their ship. The explosion came off as timed. The next day, from the *Bass* they could see that one span of the railroad bridge had dropped into the river and the highway bridge was blasted.

Within ten days after the North Koreans had attacked South Korea, General MacArthur had begun planning a counterstroke, an assault that would cut the North Korean troops in South Korea from the air supply lines. The place chosen was Inchon, the port of Seoul. When MacArthur announced the choice, the Navy said it would be impossible because of the extremely high and low tides for which Inchon was infamous. But MacArthur persisted and insisted, and ultimately he had his way.

The Inchon amphibious landing was planned.

But before the landing, the raiders were to make some feints. One of the feints was to be made at Kunsan, about halfway up the western coast. On the night of August 20, in bright moonlight, two landing craft and seven rubber boats moved into a bay north of Kunsan; not a shot was fired at them.

The group made another reconnaissance a few miles away and then landed on the beach at Kunsan, measuring the depth and making efforts that would appear to presage a landing. The Marines set up a sixteen-man perimeter. Suddenly machine guns began firing on the Americans. The boat radioed all hands back. Two men were wounded and one boat was riddled with bullets and sank. Two other boats were abandoned when they began drawing heavy enemy fire. When the men had gotten away, it was discovered that nine Marines were missing. One landing craft turned and sped back to the beach, dropping a rescue boat crewed by Marines and UDT men. They paddled into shore under heavy rifle and machine-gun fire and found the Marines standing in water up to their necks. None of the Marines could swim. The Marines were picked up and clung to the sides of the rubber boat and were ferried to the landing craft and safety. The two wounded men were flown to Japan for treatment.

The Inchon landings came next. The UDT men were not used to making preliminary checks here, largely because the Navy did not want to sacrifice the element of surprise. Besides, a naval officer, Lt. Eugene Clark, had been making studies of the tides and the currents for several weeks.

The attack came first on the harbor island of Wolmi-do, which was the key to the North Korean defenses. After the Marines captured Wolmi-do, they prepared for the landings at Inchon. The UDT men came in then to scout the low tide and flats and to prepare for the invasion. By this time about a hundred UDT men were in Japan and Korea, members of Teams No. 1 and No. 3. The men from Team No. 3 came from Coronado and from the Arctic. Lieutenant Commander Welch commanded Team No. 1, and Lt. Comdr. W. R. McKinney commanded Team No. 3.

The UDT men acted as guides for the Marines on September 15 when they made their landing, taking them up to the seawall, which had been breached in a few places by the bombardment. There the Marines scrambled over or used ladders to get up from the beach. They moved quickly, and the element of surprise was not really lost. A few North Korean tanks and some infantry tried to stop them, but the drive was too much for them. It was not long before the Marines had driven to Seoul and cut the North Korean Army down by Pusan off from its supply routes. Then the North Koreans began retreating in what was really a rout.

The UDT men spent several days cleaning up Inchon Harbor, blowing up wrecks, buoying channels, and exploding a few mines they found.

The week after the landing, Team No. 3 sailed halfway down the western coast to Katsup-po, where the *Bass* anchored two miles off the beach so the men could investigate the possibilities of a landing there. The landing craft went in and dropped five rubber boats. They passed into the beach, and the first boat paddled close to a cliff. Suddenly firing began from the cliff: The North Koreans were firing directly into the first boat. The second boat had just dropped a swimmer who swam to the edge of the beach when the firing began and was just beginning to take soundings. The second boat paddled out away from the firing and began picking up swimmers. Two landing craft came in with .30-caliber machine guns to support the swimmers. Using pencil flashlights to find the swimmers, the boats began picking the men up and then went over to the first boat, which was still afloat, though badly holed, and took off three of its crew. Another boat picked up two more men, but two were still missing. Finally they, too, were rescued. Once the swimmers were all picked up the *Bass* lit up the area with star shells and began bombarding the cliff from which the automatic-weapons fire had come against the boats.

After all that work it was decided that no further landing was necessary, since the North Korean Army was disintegrating rapidly. Instead, the UDT men faced a new challenge. To help the North Koreans in their flight from disaster, the Soviet Union had sent a large number of mines to North Korea, and the North Koreans began placing mines in Wonsan and Chinnampo harbors. On the eastern coast the Republic of Korea forces were pushing toward Wonsan. Maj. Gen. Edward Almond, the commander of X Corps, decided to make another amphibious landing at Wonsan with the Marine 1st Division, with the Army 7th Infantry Division landing later farther north, around Iwon. The Americans were then to drive to the Manchurian border. Meanwhile, the 3rd Infantry Division would link up with Gen. Walton Walker's Eighth Army, which was moving north along the western coast from Seoul.

But the whole plan was threatened by those mines in Wonsan Harbor. The harbor was too shallow for the big destroyer-minesweepers to work, so the job was given to the twelve-hundred-ton minesweepers *Pirate, Pledge,* and *Incredible,* plus some wooden auxiliary minesweepers. They would be assisted by a helicopter and a UDT to spot mines.

On October 11, Lieutenant Commander McKinney's Team No. 3 approached the outer channel of Wonsan Harbor in the *Diachenko*. Two outer islands stood off the channel, Ko-to in the north and Rei-to in the south. No one knew who held these islands, and it was important to know.

Two landing craft from the *Diachenko* were loaded with the UDT men and set out to explore. Almost immediately they encountered two horned mines, just under the surface, within half a mile of the ship's anchorage. After this all the team members were brought to examine the mines and to recognize the type. Then the men began searching for mines. By the end of the afternoon they had found and buoyed fifty mines. The closest one to the *Diachenko* was only a hundred yards away. The ship moved cautiously out of the area to a new anchorage in safer waters.

On October 12 the UDT members participated in the assault on Rei-to Island. It began with air and naval bombardment. Then Lieutenant Commander McKinney and his men went in. They wore two-piece rubber exposure suits that covered them from top to bottom, with only their mouths exposed below the mask. The suits leaked at the zippers in the back, but they were still lifesaving by preserving body warmth.

The swimmers went into the water and searched for a network of mines that might be there but found none. Lieutenant Commander Nowack's landing craft intercepted a North Korean sampan from Ko-to Island. They questioned the men on the sampan and were told that only a handful of troops were on Rei-to, and that they were all on the southern side of the island. Nowack towed the sampan toward the *Diachenko* for further questioning of the crew, while Lieutenant Commander McKinney and his swimmers started for Rei-to.

Meanwhile, the Air Force and the surface Navy were combining forces to find and destroy the mines. The Air

Force made bombing raids along the channel to explode mines. The three minesweepers approached in a staggered line, with two wooden minesweepers between them. The sweeper *Pirate* led the way, and a helicopter whirled overhead. Suddenly the helicopter pilot spotted three long rows of mines and radioed to the sweepers. The minesweeper's sounding gear began getting echoes in all directions. The *Pirate*'s bow lookout shouted that there was a mine close on the starboard bow, and the rudder was slammed hard left and then hard right, but the mine hit amidships, throwing up a column of water and debris 250 feet in the air. The *Pirate* sank stern first in a few seconds and six men went down with the ship while more than forty men floundered in the icy water.

The *Pledge* was next in line. The skipper stopped engines, and lowered a whaleboat to rescue the men of the *Pirate*. Just then the hidden gun batteries on the shore opened fire from the island of Sin-do, and automatic fire began to come from Rei-to. The *Pledge* fired its three-inch gun. But trying to turn inside an area swept by the *Pirate*, the *Pledge* hit a mine. The captain's leg was broken, and on the bridge all the men were seriously injured or killed. The skipper ordered the crew to abandon ship. The ships of the flotilla all opened up their guns on the North Korean batteries on Sin-do. The UDT landing craft sped to the area. Lieutenant Commander McKinney took his landing craft alongside the *Pledge* and began taking men off. Soon the craft was full and men were clinging to the sides and to the rubber boats the landing craft was towing. Nowack's boat went to the *Pledge* and took off more men. One man was trapped in the radio shack, and they went to find him. It looked as though his body was in three parts; he was mortally wounded, if not already dead. As they stood there, the *Pledge* shuddered and began to take her last plunge. The UDT men leaped into their boat and cast off just in time. The two landing craft took twenty-five men to the destroyer-minesweeper

Endicott. In all, seventy-five men and eleven officers were injured and twelve men went down with the ship.

The next day, the *Diachenko* boarded Rei-to Island. Two UDT craft went in to the area where the *Pirate* and the *Pledge* had been sunk, to buoy the wrecks and the lines of mines, but they could not locate the sunken craft.

On the following day, the demolition teams found two streams of air bubbles coming up. UDT diver William Gianotti, in a rubber suit and mask and an Aqua-Lung, went into the water, thus making the first American combat operation with a diving apparatus. He swam down, trailing a line with which he would mark the wreck if he could find it. He saw the sunken *Pledge* lying on its side and secured the line to it. A buoy was fastened to the line on the surface. No attempt was made to dive to the *Pirate* because the oil slick was too dense. So the underwater men spent the rest of the day locating and buoying moored mines. Five sampans from Ko-to came up, and the fishermen volunteered to help buoy the mines.

For the next few days from morning to night the UDT men and the small sweepers pushed farther into the harbor. The helicopter flew overhead, spotting mines. The wooden minesweepers sank some of the mines by cutting the moorings and then firing on the mines. The UDT men offered to take out all the mines at one time with a giant explosion of the line, but the idea was overruled by the minesweeper commander, who preferred the traditional approach.

The UDT men made several Aqua-Lung dives to salvage the sweep gear from the two sunken minesweepers. Lieutenant Commander McKinney made a helicopter survey of the landing beaches on Kalma Peninsula, near Wonsan.

The underwater men were assigned to take over Sindo Island, from which the North Koreans had harassed the minesweepers with artillery. Lt. Daniel Chandler and twenty volunteers went to the island in rubber boats loaded with weapons. They saw the smashed guns but no North Koreans. Two families came running down to the shore asking for food and first aid. They told the Americans that the North Korean soldiers, about two hundred in all, had left the island the night before.

The landing party paddled to a nearby island where a white flag was flying. It was a leper colony, they discovered, and hundreds of lepers crowded down to the shore, begging for food. The boat did not land but went back to the destroyer-transport and brought back a load of food.

So many were the mines in North Korean waters that the American Navy had found it could not deal with them, so it had employed a number of Japanese minesweepers and Japanese crews of former naval men to help with the job. One of these Japanese minesweepers hit a mine and sank in seconds. The nearest UDT boat hurried to the area and picked up seventeen survivors.

The minesweepers had pushed into the channel, and the landing force could land, although the shore was still held by the North Koreans. The UDT men charted six hundred yards of offshore approaches.

A group of ROK minesweepers came in and began to move through the swept waters when suddenly an explosion rocked the harbor, then another, and finally a third explosion blew up the ROK minesweeper *YMS-516*, which disintegrated into a mass of wreckage. The UDT landing craft headed for the area and rescued seventeen more survivors, who were taken to the sick bay of the *Diachenko*.

No one knew what had caused the explosion. Had the North Koreans gotten through in the darkness of night to sow more mines? Had the Soviets provided them with some new sort of mine that was not easily detectable and was actuated by some force with which the Americans were unfamiliar? Until they knew the answers to the questions, the landings could not be risked.

Lieutenant Commander DeForest of the UDT

found the key that following day. He went behind enemy lines and discovered some mine parts that proved the mines were magnetic mines, capable of destroying or damaging any ship. Then a Korean sailor who had escaped from the North Koreans volunteered to show the men where the mine lines had been sowed.

So the UDT men continued to look for mines and to buoy them for the minesweepers to destroy.

On October 26, a week behind schedule, X Corps brought in the Marine 1st Division to Wonsan, with the UDT craft acting as guides through the swept channel to the beaches. So the Marines started for Hungnam and Hamhung and for Chongjin Reservoir.

On October 27 the UDT detachment went into Iwon in rubber boats to prepare the way for the 7th Division landings on October 29. At Hungnam a detachment of the UDT made a mine search of Hungnam Harbor, which would be the supply port for the Marines driving northwest.

Lieutenant Commander Welch was assigned to check on Chinnampo as a port and report on its availability and usability; three UDT boats searched the area in combination with a helicopter. They found two lines of mines in the harbor and more mines nearby. The Chinnampo operation lasted from November 2 to December 1, 1950. UDTs cleared two hundred miles of channels and finally made a reconnaissance trip to the Chinnampo docks.

During this same period one element of Team No. 1 was attached to a group of British commandos, and on October 7 this combined unit attacked and destroyed railroad bridges and tunnels in two different locations, one sixteen miles south of Kyongsong and the other four miles south of Songjin, both well behind enemy lines.

Late in November the whole character of the Korean War changed when the Chinese entered the war. They began with a rush of two hundred thousand troops who overwhelmed the U.N. forces and caused an immediate and rapid retreat and withdrawal from North Korea. The UDT men were employed trying to find suitable beaches for the rapid withdrawal of troops.

When it became obvious that the United States was engaged in a war of attrition, the role of the UDTs also changed. Lt. George Atcheson was sent back to Japan to train South Koreans as guerrillas, whose major work would be to rescue downed Allied airmen. After training a team, Atcheson was returned to other UDT duties, but other UDT men took over this same sort of work, mostly associated with the CIA in covert activity, reactivating a pattern begun in the days of General Donovan and the OSS. Ultimately this pattern would develop into the establishment of the Navy SEAL. Associated with Marine officers, they undertook to teach the South Korean guerrillas many skills, from map reading to survival. The organization was known as E&E—escape and evasion. UDT men took charge of several missions to insert guerrillas into needed areas. On one mission from the APD *Begor,* Lt. Dave Gleckler sent first a pair of UDT scout swimmers from Team No. 3 to look over the area. When they did not return in proper time, he decided something had happened, and he decided to go in and examine the beach. He and another UDT man swam to the beach and it checked out, so he told his companion to flash the signal for the boats to come in, but his partner had lost the signal light on the way in, so they had to swim back to the *Begor.* Gleckler picked up another UDT man and swam back to the beach. The area checked out again, and this man did have his light. So they brought the boats in. The guerrillas arrived on the beach disguised as Chinese Communist troops and headed for the hills. Gleckler and his partner swam back to the *Begor.* The original team, which had gotten lost, had then arrived, so the mission was a success, although a little confused.

But not all the cloak-and-dagger operations were so

successful. Lieutenant Atcheson was brought back to the E&E unit, and he had some problems. His first new mission was to train a small team of guerrillas and insert them into a mountain region on the eastern coast of Korea between Hungnam and Chongjin. The area proved to be a sort of no-man's-land, full of Buddhist monasteries whose monks did not approve of the Communist government of North Korea. But before making any decisions, a preliminary reconnaissance had to be made to check out the stories and to make contact with one of the "dissident" monasteries.

Atcheson trained half a dozen guerrillas for four weeks in UDT techniques. Then he took the guerrillas to the target beach and left them. A week from that time he would return and pick them up. Meanwhile, they would go inland, contact the monasteries, and examine the lay of the land.

When it came time for the pickup, the guerrillas were late in coming and arrived at the beach at sunset, having to climb down cliffs in the dark. They had been chased by enemy patrols earlier in the day and were very nervous lest they be caught on the beach.

Atcheson violated his own security rules and signaled to the guerrillas from the ship. They thought it was a trap and refused to move. Finally Atcheson got his interpreter to shout at them and calm them down. But when they got back to the ship safe and sound, Atcheson learned that the whole mission was a failure. There were no dissident monasteries in the area, and there were many enemy troops and patrols. The whole idea of using this place as an E&E base was then abandoned.

Atcheson also led a number of guerrilla raids in which the UDT men did the scouting and the planning and put the guerrillas into the area, then got them out again. But the Koreans actually did the demolition, often far behind the enemy lines. Some of these missions were successful but others were failures, as in one raid on an area that had been successfully raided once before. Perhaps for that reason Atcheson and his men were not as careful as they should have been. They scouted the beach, found it safe, and brought the Koreans in. As they did so, a force of North Koreans who had been concealed and were waiting charged forth with automatic weapons, making an attempt to capture the raiders and their boats. Atcheson brought his landing craft in very close and picked up one raider. Other boats rescued others, but in all, nine men were lost on this raid, and Atcheson very nearly was captured. His interpreter was killed, and grenade fragments were found imbedded in the hull of Atcheson's boat.

UDT operations in Korea were important enough that a new team, UDT No. 5, was commissioned to go to Korea. The joint operations with the British were considered very successful, and Lt. Ted Fielding was the most successful of the UDT men with the British; he was involved in a number of operations with commandos and the Royal Navy. On one, a British naval command wanted to find out if a destroyer could operate successfully in the Han River estuary. Fielding and the UDT men set out to find out, using the APD *Bass* as if it were the destroyer. They ran a hydrographic survey of the river and were able to penetrate far enough inland that Fielding thought the British could do the same. Having taken the *Bass* upriver as far as it would go, Fielding then set out to scout the area, and while collecting information noticed two children from a nearby village standing by a haystack in a field and beckoning. Fielding told his men to ignore the children. The children continued to make signals. Then one of the men noticed that the haystack moved, and Fielding told his men to drop; they had no sooner done so than the haystack erupted with machine-gun fire. It was a Chinese trap. The UDT men were stuck on the beach. If they moved, the machine gun would track them. Fielding called for fire from the *Bass*'s five-inch guns, and in a few minutes the haystack disappeared. The UDT men went back to their ship.

The war dragged on through 1951, 1952, and into 1953.

The UDT men were occupied with all sorts of chores, including the demolition of North Korean fishing nets to deprive the enemy of one of their major food sources. When the war came to an end at the end of July 1953, the UDTs had participated in sixty-one assault landings and carried out many other forms of clandestine activities. They were not just Underwater Demolition Teams anymore but were recognized by the Navy as capable of operating on land as well, having participated in more than a hundred reconnaissance missions, most of which involved land operations and many special missions, some of them far behind enemy lines. The nature of combat had changed in this war, and the Navy had adjusted to it. There would be much more adjustment in the future.

SSSS
SSSS Some of the thinking of the UDT men during World War II and certainly the experience of the Korean War combined to change the Underwater Demolition Teams during the 1950s. To start, in 1954 the Navy changed the names of the teams. Teams No. 1, No. 3, and No. 5 became Teams No. 11, No. 12, and No. 13, stationed on the West Coast, at Coronado, and Teams No. 2 and No. 4 became Teams No. 21 and No. 22. These were not to be confused with the World War II UDTs of the same numbers.

The mission of the UDTs was expanded considerably. The men would still look for underwater obstacles and clear harbors and channels for amphibious landings, but they would also penetrate enemy waters to attack ships at anchor, demolish antisubmarine and other nets, and create confusion in the enemy forces. They would be responsible for mine clearance, but also dissemination of intelligence. They would guide assault waves to the beaches as in the past, but they would also make inland penetration for intelligence purposes and would land and supply raiders and guerrilla fighters. They would improve channels and harbors as they did in World War II and in Korea, but they would also destroy port facilities during withdrawals.

In other words, the mission of the UDT men had expanded broadly to make of them a special force with the capability of the raider and guerrilla added to the frogman activities underwater. And as their mission expanded, so did their range of weapons and their skills. Particularly during 1954, the UDTs became adept at working in cold waters, since exercises were staged in Dutch Harbor and Kodiak Island in Alaska.

Team No. 11 was called on for a very special mission in February 1955. The United States was still protecting the Chinese Nationalist government on Taiwan, and that government decided that its occupation of the Tachen Islands near the Chinese mainland was untenable. But how to get the troops out? If the Nationalists sent in ships, the Beijing government might attack them. So the Chinese called on the Americans for help, and the U.S. Seventh Fleet undertook the task of protecting the Nationalist evacuation of the islands. A Team No. 11 unit was given the responsibility of charting a safe passage for the ships into deep water, and after the Nationalist Chinese had left the islands, of blowing up the installations and supplies that might be useful to the mainland Chinese.

The UDTs also worked with the Distant Early Warning System, again in the frigid waters of Alaska and Canada, making surveys and doing demolition work. This cold-water experience led to the creation of a new foam rubber wet suit that soon became standard cold-water equipment.

The absence of wars and serious threats of a traditional nature (except the Cold War threat of the Soviet Union, which lasted for decades) brought about cuts in naval appropriations, and the UDTs were cut down. Five teams were reduced to three, with Teams No. 13 and No. 22 being decommissioned, but the idea of underwater warfare was not abandoned. By this time it had become an essential element in any amphibious operation, and the Americans were learning a fact the Europeans had known for a long time: There is a place for special operations, such as the mining of ships in harbor, in naval warfare. The area of operations was extended. On one exercise, underwater swimmers staged an attack deemed successful on the Panama Canal. In another exercise, demolition men in fatigues got past the guards on a moored vessel in harbor by pretending to be a garbage detail, but instead of garbage, their trash cans were filled with explosives, and they "sank" the ship that was their target. In this operation the UDT men stole the ship captain's keys, unlocked a cabinet in which the gunnery officer's keys were kept, unlocked the ship's powder magazines, and planted their timed charges in the magazines. Then they returned the keys, picked up their trash cans, and left the ship with no one knowing they had been doing anything untoward there. When the captain was told that his ship was officially "sunk," he protested that there was no sign of any explosives having been laid anywhere. The UDT men then showed the captain their charges in the magazines and told their story.

So the UDTs became checks on ship security. These operations certainly called for skills that were not taught in seamanship classes, and the UDTs were constantly trying to improve their capabilities for special warfare, although there were many in the "regular" Navy who thoroughly disapproved of the UDT tactics and sometimes of their behavior. Because of their special training, which since the earliest days had included testing of the limits of endurance in UDT "Hell Week," and their close association with one another and with few others, the UDT men were a group apart in the Navy of the 1950s. They already had a special-warfare role, and in that capacity were with the fleet units that shipped to the coast of Lebanon during the crisis of 1958 when President Eisenhower alerted the Marines during the Syria-prompted rebellion. UDT men were also involved in actions around Quemoy and Matsu islands near the China coast. These islands, held by the Nationalists, had been used by them for harrying attacks on their Communist enemies on the mainland. In 1958 the mainland Chinese retaliated by shelling the islands. American policy was still hitched to the Nationalist Chinese Kuomintang star. So the U.S. Seventh Fleet was again called to action to protect the Nationalists. A UDT group came in with the fleet, and the UDT men conducted surveys and reconnaissance to determine the method of evacuating the islands if the mainland Chinese attacked.

Underwater Demolition Teams also participated in various service tests in connection with the space program. The most important of these was investigation of weightlessness as a factor in space travel. So by the end of the 1950s the underwater men had branched out into many activities that had little to do with their original assignment of preparing beaches for invasion. At the same time, all the American armed forces were recognizing a basic change in styles of warfare and the needs of the military to cope with these changes. The discovery that a small group of guerrilla fighters could even take over a nation had been proved in Cuba, where Fidel Castro's revolution had succeeded, much to American chagrin. Castro and Che Guevara had become heroes in the eyes of many Third World countries, and Guevara's book on guerrilla warfare was studied as avidly as was that of Mao Zedong. In the American military a previous distaste by the high command for extraordinary units to conduct special warfare was expanding. Even as the 1960 presidential election was being fought in America, the CIA and the American military were making preparations for the Bay of Pigs invasion of Cuba, which was to be orchestrated by the American military but carried out by Cubans. In this atmosphere the American military was ripe for some changes in its approach to unconventional warfare, and among the units in the forefront were the Underwater Demolition Teams.

Surveying the world around him in 1961 after taking office as president of the United States, John F. Kennedy saw country after country enveloped in struggle, most of it involving irregulars of one sort or another, and a world atmosphere in which terrorism and small-scale violence were taking hold.

His reaction was to order the U.S. armed forces to increase their capability for limited action and unconventional action to meet unconventional challenges. He also wanted the United States military to be able to train guerrillas from other countries.

In the winter of 1961 the U.S. Navy moved to comply with the presidential directives. New designs for shallow-draft boats for use in riverine warfare were presented. As for the units capable of meeting the presidential demand, one already existed: the Underwater Demolition Teams, whose members had already trained guerrillas in Korea and had already been involved in the Vietnam War, in the Gulf of Tonkin, and in Laos. The office of the chief of naval operations began consideration of a plan that would create for the Navy the closest thing to the Army's Green Berets that was possible. The unit would be called the Navy SEALs. The name was an acronym for Sea, Air, and Land teams. Their responsibility would be to develop naval guerrilla and counterguerrilla capabilities. The emphasis of the moment was on operations in bodies of water or onshore. They would also be prepared to send advisory groups to friendly nations to teach them and even participate in maritime special operations. And so in December 1961 the Navy SEALs were born.

The SEALs took many leaves from the book of the

UDTs. They would be stationed at the same places, Coronado on the West Coast and Little Creek, Virginia, on the East Coast. In January two SEAL teams were commissioned, Team No. 1 on the West Coast and Team No. 2 on the East Coast, as "Navy fleet tactical units tasked with conducting naval special warfare." Almost all the members of these two teams were volunteers from the Underwater Demolition Teams—five officers and fifty enlisted men for Team No. 1 and ten officers and fifty enlisted men for Team No. 2. The teams had scarcely been formed when the American involvement in Vietnam became serious. It had been building for more than five years since the Eisenhower administration's decision to prop up the French colonial empire and then the French defeat at Dienbienphu. All this was tied closely to Secretary of State John Foster Dulles's notion of a domino theory, in which once a government fell, particularly to a nationalist group (and almost everywhere in these years that meant a Communist group), then governments around it would also begin to topple. The only antidotes for this, according to the conventional American view at the time, were large infusions of American military assistance, American military advice, and (although it was not then stated) American military involvement.

America had been deeply involved in Vietnam on land since the late 1950s, when the Green Berets moved into Laos and South Vietnam. Ostensibly they were present only as advisers, but actually they were more involved than the American public realized almost from the beginning. The Navy involvement was much more open and less demanding—five LCVPs and five LCMs were given to the Royal Laotian government for its riverine forces. In June 1960 a detachment of UDT No. 12 came down from Yokosuka, Japan, to deliver the boats up the Mekong River. The journey was 430 miles, and it was successfully completed on July 4. Having delivered the goods, the Navy men took a plane to Saigon and went back to Japan.

The actions and statements of the Kennedy administration clearly indicated that the U.S. involvement in Vietnam was going to increase. So late in 1961 the U.S. Navy's commander in chief in the Pacific decided that hydrographic information about Vietnam waters was going to be essential for the future. He sent the APD *Cook* to Vietnam with a detachment of UDT men. They finished their survey without difficulty on January 27, 1962. By that time the miring of the United States in Vietnam had significantly progressed, and the Military Assistance Command had been formed. So as the SEAL teams were formed, their active involvement in Vietnam was already a certainty.

One might say that the SEALs had their birth from the UDTs. Their training program of basic underwater demolition BUD/S had its inception in the early days at Fort Pierce, as did its program of ferocious physical involvement culminating in Hell Week. The result for the UDT men had been a high esprit de corps, and this was handed down to the SEALs intact. From the outset the SEALs knew they were a special sort of outfit, and it was their ambition to make the SEALs the prime special-warfare organization in the world. SEAL Team No. 1, which was assigned to the Pacific Fleet, was commanded by Lt. David del Guidice, who had been one of those involved in the trip up the Mekong River to Laos. Hardly had the team been formed when two officers were dispatched to Vietnam to investigate the type of support the SEALs could provide. On March 10, 1962, two SEALs arrived in Vietnam to begin teaching the Vietnamese clandestine warfare. For six months they taught the South Vietnamese and then almost immediately began another six-month course for more men. At the same time more SEALs, functioning as Mobile Training Team 10-62, began to train Junk Force commandos of the South Vietnamese Navy. Their course was frogman materials for the most part. In the fall of 1962 they graduated sixty-two men from the course, and then they took on another session of six months. The Vietnamese they had taught were sent out to teach others.

The direct involvement of Americans in Vietnam was delayed for a time, but the direction was clear. The concentration of American effort and thinking was on unconventional warfare because of the nature of the enemy and the nature of the war. It had been decided that the Vietnamese would run their own war with American assistance, but as was proved early in the war, this was virtually impossible because of the nature of the South Vietnam regime, which was riddled with corruption and self-serving. This regime was established by the French in the French pattern, and even by 1962 it could be seen that there was very little of the spirit of nationalism that drove their enemies, the North Vietnamese and the Viet Cong guerrillas. This was the cross that Americans involved in Vietnam would bear during the entire conflict. Almost from the beginning, some of the SEAL team members wondered if the United States was on the right side in the conflict, but the essential factor for the SEALs was that they were Navy men and they were professionals. They would do the job assigned to them as well as they could do it.

By the beginning of 1963 the American involvement in Vietnam had again risen, and now twelve thousand Americans were in Vietnam, most of them in specialist roles, a fact that maximized their efforts. By this time, public detestation of the regime of President Diem and his family even reached Washington, D.C., Diem's strongest prop, until finally the United States disassociated itself from the Diem regime and did nothing to stop his downfall and murder in the coup of November 1963. Was the new regime any better? The Americans convinced themselves it was. But then John F. Kennedy was assassi-

A member of the SEAL team is picked up in an inflatable recovery boat after parachuting into the water during an exercise near Naval Air Station, Rota, Spain. *(U.S. Navy)*

Navy SEAL trainees carry rubber boats up a sand dune during a Hell Week exercise at the Naval Amphibious Base, Coronado, California. *(U.S. Navy)*

Teams of SEAL trainees struggle in a mud pit during a Hell Week exercise in Coronado, California. *(U.S. Navy)*

During exercises at Little Creek, Virginia, underwater demolition men are picked up from the sea by helicopter. *(National Archives)*

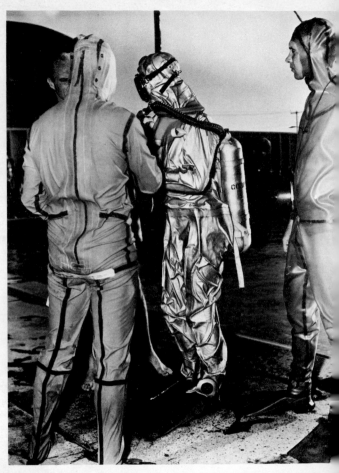

Underwater demolition men in divers' suits. *(National Archive*

Navy corpsmen crawl under barbed wire on a smoke-covered obstacle course during a simulated firefight. They are undergoing combat training at Camp Pendleton, California. *(U.S. Navy)*

SEALS prepare with white phosphorus fire for operations at West Beach, Iwo Jima, during World War II. *(National Archives)*

UDTs measure water depth along the beach at Twon, Korea.
(National Archives)

Members of a SEAL team aboard a mechanized landing craft fire on Viet Cong huts during a Vietnamese/American operation approximately fifteen miles south of Saigon in 1967. Four Viet Cong were killed and some 90,000 pounds of rice and other supplies were captured. *(U.S. Navy)*

SEAL team members ready their weapons as they prepare to conduct an operation from a riverine craft in Vietnam. *(National Archives)*

nated, and President Lyndon Johnson, in his efforts to keep the Kennedy policies going, was willing to accept statements attesting to the probity of the South Vietnamese. The American commitment in terms of numbers was not yet so very high, but the commitment in terms of its depth was already complete.

The Johnson administration believed that the war in Vietnam could be won. President Kennedy had set the wheels in motion for further expansion of special-warfare units, and the Johnson administration continued to support this policy. More SEAL detachments were sent to Vietnam. At Danang the SEALs set up a base to train South Vietnamese in maritime command operations. Meanwhile, the CIA was conducting several kinds of covert operations. In 1963 the Navy recommended the use of UDT and SEAL personnel in commando operations into North Vietnam. This was a far cry from "advisory capacity," but it was the direction in which the U.S. forces were steadily moving. Since the Vietnamese were not effective in fighting their battles, many of the Americans involved wanted to fight them for the South Vietnamese and win them. But there the American high command drew the line. The United States was not going to try to win the war in Vietnam in any conventional fashion. Instead, its aim was to punish the North Vietnamese to the extent that they would withdraw from South Vietnam, and more and more this punishment demanded special tactics and special forces. In September 1962 the Navy recommended involvement of the SEALs with high-speed PT boats against the North Vietnamese in covert operations. They would attack the rail and highway routes that ran down through North Vietnam to the Ho Chi Minh Trail. That recommendation was not then accepted by the high command; they were not quite ready for the use of Americans in combat. However, the idea was accepted, but the boats would be manned by South Vietnamese. So the first of the high-speed shore boats were brought to Vietnam, ostensibly for the use of the Vietnamese. They were a combination of old American PT boats, and boats bought from a Norwegian shipbuilding company and called popularly Nasty boats after a Norwegian boat. They were aluminum-hulled, could reach speeds of forty knots, and had a range of a thousand miles. They were armed with machine guns and later with mortars. By April 1962 several SEAL teams had been put in motion to go to Vietnam. The mission of SEAL Mobil Training Team 10-62 was to train a group of Vietnamese coastal force personnel in sabotage and guerrilla warfare. Six months later, MTT 4-63 relieved that team. Its commander was Lt. Alan G. Routh of SEAL Team No. 1, and he had one officer and seven enlisted men in the team.

The SEALs were becoming more involved in Vietnam and so were the UDTs, which were training for operations with submarines. The USS *Perch* was to be brought to Subic Bay in the Philippines, which would serve as its home port, to take part in clandestine operations in Vietnam.

In 1963 the Navy decided that it needed more information about South Vietnamese waters and sent the APD *Weiss* to make surveys of the beaches from Danang to Bac Lieu. The surveys would be made by the UDT men, who would carry small arms for protection, although theoretically they would not be involved in any combat operations. Nor would the UDT men go beyond the high-water mark, which left land reconnaissance and activity in the hands of the Marines.

SEAL men by this time were attending Army special forces schools and other specialist schools to learn all they could about clandestine operations. They also attended Fort Benning's parachute school. They learned new techniques of escape and evasion, jungle warfare, and unconventional warfare equipment use.

SEALs from the East Coast team were working with

NATO units in Europe to better their skills. Their mission now was described as perfecting their skills for sabotage and the training of "indigenous personnel" in guerrilla activity. They went to Norway, Turkey, and Greece. In Norway they went to school at the Norwegian frogmen's school in Bergen. Afterward they held an exercise in which their mission was to penetrate twenty-four miles of "enemy" territory to reach a friendly base. The Norwegians played "enemy." The SEALs started out and finished the job without being intercepted, and thus proved to their NATO allies that the American unit was extremely capable.

At Volos in northern Greece the SEALs played the role of teachers, not students. They taught the Greeks maritime sabotage techniques. In an exercise, the SEALs parachuted into the area and then participated in a combined attack on a fuel pier, radio station, and other facilities.

In Turkey they worked with submarines and guerrilla tactics, putting a Turkish guerrilla unit ashore from a submarine.

By this time, then, the SEALs had achieved a worldwide reputation for excellence after only a year of operations. This obviously was a result of the buildup of personnel over the years, with some of the men having served in World War II and Korea in the parent UDT organization.

In 1963 the SEALs had a new directive that took them further into the field of special warfare than any Navy unit had gone before. They were now unashamedly involved in clandestine operations of a sort that had previously been the province of the CIA and in World War II of the OSS.

"To develop a specialized capability for sabotage, demolition, and other clandestine activities, conducted in and from restricted waters, rivers, and canals. Specifically to be able to destroy enemy shipping, harbor facilities, bridges, railway lines, and other installations in maritime areas and riverine environments. Also to protect friendly supply lines, installations, and assets to maritime and riverine environments from similar attack," said their official designation. It also enjoined them to insert and exfiltrate agents, guerrillas, and other intelligence agents, and to conduct varied intelligence activity. They were also to be ready to carry out counterinsurgency tasks and to educate indigenous populations in these matters. To do this they were to develop tactics and equipment for the jobs at hand.

So the SEALs began to move away from the limited capabilities of the Underwater Demolition Teams, which still held the responsibility for aquatic reconnaissance, and which would work with the SEALs for the next few years. The BUD/S training was the same, but by the 1960s the SEALs had gained a new set of capabilities and a new spirit that made them unique in the special-warfare field as far as the Navy was concerned. It was dangerous work under the best of conditions, a point brought home in the spring of 1963, when one SEAL man was lost in a diving accident in the Bosporus. He had been instructing a group of Turkish students in buoyant ascents and put on an Aqua-Lung to observe his students' activities. He surfaced from his first dive, then went down again and did not come back. The body was never recovered in the swirling waters.

By the fall of 1963 the number of SEALs was increasing so that the organization was reformed on a fleet basis, as it had been earlier with the UDTs. Later the UDTs, boat groups, and SEALs would all be brought under the Naval Special Warfare Command. Because of the organization, from that point on SEAL operations in Europe and the Atlantic would emerge from the Little Creek, Virginia, base, and SEAL operations in the Pacific would come from the Coronado, California, base.

The SEALs were active in NATO exercises in these

years and in hemispheric activity. They trained with Canadians and in the Virgin Islands. They participated in activities in Italy, where there was much to be learned from the Italian underwater men.

They were involved in various American forays into Latin America. At the end of April 1964, SEALs were sent to the Dominican Republic aboard the USS *La Salle* when the United States was involved in settling troubles there. Later another SEAL detachment was dispatched for reconnaissance work off the Dominican Republic. The SEAL team was under command of Lieutenant Kochey, and it was told to look for suspicious activity that might indicate rebels working in the Samona Bay area. The SEALs decided to take on protective coloration and pretended to be tourists on a fishing trip, dressed in civilian clothes and carrying the proper rods and reels and other equipment. They searched the coastal areas, including a number of caves, but came up with nothing. But that did not mean the rebels were not there. The SEALs were involved in several firefights with them before they were through with the activity, one of the fights occurring in the streets of Santo Domingo. It became apparent that where units of the fleet would be involved in any sort of activity that concerned rebels or guerrilla activity, the SEALs would be there, too.

15   Vietnam—The American Involvement

ꝯꝯꝯꝯ
ꝯꝯꝯꝯ In the years of the Eisenhower administration the United States government elected to replace the French as the primary instrument of power in Indochina, and the deep involvement of the American military became assured, although at first an effort was made to cloak its role in euphemisms such as "advisory" and "cooperative." In fact, from the time of the Bucklew Report on conditions and possibilities in Vietnam, made in the winter of 1964 by the legendary Capt. Philip H. Bucklew, the U.S. Navy was deeply involved in clandestine warfare in Vietnam.

That had been Bucklew's recommendation to the Joint Chiefs of Staff, and that recommendation was given favorable action during the years that followed.

In the spring of 1964 the North Vietnamese began moving some of their regular Army units south to extend the fighting. A SEAL adviser discovered that only a handful of the South Vietnamese who had been trained in underwater and sabotage work remained in the services; therefore a new training program was introduced based on the SEAL BUD/S program. The first class was graduated at the end of September, after paddling over a hundred miles, running seventy-five miles, carrying rubber boats for twenty-three miles, and swimming ten miles during "Hell Week."

The South Vietnamese were pushed immediately into operational missions, for by that time, the fall of 1964, the United States had quietly taken control of covert military operations under the Military Assistance Command in Vietnam. Of course, covert military operations had been going on from the beginning of the American involvement, but hitherto had been the province of the CIA, and although the CIA continued to be very active in Vietnam, the command structure changed. The Military Assistance Command had its overt activities, which were reported in the press as fully as the media wished, but in addition it had its covert side, under the innocent name of Studies and Observation Group. This meant there was covert warfare conducted by Americans long before the public was aware of any such change.

The Studies and Observation Group masked many activities under its operations sections (OPS). OPS-31 ran all maritime operations; the SEALs were particularly involved here. OPS-32 ran air operations; OPS-33 ran psychological warfare; OPS-34 ran espionage and sabotage in North Vietnam; and OPS-35 ran direct raids into North Vietnam, Laos, and Cambodia. The maritime OPS-31 was centered at Danang. The South Vietnamese attached to this organization pretended to be a coastal survey service, and the Americans operated under the innocent name of Naval Advisory Detachment. Their major role was the training of Vietnamese commando forces in six-man teams, carried out by SEALs and Marine Reconnaissance Units, which were the Marine equivalent.

By the spring of 1964 the fast boats for work along the shore were beginning to arrive from Subic Bay in the Philippines—Nastys and Swift boats, with fifty-foot aluminum hulls and carrying an 81mm mortar and light machine guns. These were to insert and bring out Vietnamese commandos on their raids into enemy territory to capture prisoners and gain intelligence. When they had prisoners the Americans of the security section would be standing by to receive them at Danang.

But the Americans were also involved in direct action under approval from President Johnson in 1964. Under the code name "Timberlake," the Swift and Nasty boats were used for raids into the North. But in 1964 the Americans, concerned with operations in Vietnam, became frustrated by the slow pace of their involvement. Adm. U. S. Grant Sharp, the commander of the Pacific Fleet, had some serious reservations about the South Vietnamese capacity to carry on this sort of warfare, but they had some successes. On June 12 the Americans and South Vietnamese destroyed a storage area on the coast.

Not long afterward, American Swift and Nasty boats brought a Vietnamese team to the bridge on Route 1 near Hao Mon Dong, and another team to the south of the Kien River. The Kien River group ran into North Vietnamese fire; the Nasty boats moved in, and the Americans provided fire support for the South Vietnamese.

That summer the North Vietnamese made several attempts to destroy both Nasty and Swift boats, but the crews fought back. In addition, they made several strikes, such as one at a radar site on Hon Me Island, and another near Vinh. By midsummer, then, the Americans were used to being involved in shooting situations with the North Vietnamese and the Viet Cong, and claims made publicly about the "advisory" capacity of the Americans in Vietnam no longer had much validity. It had been a gradual process, but from the outset the American government's policies had been belligerent.

The result of this belligerence was the North Vietnamese apprehension that every American vessel in the area was engaged on a warlike mission, and this fear led to the celebrated Tonkin Gulf incident. On one night in August, American Nasty boats with Vietnamese commandos aboard shelled a radar site at Cape Vionh Son, and a security post south of the Ron River. The mission was successful.

The North Vietnamese were convinced that these boats were operating from larger American vessels offshore and not from Danang, where they actually were. Thus when the American destroyer *Maddox* was operating in international waters along the North Vietnamese

coastline on an intelligence mission, it was attacked by
North Vietnamese gunboats in broad daylight in the Gulf
of Tonkin. On August 4 the *Maddox* and the destroyer
Turner Joy were ordered back into this area by a provoca-
tive American high command, and the two reported a
second attack. This was precisely what President Johnson
was looking for —a reason for the Americans to escalate
their war effort. He made much of this Gulf of Tonkin
incident and secured from the U.S. Congress a resolution
allowing the American government to escalate the war
and participate in it openly, on a "defensive" basis. From
this point on, the involvement of the SEALs grew rapidly,
although CINCPAC did its best to hold the special-warfare men in check. For example, on August 11 the Military Command in Vietnam suggested infiltrating a team
of 80 frogmen onto the islands of the Fai Tsi Long archi-
pelago, using American submarines and Vietnamese
frogmen CINCPAC disapproved the plan as being too
drastic an escalation of U.S. participation. But authoriza-
tion for an additional eight Nasty boats was given.

In that fall of 1964, American-trained Vietnamese
frogmen participated in many operations with American
support. The North Vietnamese responded with a strike
at the U.S. air base at Bien Hoa, killing five Americans
and destroying six bombers. This was the excuse the
Johnson administration needed to order further escalation of American efforts, particularly in raids conducted
by special-warfare forces and particularly hit-and-run
raids by high-speed boats.

After the November American elections in which
President Johnson was elected president in his own right,
he saw his victory as an endorsement of his policy in Vietnam, and the further escalation of the American war effort continued. These coastal raids against the North
Vietnamese did very little to change the military balance,
but they did strengthen the North Vietnamese resolve to
win the war, and their recognition that the United States

was their enemy. The North Vietnam reaction was to start a series of terror raids against American installations in South Vietnam. First was a raid on American billets in Saigon on Christmas Eve 1964, in which two Americans were killed. This brought about American raids against the North, including nine maritime operations that involved SEALs and others. In February 1965, Operation Flaming Dart, the first of a series of bombing raids against North Vietnam, was begun by American aircraft. The Americans were very definitely at war against the North Vietnamese. It was now no longer a question of taking over the French commitment to help the South Vietnamese resist the North. The Americans were now fully committed to this war in Southeast Asia. They had walked into the trap of committing themselves to a foreign civil war where the enemy had a strong sense of right on its side, and their ally was an artificial government with relatively small public support and that had been established by the French to serve their own interests. This government continued to exist because of the support of foreign powers. America had made itself the principal prop of the South Vietnam government in the Vietnamese civil war.

The fiction of South Vietnamese responsibility was maintained early in 1965 at the Danang naval support base, where the boats sent out against the North Vietnamese were manned by South Vietnamese, but when the boats came back to Danang, they were the responsibility of the Americans, who did the planning and support for all these missions against shores in the North.

The reaction of the Americans in 1965 was to seek proof of North Vietnamese infiltration into South Vietnam and to punish the North Vietnamese. Thus when an American helicopter discovered a North Vietnamese trawler at Vung Ro Bay on the South Vietnamese coast south of Qui Hjon, the trawler was attacked by American aircraft and finally capsized. American trained guerrilla then surrounded the area and discovered a shipment of Chinese and Soviet arms that were scheduled to be delivered to Viet Cong forces. Much of the shipment was in fact delivered to Viet Cong who got away with it during the fighting in the area. A SEAL adviser was with the South Vietnamese force and helped salvage the shipment and identify it as North Vietnamese.

On March 8, 1965, the first American combat troops came into Vietnam, the 3d Marines, who came into Danang. They were greeted by UDT No. 12 with a sign erected between two paddles, saying "Welcome Marines." This incident received much attention in the United States where the media were beginning to discover the Navy's underwater capability.

Soon the Marines were involved in offensive activity in Vietnam, and this meant that the Navy had to begin to chart the shores of South Vietnam for operational problems of the future. It was not long before there were a number of UDT units in the country operating from submarines from the shore and with boat elements.

The men of the Navy were now committed to offensive action in Vietnam.

Detachment Alpha of the Underwater Demolition Team was the headquarters unit at Subic Bay. Detachment Bravo was directly a part of the Far East Amphibious Squadron of the Seventh Fleet and did many surveys for the fleet. Detachment Charlie operated from the submarine *Perch* in combat operations. The frogmen would surface by swimming upward out of the escape trunk or by being launched in rubber boats when the submarine descended beneath them.

Detachment Delta was stationed at Camp Tien Sha near Danang and served as a rest and recuperation center for UDT men. Detachment Delta's usual job was to knock out and blow up enemy bunkers. Detachments Echo and Foxtrot were part of the amphibious ready group and as such carried out hydrographic and reconnaissance missions. Detachments Golf, Hotel, and India were with the riverine forces in South Vietnam involved with bunker destruction and commando operations against the Viet Cong in river and swamp country.

The Marines and the UDT men staged four major amphibious operations in 1964: Operation Piranha in August, Operation Starlight in September, Operation Dagger Thrust in October, and Operation Blue Marlin in November.

Operation Dagger Thrust was typical of the involvement of the UDT men. This operation was coordinated by Rear Adm. D. L. Wulzen, amphibious commander of the Seventh Fleet. It involved the submarine *Perch* and men of Detachment Charlie. The frogmen inflated their boats on the afterdeck of the submarine when it was on the surface. Lines were connected to the periscope. The submarine went down just below the surface, and the frogmen's boats were still attached by the lines, towed until they were near the beach, and then released. The UDT men then paddled in the rest of the way to carry out their mission, and the *Perch* stood by to provide support. The hydrographic information and intelligence were collected and sent back. The frogmen then remained ashore to provide security for the Marines who made their amphibious assault at dawn.

So the American commitment was complete, and it drew into the war servicemen from other countries. By 1965, Australia, New Zealand, and South Korea had forces in Vietnam.

The increasing American involvement was known to the North Vietnamese, and they began to react. On October 28, 1965, Comdr. Robert J. Fay, the chief of security of the Danang base, was killed by a mortar shell when making inspection rounds in a jeep. He was the first UDT man to die in the Vietnam War.

By January 1966, after a carrot-and-stick effort that involved the bombing of North Vietnam and then cessa tion with a peace offer to the North Vietnamese (which was rejected), the volume of American attacks escalated on land and at sea. Back at Coronado in BUD/S training, the underwater men began looking forward to assignment to Vietnam.

In Vietnam, January 21 saw the beginning of the largest American amphibious operation since the Inchon landing in Korea. UDT men aboard the *Perch* went in first. The *Perch* sat on the bottom about a thousand yards offshore, and the UDT men left the boat through the escape trunk, boarded the boats that were sent up, and moved toward the beach. The *Perch* directed them to the proper landing point. After the reconnaissance, the UDT men paddled back out to sea, attached a line between their two boats, and signaled the *Perch*, which came up, snagged the line on its periscope, and towed the boats farther out to sea, where observers from land could not make out the activity as the frogmen rejoined the submarine.

In February 1966 the Marine 1st Regiment of the Marine 1st Division went to Vietnam, as did a group of SEALs from SEAL Team No. 1, three officers and fifteen enlisted men. Their assignment was to carry out direct-action operations as directed by the commander of naval forces in Vietnam.

Ashore in Vietnam, the command had no idea at the moment about how they would use the SEALs. But a decision had to be made and was. The SEALs would be used against Viet Cong guerrillas in the Rung Sat special zone near Saigon, one thousand square kilometers of mangrove swamp that was a major operating ground for the Viet Cong because of its difficult nature and proximity to Saigon. The shipping channel on the Mekong River ran directly through this territory, and the Viet Cong harassed many a ship with gunfire and mortar fire. It was the sort of area for which the SEALs had trained and the sort of operation for which the group was invented.

16   The SEALs in Vietnam, 1966

〽〽〽〽
〽〽〽〽 Rung Sat was just the sort of job for which the Navy SEALs had trained in the mud flats of Coronado—stinking, greasy jungle and twisted mangrove roots that caught a man's ankle and stopped him abruptly. The whole thousand-square-kilometer operating zone was honeycombed with rivers and streams that meandered through the jungle and masses of nipa palm. The tides ran at four knots and raised the water level by eight feet from low to high. At low tide the mud was often chest-high. The delta was full of crocodiles, snakes, jungle cats, and monkeys. Spiders, scorpions, and leeches seemed to linger on every blade of grass or bit of vegetation, and if the spiders or the leeches did not get to a man, then the stinging ants would.

The Vietnamese called this area the Forest of Assassins, for long before the Viet Cong had come, the place had been the home of river pirates, smugglers, and fugitives. In the villages of the Rung Sat, sixteen thousand Vietnamese subsisted by rice farming, woodcutting, and fishing. In 1964 Rung Sat became the center of activity for about two hundred Viet Cong, but as the war escalated, so did the population, and by the time the SEALs began to arrive, several thousand Viet Cong were in this area, equipped with rifles, automatic weapons, and heavy machine guns and mortars.

The SEALs went to the Nha Be naval base, where Detachment Golf of the UDT was operating. Nha Be is on the Mekong River between Saigon and Rung Sat. From here the SEALs would operate. So now two elements of the Naval Special Warfare Command were working in Vietnam.

The first SEAL operation was Operation Jackstay, conducted in conjunction with the UDT men of Team No. 11 and the 5th Marines. It was to be an amphibious landing, starting on March 26, 1966.

First the swimmers of UDT No. 11 made a beach reconnaissance from the APD *Weiss*. That began at three-thirty in the morning. The area checked out. Red Beach was on the southern tip of Long Thanh Peninsula, that point of the Rung Sat that juts out in the waters of the South China Sea.

The UDT men did not find any mines or obstacles and so told the Marines, who started going ashore at seven-fifteen that morning. SEALs from Detachment Golf and Force Reconnaissance Marines put together twenty-four teams to find the Viet Cong. They moved into the deepness of the Rung Sat jungle and set up surveillance points. By afternoon on March 26 they were in place, watching and waiting for the enemy to appear. And they did appear, although they were not seen. But they were heard. Some of the SEALs reported that the Viet Cong were so close to their positions that they could hear their breathing. Four Viet Cong were unlucky enough to stumble on the Americans, who had orders not to engage the enemy while on reconnaissance unless it was necessary for security. So the four Viet Cong became the first casualties of Operation Jackstay.

Next morning the teams were taken out by boat, but that was only the beginning of operations for the next two weeks. The SEALs, the UDT, and the Marines routed the Viet Cong from this area, destroying bunkers and munitions. There was not a casualty among the SEALs or the UDT men.

Combat was new to the SEALs if not to the UDT men. They had to devise their operating procedures and get used to working in this environment. So they continued to operate in the Rung Sat in fire teams of seven or units of three. Supposedly they were making reconnaissance, but actually they were beginning to specialize in ambushes.

The critiques of Operation Jackstay determined that its greatest failure was in intelligence before the operation began. If they could not find the enemy, they could not come to grips with him. This was always to be a problem in dealing with the Viet Cong, but the SEALs set out to solve it as best they could. They were successful enough that Detachment Golf was increased in size that year to five officers and twenty enlisted men in two platoons.

In the spring of 1966 the SEALs participated in many operations into the interior, designed to surprise the Viet Cong. The program was designed to stop the flow of the enemy across the demilitarized zone. The Americans and South Vietnamese started the Deckhouse operations, which were planned for that purpose. But they failed; the North Vietnamese were interested in escalating the war, not in diminishing it. Their aim, unlike that of the Americans, was total victory, and they never lost sight of it.

This was the major aspect that made the SEAL efforts so frustrating. President Johnson would increase the pressure on the North Vietnamese by bombing and then decrease it by stopping the bombing. All the American talk of "peace" went for naught, because of the North Vietnamese conviction that they would win in the end.

Meanwhile, the SEALs made one mission after another, often skimpy in their results. For example, in June a SEAL ambush resulted in one Viet Cong soldier killed and one wounded, while a third escaped. It was a great deal of effort for minimal gain. But that was the sort of war it was.

On July 15, 1966, Lt. Comdr. Franklin V. Anderson took command of SEAL Team No. 1. He authorized an extension of SEAL activities in Vietnam. By midsummer the SEALs had developed a powerful reputation among the Viet Cong, basically because of their ambushes. These had not resulted in a great number of enemy killed, but they had put a definite curb on Viet Cong travel through the Rung Sat.

Lieutenant Bell was one of the officers assigned to Detachment Golf; he served as its executive officer. That summer and fall Lieutenant Bell did thirty combat operations, from ambushes to simple observations of enemy movements. On August 7 Lieutenant Bell led an ambush on a Viet Cong convoy consisting of a junk and two motorized sampans. The SEALs had to stand in hip-deep water and expose themselves to enemy fire to carry out this ambush, but it was successful, resulting in the killing of seven Viet Cong and the capture of valuable enemy documents about Viet Cong operations.

On July 27 the SEALs sent three six-men squads into the area west of Can Gio in the middle of the day. One unit followed a trail they discovered that had fresh tracks, as though it had been quite recently used. At three-thirty that afternoon the point man came face to face with three Viet Cong soldiers. He fired his grenade launcher, killing one of them, but the other two disappeared. While they were searching the area, the SEALs discovered what had been so often discovered before, a base camp that had housed a full platoon of Viet Cong, but they had gone. The mess hall could accommodate eighty men. They destroyed two hundred pounds of rice and five hundred rounds of ammunition along with some weapons and captured some documents that showed Viet Cong disposition on the Long Thanh Peninsula. That last was most important, but by the time the authorities would act on the intelligence, the Viet Cong would have changed its dispositions.

On August 5 the SEALs laid an ambush and captured three sampans that were carrying six thousand pounds of rice. An enemy soldier in the lead sampan sensed that there was something wrong as the SEALs closed in and fired a warning shot. Three Viet Cong then leaped into the water and escaped, pursued by the SEALs.

Two days later a six-man patrol was out on another ambush. The Viet Cong retaliated by staging ambushes of their own, and in one of them the SEALs ran into trouble. This patrol was led out by Lieutenant Truxell, an eight-man patrol deep in the enemy jungle. On August 18 the patrol had discovered two buildings that contained a cache of more than a quarter of a ton of rice. The destruction of the cache was quite a blow to the Viet Cong, and they set out to retaliate. The patrol was moving through the jungle the next day, August 19. They had received reports of some Viet Cong sampans in the area, and they had reached a clearing and stopped. Suddenly the point man, PO Billy W. Machen, opened fire. He had stumbled on a Viet Cong ambush. The Viet Cong opened fire on him, and he was killed. Lieutenant Truxell and Petty Officer Moscone organized the men to combat the Viet Cong. The enemy were estimated at thirty to forty men. The SEALs put out a hail of fire, drove the Viet Cong off, and then recovered Machen's body and finally were able to be evacuated. Petty Officer Machen became the first SEAL casualty. He was awarded the Silver Star for gallantry.

The Underwater Demolition Teams were as active as the SEALs in this period. UDT No. 11 men played important roles in the Deckhouse operations in Binh Thuy Province, making reconnaissance missions and leading the Marines ashore. On August 20 the submarine *Perch* was again in action, in an attack on a Viet Cong base north of Qui Nhon. Detachment Charlie was told to conduct clandestine beach surveillance from the submarine *Perch*. Although it was presupposed that the Viet Cong had advance word of their plans, the plans were not changed. On the night of August 20 three rubber boats were used by the UDT men to get ashore and carry out their mission. The next night they did the same, but this time the Viet Cong had set up an ambush. Even so, they could not find the frogmen, and their fire was dispersed and ineffective. But the confusion was immense, and in that confusion several swimmers got separated from the others. A search was launched, and the *Perch* lay on the surface a little over a mile offshore and waited.

The first search party turned up missing. The UDT commander took two men in a rubber boat and went to find them. Halfway to shore the commander lighted a flare to guide the missing men, who saw it and soon joined their rescuers. The Viet Cong also saw the flare and began firing toward it. The *Perch* closed in, and the deck crews manned .50-caliber machine guns and a 40mm antiaircraft gun. The heavy fire discouraged the Viet Cong, and all men were recovered. On August 21 the *Perch* was operating with the UDT men and an eighty-five-man South Vietnamese Army force. The Vietnamese camped on the beach and the *Perch* stood offshore about a quarter mile for protection. That night the Viet Cong attacked, and the *Perch* opened fire. A lucky shot hit the Viet Cong ammunition supply, and the result was a number of explosions. The attack fizzled out, and next morning the Vietnamese were evacuated by Swift boats while the UDT men and the *Perch* dealt with the Viet Cong.

That summer the *Perch* was replaced by a converted missile submarine, the USS *Tunny*, which had been equipped specially to manage as many as seventy frogmen and had a dozen inflatable boats. That fall the *Tunny* began work with UDTs to carry out reconnaissance missions in support of amphibious operations.

Since nobody in Vietnam seemed to know what the mission of the SEALs was supposed to be, they made their own rules. Their procedure was to go on a mission, seek contact with the enemy, and kill as many of them as possible. The SEAL performance is a repetitive story of missions, all of them dangerous, that seemed to have no particular point except to kill. There was, however, one exception: the SEAL preoccupation with intelligence, which caused them forever to be on the lookout for documents and to bring back many important bits of information. But since the high command persisted in its policy of body count as the yardstick for success in a war in which bodies were not very important to the enemy, there could be no markers for SEAL success outside that system.

One of the problems the SEALs shared with all other elements of the American forces was their extreme visibility in camp. Everything they did at the Nha Be camp was known to the local people. The foreigners stood out like beacons in a night sky. Every time they went on a mission everyone in the area knew about it, and so, of course, did the Viet Cong, whose agents were everywhere. Thus many of the SEAL operations in the early months of 1966 were failures. The SEALs began to become more secretive in their approach. They would have the equipment for a mission loaded into the boats at Nha Be, but the team members would go into Saigon and the boats would pick them up there.

Another problem was the bad coordination between South Vietnamese intelligence and American intelligence, neither trusting the other too much. This failure led to the SEALs sometimes killing South Vietnamese intelligence agents.

Toward the end of 1966 the loss of five of the attack boats in operations brought a change. The Navy commissioned the building of a new type of boat, the *Osprey,* which had a ninety-five-foot aluminum hull and could make forty knots. The South Vietnamese frogmen continued their attacks in the North, and the SEALs continued their commando raids in the Saigon area. The results were usually sparse, as on September 1 when an operation was staged carefully, but ended in the killing of two Viet Cong. Sometimes it seemed to be a great amount of effort for little return, as on October 3, when a SEAL patrol ambushed a sampan. The SEALs grouped in two-man positions. They held their fire until the sampan was only twenty-five feet from them and then opened up; the three Viet Cong on the sampan were killed.

But sometimes the action involved much more. On October 7, 1966, two squads of seven men were moving in a landing craft for a mission when they encountered a whole battalion of Viet Cong, which was waiting along the shore to attack traffic on the Mekong. A Viet Cong mortar shell made a direct hit on the SEAL landing craft and wounded sixteen of the nineteen men aboard. The SEALs then leaped into action. Two men were manning a .50-caliber machine gun; the gun barrel turned white-hot from the rate of fire. The SEAL counterattack was so aggressive that the Viet Cong battalion broke and ran. The SEALs estimated that forty men were killed and many others wounded by their fire. For the next two weeks this battalion was out of action.

The SEAL buildup continued at the end of 1966 along with that of the rest of the American forces. President Johnson visited Vietnam, giving an indication of his intent to pursue the struggle. One result was the commitment of men from SEAL Team No. 2 at Little Creek to Vietnam for the first time. Five officers and twenty enlisted men were sent to Vietnam.

By this time the SEALs had achieved such a reputation in the area that in the celebration of South Vietnam's national day, a SEAL-trained guard of Vietnamese frogmen was selected to protect the South Vietnamese prime minister.

In the last months of 1966 the SEALs rolled up many victories—some small, some large. They captured a large cache of Viet Cong arms and ten thousand rounds of ammunition in one raid. They were continually finding and destroying caches of rice, the Viet Cong's staple food. In these operations they did some pioneering, using helicopters, which were not much used at that time by other units, to get into and out of their raid areas.

As the year came to close, the Navy began an assessment of the operations of the Special Warfare units in Vietnam. The Underwater Demolition Teams had been there for several years. This year they received the Navy Unit Commendation for their operations.

For the SEALs this was the first stage of their employment in combat. They had carried out 153 combat operations during the year, killing 86 Viet Cong and perhaps killing another 15. They had destroyed 21 sampans and 2 junks and 33 huts and bunkers used by the Viet Cong. They had captured and destroyed more than 500,000 pounds of rice. This does not sound like much of an accomplishment, but in terms of the total impact on the war effort and the total amount of money expended in Vietnam (by the end of 1966 the United States had 385,000 troops stationed in Vietnam), the impact of the SEALs operation plus that of the UDTs was enormous. No more than forty SEALs were present in Vietnam at any one time during this year, yet their presence was a constant threat to the Viet Cong. The reason for this was that the SEALs were defeating the Vietnamese guerrillas at their own game. The Viet Cong reputation for striking swiftly out of nowhere and then vanishing was overpowered by the SEAL reputation for emerging from a swamp like the primeval statue of the frogman that stands in the courtyard of SEAL headquarters. The impact of the SEALs in this first year of operation in Vietnam had been to put a new emphasis on the riverine war. In this first year, the SEALs had already made their mark.

Welcome to the Nha Be Summer Resort
For your pleasures we provide:
SWIMMING FACILITIES:
Delightful frolics under the ships in the harbor.
BOATING EXCURSIONS:
Try one of our famous moonlight cruises down the river.
CAMPING TRIPS:
Enjoy a night out in the open air as you sit comfortably and companionably beside a trail or a stream.
—Sign posted by the SEALs at Nha Be

In the beginning of 1967 the U.S. government was still escalating the Vietnam War in the hope of overwhelming the North Vietnamese by a show of force. Four hundred thousand Americans were in Vietnam by that time, about sixty of them Navy SEALs, for Team No. 1 had now been joined in the conflict by elements of Team No. 2 from the East Coast of the United States.

By 1967 the Navy SEALs had built a larger-than-life portrait that was etched in the minds of the Viet Cong. They would appear out of the mist and murk, dripping mud and clutching fearsome weapons, of which they had a plethora, in their uniforms with the tiger stripe or the green leaf pattern and their faces black and green with paint. It was enough to strike terror into the heart of any simple villager, and the Viet Cong as well, even before the men began using their awesome weapons.

Those weapons included the K-bar frogman knife with a plastic sheath that would not fall apart, and the Ithaca Model 37 shotgun, which fired a 12-gauge shell, or a rifle. It could be the standard M-15, or a special version developed for the SEALs without storage space in the butt, or a 7.62mm Heckler & Koch G-3 assault rifle. Accommodating themselves to the mud of the Mekong delta, the SEALs developed mud plugs for their weapons. These plugs would protect the barrel from fouling during the often difficult approaches to action, and when the weapon was fired, the plug would be blown clear of the weapon. Some SEALs liked the .45-caliber M-3A1 submachine gun or "grease gun," which was a holdover from World War II. But more preferred the M-63 Stoner, produced by the designer of that name, which could be converted to an assault rifle or a light machine gun. It had the great advantage of feeding from either side, which appealed to left-handed men.

Another advantage was the fact that it could carry a box or drum with a hundred rounds ready to fire. The disadvantage was that it was a cranky weapon that required much maintenance, and some SEALs tried and discarded it.

The 40mm grenade launcher was the favorite of some for ambushes, and a single-shot version was later supplemented with automatic versions, one of which could be fitted to an M-16 rifle barrel.

On their boats they liked the 7.62mm minigun, which had a rate of fire of six thousand rounds per minute. Since much of the impact of a SEAL operation lay in its shock value, the ability to put an enormous amount of fire into an area was very important.

For close infighting the SEALs used submachine guns and handguns, particularly the Smith & Wesson M-39. Equipped with a silencer, this weapon and the Smith & Wesson M-76 submachine gun were often used to eliminate barking dogs or other animals that might "spook" the enemy. They were equally effective in disposing of sentries quietly. The fact was that a SEAL could employ just about any weapon that made him comfortable and secure. A team would go into the field with perhaps a quarter of a million dollars' worth of weaponry, all kinds, all sizes, for specialized use in special situations, and the SEALs prided themselves on their ability to make optimum use of these weapons.

Although the original concept of SEAL operations called for insertions by water, more and more often they would be going in by helicopter. The emergency way of bringing them out in a hurry was to employ the Jacob's ladder, an adaptation of a naval device. The helicopter would hover over the team and drop ropes with loops or a rope ladder. The advantage was that men could be taken out of an area in a hurry, but the disadvantage was that unconscious or badly wounded men could not be handled in this way.

A new method of bringing SEALs out of trouble was also adapted from the Army Special Forces, the McGuire rig. This consisted of a number of ropes and harnesses attached to a helicopter. The rigs would be dropped from both sides of the helicopter when it came down to pick up SEALs who were in danger and in a hurry to be extracted from the troubled situation. The helicopter would hover fifty feet above the ground, and each man would grab one of the harnesses (three harnesses on each rope) and secure himself. The helicopter would then rise and carry the men suspended beneath the aircraft. When they reached a secure area, the helicopter would land gently and the men would disengage from the harnesses and board the helicopter for a normal flight back to base.

The area of SEAL operations was also expanding. The force increased and moved afield from the Rung Sat special zone in Vietnam. However, there was still reason to be active in the special zone in those winter months because the Viet Cong increased its attacks on Saigon shipping, which had to move up the Mekong past this fortress. In January the Viet Cong made a dozen attacks, some of them involving the mining of ships and some involving ambushes. The SEALs countered with ambushes of their own and constant patrols to find and destroy enemy encampments.

In the first week of January the SEAL *LCM-3* was attacked by heavy machine-gun and antitank rocket fire from the riverbank. The SEALs were using two landing craft to support a South Vietnam Army sweep in the Rung Sat, and their task was to block the Viet Cong from escaping from an island in the river while the Army moved in. As the SEALs approached a village, it began to erupt fire from hidden machine guns and rockets.

In the firefight that followed, three SEALs were wounded and one South Vietnamese Army officer aboard the *LCM-3* was killed. But the landing craft fought off the enemy and soon gained fire superiority. Later it was determined that four Viet Cong had been killed in action, and many supplies and documents were captured. On the basis of these documents, 360 Viet Cong suspects were detained, and questioning indicated that most of them were active Viet Cong members.

On January 9 a SEAL team was nearly overwhelmed by enemy forces when it came upon an enemy camp out of Nha Be. The Viet Cong attempted to surround them but the SEALs, true to nature, slipped into Rach Cat La Be Creek and swam downriver, passing an even larger base camp without detection, to the point where they were to be taken out by helicopter. Once in safe hands they called in air strikes on this area.

Lt. J. H. McGee commanded the SEAL Golf Detachment that winter and spring. It was an exciting time. During December the SEALs had captured a number of Viet Cong documents. They were sent to intelligence for translation, and in January began to come back with information that would govern future SEAL activities. The documents, supplemented by aerial photographs, showed that the Viet Cong were using a number of freshwater wells in the southern part of the Rung Sat. On January 1?

the SEALs set out to destroy these one by one. They were successful, as later intelligence reports indicated. After the raids, the Viet Cong had to travel to other villages to get fresh water.

The enormous buildup of American activity in Vietnam this year, 1967, also affected the SEALs, the demands causing SEAL Team No. 1 to grow shorthanded and resort to drafting whole classes for the SEALs instead of letting some of the men go into UDT. About 20 percent of the SEALs in the continental United States were undergoing some sort of special training at an outside school, which also contributed to the shortage of personnel to meet the needs in Vietnam.

Men of SEAL Team No. 2 from the U.S. East Coast arrived in Vietnam on January 31. They had stopped off for two weeks in Coronado on their way to confer with SEAL Team No. 1 and to learn what they could in advance about operations in Vietnam. They brought with them a scout dog named Prince. They stopped at Nha Be to run some missions with SEAL Team No. 1 men and thus learn the ropes before starting out on their own. Their operating zone would be the Bassac River area in the Mekong delta.

One fact the new men learned quickly was that the elements could be as much their enemy as the enemy soldiers. On February 13, men from UDT No. 12 left the deck of the submarine *Tunny* in a motorized rubber boat. They were operating off Sa Hunh in II Corps territory. As the boat left the deck, it was hit by large swells; they moved to just outside the surf zone, and two swimmers were sent into shore to scout. In the darkness the command boat was hit by an unseen twenty-foot breaker and capsized. The three men on board were dumped into the water, and they struggled for the beach. The other boat was hit by the high surf, and the crew fought to keep the boat afloat. They shot off a flare to notify the submarine that there was trouble, and the *Tunny* launched a third boatload of men to try to help out.

The men from the sunken command boat could hardly make it to shore, but they did and linked up with the swimmers stranded on the beach. They buried their radio and the wreckage of their boat and then tried to swim out through the surf. Just before six o'clock in the morning three of the men made it to the second boat.

By this time the *Tunny* had come to within fifteen hundred yards of the beach and anchored. She called up an LST for help, and the LST launched a landing craft to help recover the other swimmers. One of them was found by the second boat. Eventually all the swimmers were brought in and recovered by the *Tunny*.

Wildlife could be a menace, too, as one SEAL team learned on a mission. All was going well on this mission until one SEAL saw what looked like a stump in about three feet of water near the shore where he was in hiding. Then he saw the stump move, and it moved in on him steadily. When the stump was about six feet away, it pointed its snout toward the SEAL and began to move in faster. He saw the eyes gleaming and moved back about three feet and fired his M-16. The noise of firing compromised the whole mission and the team had to get out of this action without accomplishing anything but killing one crocodile.

The SEALs were getting more recognition now than they had been in Vietnam for a time. On March 15 Admiral Sharp, the commander of the Pacific Fleet, and General Westmoreland, the Army commander in Vietnam, visited the Golf Detachment.

In April the SEALs proved several new capabilities adjusting to local conditions. One was to be able to conduct an extended reconnaissance without any support. They set up a new sort of listening post in the Rung Sat watching several waterways to observe patterns of Viet Cong resupply to the area. One platoon held the post fo four days, and three other posts were operated for a seven-day period. Juliet Platoon was involved in this operation, but a few days later Kilo Platoon arrived, bringing fourteen more SEALs to Golf Detachment. Within the week Lima Platoon also arrived, bringing another eleven men.

The second new capability was to get rid of their boots and go barefoot in the jungle. That is what the Viet Cong did, and the bootprints of the foreigners were a dead giveaway. So the SEALs abandoned their boots, and when they wore shoes at all, they were lightweight sneakers of the type that the Viet Cong sometimes wore. Going barefoot, the SEALs found that they were better and quieter in moving through the terrain and that they could sense trip wires of ambush and booby traps with their bare feet and legs.

The Viet Cong were a canny enemy, and the SEALs constantly learned new techniques in dealing with them. Their main effort was to preserve the element of surprise, which could be lost by a simple movement that seemed out of place. In moving into an area they learned not to go inshore by the conventional motorboat method. The change in pitch of engine noise was an indication that something was happening aboard the boat, and that would "spook" the Viet Cong. So the SEALs learned to jump off the stern of their boats if they went in by motorboat. They also learned to go in with minimal equipment. They took no sniper rifles, for these were too big and too cumbersome to be effective on SEAL patrols. Many times radios were a definite disadvantage, although they were necessary on missions where some third party was to recover the SEALs. If they were moving in helicopters, they learned to coordinate the overflights so that the noise and distraction confused the enemy.

Coming in by river, the SEALs and UDTs learned to pretend to put men ashore at various points to make the Viet Cong nervous. Their ambushes became ever more competent and more complicated. One action was the double-back ambush, in which the team pretended to move out of the area, then doubled back and around their own tail, and lay in wait for anyone tracking them.

In April the SEALs had one shock when operating with other units in a joint operation. The SEALs of Kilo Platoon were traveling along the Vam Sat River when their LCM was attacked by heavy fire from bunkers along the shore. Aboard the boat were Kilo Platoon men and some South Vietnamese undergoing training. They began firing back at the enemy. Suddenly there was an explosion overhead that caused a number of casualties in the boat. It came from a Viet Cong mortar shell that had been fitted with a proximity fuse. Twelve SEALs were wounded and two were killed by the blast. Two Vietnamese military personnel were wounded, too. (One of the wounded SEALs later died from his wounds.) The LCM still managed to fight its way clear of the battle, the wounded were evacuated by helicopter, and then the boat returned to base.

This incident happened four days after the arrival of Kilo Platoon in Vietnam. Killed were Lt. (jg) D. Mann, IC-3 Boston, and RM-3 Neal.

After the April disaster the SEALs stopped using their larger craft for support operations. Too many SEALs were being exposed to little purpose, or at least not the purpose for which the SEALs were in Vietnam, which was to provide a riverine and jungle covert ability in answer to the Viet Cong.

The SEALs continued to operate as they had until the monsoon season in June caused a slack-off of ambushes and patrols. But during the first week of July the SEALs participated in a joint operation with the 1st Air Cavalry, the U.S. destroyer *Brush,* and the Coast Guard cutter *Point White.* The operation was called Operation Shallow Draft II A. Their target was a Viet Cong strong hold northeast of Nha Trang, and their intention was to abduct several Viet Cong leaders from this area.

This was the first time the SEALs had the use of a destroyer to support any of their operations. The *Brush* stayed with them for three days to provide radio communication and fire support with its five-inch guns.

The SEALs moved to within range of the shore in their rubber boats, and then swimmers entered the water to scout and make the beach reconnaissance. This done, the SEALs went ashore. They went to Nui Binh Hwon Hill, where they established an observation point. All the next day they watched the region. Just before dark a four-person Viet Cong unit was seen to leave the tree line and go to a well that the SEALs were watching. That night the six-man abduction patrol moved. The four Vietnamese were two men and two women. The SEALs interposed themselves between the well and the party and through their interpreter hailed them. The Vietnamese began to run, and one of the women was shot and killed. One of the men received a flesh wound. The SEALs called for helicopters to come in and get them and for supporting fire from the *Brush*. Both arrived on time, and the SEALs and their prisoners went out of the area, protected by the firing from the *Brush* as they went. The woman who had been killed turned out to be the head of an important Viet Cong women's organization. The male prisoners were Viet Cong cell leaders, and they had on their persons important papers that related to these cells.

This operation was quite successful, a fact the SEALs attributed to good intelligence, newly acquired and accurate. That was one of the keys to their successes. When they had good intelligence, their organization was such that they were able to act on it. Without good intelligence, they were almost helpless.

In August the SEALs were called on to make a number of special missions with the Army 199th Brigade and to carry out forty-eight-hour ambushes. They managed to

ambush and kill a Viet Cong courier who was carrying ten
pounds of very important documents.

In September the monsoons began to slow down,
and in October the skies cleared. On September 21 the
SEALs made a successful ambush of a Viet Cong squad
of combat engineers who were preparing to mine the
Long Tau River, and they captured a number of mines
while killing seven Viet Cong. In November and December the SEALs of Team No. 1 conducted eight successful
ambushes. By this time Echo Platoon, which had served
six months in Golf Detachment, was relieved by Bravo
Platoon. This was standard procedure. Because of the
high tension of SEAL duty, a tour was only six months.

Bravo Platoon got into trouble on December 2,
while patrolling in the Viet Cong headquarters area.
They blundered into the perimeter of a Viet Cong base
camp, proving that with all their skills the SEALs still
could make human mistakes. During the fight one SEAL,
F. G. Antone, was killed, and so was a Vietnamese scout;
three SEALs were wounded.

By the end of 1967 the American war effort in Vietnam had escalated until more than five hundred thousand
Americans were serving there. Because the numbers of
SEALs and UDT were so limited, by the end of the year
most SEALs had seen service in the Vietnam War and
would see it again, for as the rest of the American effort
continued to escalate, so did that of the SEALs in the
following year. They had been in Vietnam uninterrupt-
edly for two years now, and their reputation was established as a hard-hitting, covert operations group, while
the UDT men were now an expected part of every amphibious operation, and the Navy called on them constantly for hydrographic and reconnaissance work on the
beaches.

18   The Year of the Tet Offensive

SSSS
SSSS   As 1968 opened, the North Vietnamese increased the tempo of the war and threw more North Vietnamese troops into action in the South, while the Viet Cong's operations continued unabated. But the SEALs continued to go up against the Viet Cong with as much effort as ever.

On January 2 a SEALs unit was guided by a Viet Cong defector who had been pressed into South Vietnamese service. These people, called Hoi Chanh, were an anomaly of this war; one could never quite tell what aim or cause they were serving. The South Vietnamese authorities employed many pressures on Viet Cong who were captured, including threats to their families, to force them to work against their former comrades. On this occasion the Hoi Chanh's information and activities were punctiliously correct. The SEALs found a small Viet Cong camp on May Island in the Bassac River sector where Team No. 2 operated. They killed six Viet Cong in a firefight and destroyed two buildings and eight hundred pounds of rice. Later that day they captured a communications courier.

Team No. 1 on January 7 found a deserted Viet Cong base camp and destroyed the buildings and food supplies there. They also eliminated one motorized sampan. Four days later a SEAL Team No. 1 man became the first fatality of the new year, when his Bravo Platoon squad came across a Viet Cong bunker that housed a five-man rocket crew in Ba Xuyen Province. As the SEALs approached, one Viet Cong burst out of the bunker, firing an AK-47. Seaman Roy Keith was mortally wounded. The other SEALs then attacked the bunker, killing four of the five men and capturing the rocket launcher, rockets, and a number of rifles.

SEAL activity was stepped up that winter. On January 12 UDT Team No. 12 of Golf Detachment moved to the Mekong delta at Dong Tank, near My Tho, to work with the riverine force. By this time the Navy, in its recruiting drive for the SEALs, was seeking some controlled publicity. They managed to get a sequence on SEALs inserted into the comic strip *Buzz Sawyer,* which appealed to many young readers. They also gave access to some hitherto secret information to *Time* magazine and let a *Time* correspondent accompany a SEAL mission into combat. He was also on a riverine ambush in which two Viet Cong were killed. *Time* then published a story asserting that the SEALs had carried out 600 missions, knocking out 70 boats, 200 bridges, 200 bunkers, and killed more than 175 Viet Cong and captured 60 while losing only 6 men in two years.

In 1968 five platoons of SEALs were in Vietnam with Golf Detachment. Their basic mission was to terrorize the Viet Cong by raids and kidnappings, although they did not cavil at more mundane jobs, such as clearing a canal blocked by the Viet Cong, which they did in January, using three hundred pounds of explosives and techniques learned in BUD/S training.

On January 18 the SEALs of Team No. 2 were involved in a clandestine operation when they ran afoul of the Viet Cong in considerable number, enough of them so that the group decided to get out and call for help. They came under a hail of fire, and GM1C Arthur Williams was shot; the bullet entered his body under the arm and lodged in his spine. He died shortly afterward and thus became the first Team No. 2 casualty of the war. On that same day UDT No. 12 lost its commanding officer, Lt. Comdr. Robert Condon, who was observing tests of some new equipment when a rocket hit the LCM on which he was riding. He was killed. And then a few days later Av MM2c Eugene Fraley was the victim of a freak accident. He had prepared a booby trap for use in an operation against the Viet Cong and, when he removed it from the sandbag enclosure in which he had assembled it, the booby trap exploded.

On January 22 two small SEAL squads managed to get some of the Viet Cong to kill one another. They were operating on a canal on the Tien Gang River some seventy miles south of Saigon. One squad found a sampan that was moving at night without lights, and sure that it was Viet Cong, they began firing on it. They killed four Viet Cong soldiers. The second squad moved southeast of them and found and killed two more Viet Cong in a second unlighted sampan. Then a force of Viet Cong on the canalbank began firing in the direction of the Americans, who ducked and lay low. The Viet Cong fire was answered by a second Viet Cong group on the other bank, so the SEALs watched as the Viet Cong killed one another. After a while the SEALs also began firing, and then the Viet Cong stopped. The SEALs got another sampan with a single soldier aboard. After the Viet Cong vs. Viet Cong battle, the SEALs found eight bodies, which they checked before they withdrew.

From time to time the SEALs worked with Australian and New Zealand Special Forces, who had the same sort of training and operational methods that the SEALs used. One such occasion was on January 22, when SEALs and the Aussies made a joint mission in which they encountered Viet Cong and some North Vietnamese soldiers who had begun operating with the Viet Cong in this area. This was news—the first time they had encountered North Vietnamese in this region. It indicated a new escalation of North Vietnamese activity.

The expanded SEAL teams conducted expanded operations. On January 25 they began operation Wing Song in Kien Hoa Province. This was a Viet Cong-controlled area along the Thom and Mo Cay canals. The 6th and 7th platoons were put ashore by river to conduct a sweep against the Viet Cong. The sweep resulted in sporadic fighting in which five enemy soldiers were killed and fifty-one Viet Cong suspects captured, one of whom turned out to be the official who collected taxes from the local villagers. While conducting these operations the SEALs eliminated thirty bunkers, twenty-five sampans, and captured and destroyed five tons of rice.

This winter of 1968 the North Vietnamese were eager to bring the war to a successful conclusion, and they knew that many people in South Vietnam were disaffected with its government. They hoped that if they began an uprising, the general population would join and overthrow the South Vietnamese government, thus bringing an end to the civil war. The time chosen for this uprising was the holiday of Tet, which began on January 31.

It began with Viet Cong assaults on several cities in the South, and almost immediately the SEALs were engaged. In My Tho the SEALs helped defend American billets against Viet Cong attacks. Then three battalions attacked the city and tried to seize all the bridges. At one point the Viet Cong brought up an armored sampan, which cruised along the river, firing at government forces. The SEALs reacted quickly and pulled forth 66mm light antiarmor weapons, and two SEALs attacked the vessel with them and put it out of action. The SEALs were conducting a course of training at Hung Tau, and this was suspended so the SEALs and their students could go into Saigon, where they went to the defense of U.S. naval headquarters.

On January 31 SEAL Team No. 2's 8th Platoon was conducting a combined operation with a local Vietnamese force near the Cambodian border. At two o'clock in the morning the SEALs were outside Chau Doc on the river when they were startled to discover some fourteen hundred enemy troops massing near the city. Because they were enormously outnumbered, the SEALs and the

South Vietnamese withdrew to report what they had seen. The Viet Cong attacked about an hour later, planning to seize the city piece by piece. The SEALs linked up with a handful of U.S. Army advisers in the town, but the Army men had few weapons. The SEALs went downriver, where an American group with heavier weapons was located. They found two jeeps, mounted a .50-caliber machine gun on one of them, and then drove quietly through the town, past several Viet Cong strongholds, to get back to the command post. There they learned that several American civilians were missing, and they went out to look for them. They went first to the house of an American nurse and found that the Viet Cong had gotten there before they did and were ransacking the place, while the nurse hid in a wardrobe in the living room. As the Viet Cong came into the living room, she panicked and bolted for the back door. As she swung the door open she was met by Viet Cong in the backyard. They were as startled as she, and just stood there looking at her. The SEALs kicked in the front door, and the nurse turned to run to them. She tripped and fell, which opened a clear field of fire for the SEALs, who began shooting; but as their bullets hit the back door, they knocked it shut. The SEALs grabbed the nurse and got her into the jeep and raced down the road, with the Viet Cong running to the front of the house and firing after them.

The other missing Americans were found safe at another location and rescued.

On February 1 and February 2 the SEALs continued in the fight against the Viet Cong. South Vietnamese forces rallied and entered Chau Doc from the north but got bogged down at the marketplace in heavy fighting. The SEAL 8th Platoon split into two squads, attacked the Viet Cong from the rear, and soon reached the market area. The SEALs were using all the heavy weapons they had, including a 57mm recoilless rifle. They found that the Viet Cong had settled in a theater, which was their command post; the SEALs found a three-story building nearby that would make a fine vantage point above the theater. PO Ted Risher was hit by a bullet, and while he was being evacuated, another SEAL stood by, firing, to cover him. The SEALs found an old station wagon, which they used as an ambulance, and hurried back to their patrol boat, which had been moving up and down the river, firing at the Viet Cong. The boat had twenty-eight bullet holes in it. The nurse the SEALs had rescued came to help Risher, but he was too badly wounded and died.

The Tet offensive was a great surprise to the Americans and triggered much negative public opinion in America. But it was actually a failure for the North Vietnamese and a disaster for the Viet Cong, particularly at Hue, the center of the activity. The Marines recovered from their initial shock and engaged the enemy in house-to-house fighting, which decimated the Viet Cong forces in the area to the point that they never did recover all their strength.

But Americans did not know this because the reports from Saigon and other besieged cities made it appear that the enemy was winning. Thus the Tet offensive, while a military failure, was a political success, triggering a new movement to end the war or get the United States out of it. After Tet, President Johnson gave up. The result was deescalation of the American effort as more and more Americans began to wonder why the United States was involved in an Asian civil war, and the decision of President Johnson not to seek reelection because his popularity had fallen so low he probably could not win. As it turned out, his vice president, Hubert Humphrey, long a stalwart in the Democratic Party camp, supported the Johnson position on the war, and this became a major factor in his defeat in the autumn election.

The debris from the Tet offensive had been cleared away by the middle of February, and the SEALs went back to their usual activities. Sometimes they masked themselves as Viet Cong, wearing black pajamas and carrying AK-47s or other weapons that were commonly used by the enemy. In one intelligence reconnaissance along the Cambodian border, the SEALs successfully passed themselves off as Soviet advisers to the Viet Cong. Looking around the area in their disguise, they discovered more than four hundred Viet Cong in camps. Usually the numbers of those involved in any fighting were small where the SEALs were concerned, but on February 17 one SEAL led a sixty-man Vietnamese force, which ran into a large number of Viet Cong, twenty of whom were killed, with the loss of one South Vietnamese; two Viet Cong were captured.

The war changed somewhat. The Viet Cong began trying to confuse the SEALs by using some of their tactics. For example, one night when the SEALs were on a mission, they failed to make contact at a night ambush and used a red flashlight to signal their boat. A few minutes later, another red light appeared on the opposite bank. The SEALs threw a hail of gunfire at the light, and it went out and stayed out. But thereafter they took precautions to change the signals for extraction in each operation.

An attempt was made to use the SEALs in combination with Vietnamese elements in large joint attacks, but the SEALs were uncomfortable in these circumstances, and did their best to keep running their own operations, limited and with small groups of men who knew and trusted one another to do the proper thing at the proper time.

A very satisfactory SEAL operation was usually small and pointed. On March 10, led by a Vietnamese civilian whose father had been killed by the Viet Cong, the SEALs killed a Viet Cong hamlet security chief and two soldiers. They were then led to a hut where a female Viet Cong communications official was staying. They approached silently, captured her, and then withdrew with her from the area. That same night a squad from Mike Platoon had a similarly successful mission at a river ambush of sampans that were carrying six Viet Cong passengers. They killed three, captured two, destroyed three hundred pounds of rice, and captured an American submachine gun that one of the Viet Cong was carrying.

In March the SEALs got more than they bargained for when the 7th Platoon from Team No. 2 landed thirteen miles east of My Tho, deep in enemy territory. They patrolled northward for about a mile and then split, one squad moving northeast and the other east. The first squad suddenly came upon two Viet Cong and started firing. Then they found that there were fifty other Viet Cong descending on them. They evaded and moved north, calling for helicopter support from gunships. The guerrillas pursued them. They fought off about twenty of them, approaching from the east as they reached their pickup point. During the fighting at the end, the patrol leader killed one Viet Cong with a pistol and another in hand-to-hand fighting.

The second squad which had gone east, stumbled on a Viet Cong battalion base camp. The teams found the barracks building and stopped. Three SEALs moved up to investigate the building. At 3:00 A.M. senior chief Bob Gallagher led the men into the complex. Inside were thirty Viet Cong, asleep with all their weapons and equipment by their sides. A sentry discovered the Americans, and a firefight broke out. Half the guerrillas were killed by the SEALs' rapid-firing weapons, but the SEALs had five men wounded, including Gallagher, who was hit in both legs, and the officer in charge was hit so badly that he could not walk. The SEALs regrouped and began to evade. The Viet Cong tried to pursue them. The less seriously wounded carried their more seriously wounded SEAL comrades. Chief Gallagher took over command and led the escape to the south. The Viet Cong made a search, at one time passing within thirty meters of the

SEALs, but did not discover them. The SEALs called in helicopter support, and as they heard the helicopters coming, they fired tracers into the air. The Viet Cong saw the tracers but could not distinguish the American fire from their own. The helicopters came in, and Gallagher held off the attacking Viet Cong while they landed and began loading the seriously wounded. Gallagher was wounded one more time but managed to get the whole squad out alive. They called then for artillery and air strikes to demolish the camp. For that action Gallagher won the Navy Cross.

The activity continued on all fronts. The next night the 8th Platoon of Team No. 2 was involved in a river ambush about three thousand meters out from a South Vietnamese Army post. The men waited an hour without seeing any enemy. Then a single Viet Cong soldier appeared, and they captured him. Through questioning they discovered that he was a member of a local Viet Cong battalion. They settled into position, and a half hour later they encountered six Viet Cong, who entered the area and were shot down. The SEALs then took over a sampan and captured another. They found that they had captured the deputy battalion commander and a newspaper reporter from Hanoi.

On March 29 SEALs from Team No. 2 and Team No. 1 combined efforts in an operation led by Hoi Chanh against an area ten miles south of Ben Tre. The target area was a hamlet of four huts. The SEALs surrounded the area and prepared to storm the huts, but before they could move, two Viet Cong walked into the security guard. They were killed by hand, silently, so as not to disturb other Viet Cong in the area and upset the operation. The SEALs then attacked, killing two more Viet Cong, who had tried to escape. The Hoi Chanh apparently knew about an arms cache, and he led them to this well-camouflaged dump. Hidden in one of the huts, this cache included a complete factory for the manufacture of

hand grenades. Then a villager led the SEALs to a hut
not far away, where there was another cache. This was
the biggest they had found, including twenty-eight claymore mines, thirty water mines, two East German machine guns, three carbines, two 75mm recoilless rifles, five
120mm rockets and launchers, twenty-five Chinese grenades, nineteen tear gas grenades, fifty blasting caps,
seven boxes of Viet Cong grenades, eight cases of rifle
ammunition, a box of medical supplies, and many documents.

The SEALs loaded all this into their landing craft,
but a low tide made the boat too heavy, so they had to
destroy most of the equipment. So large and so important
was this find deemed in Saigon that the SEALs received a
personal commendation from General Westmoreland for
the operation.

Team No. 2 changed platoons on April 22: The 6th
Platoon went out and the 10th Platoon came in. In one of
the 10th Platoon's first operations, they made a ten strike.
A Hoi Chanh defector led them to a place where he said
the Viet Cong were holding a meeting. They surrounded
the area and captured all the people there. The Hoi
Chanh pointed out six people he said were Viet Cong.
They were taken to the National Police, and under torture they gave information that led to the arrest of more
than a hundred Viet Cong in the My Tho area. When
they were rounded up, it was discovered that the Viet
Cong had infiltrated every Allied agency and military unit
in My Tho. What an intelligence network it had been!
But now it was destroyed. Still, the lesson remained, and
the SEALs could understand why so many of their missions went astray, particularly those ordered by higher
authority. It was apparent that the South Vietnam government and Army were honeycombed with North Vietnamese and Viet Cong.

Pressed by the Special Forces, the Viet Cong became
ever more resourceful. One night in April the SEALs c

a mission listened to radio calls in which voices in English called for an emergency pickup, using the techniques and language they employed in such situations. This was the Viet Cong trying to lure a boat support unit into a trap. It did not work this time, but in the case of an inexperienced crew it might work. The SEALs tried to avoid such situations.

For the size of their units and the many missions they conducted, the SEAL casualties were high this spring. One SEAL was killed by friendly fire on April 29 when moving into an operational area. Another SEAL drowned during a beach operation on the Ham Loung River.

A SEAL drowned? There had to be a reason. He was David Devine, and he was the Stoner machine gunner of his squad on this patrol. When the patrol leader examined the circumstances, he concluded that Devine had been dragged down by the weight of his machine gun and ammunition during this night insertion, and had gone under before anybody could help him. From that time on the SEALs who carried heavy weight began to wear two inflatable life jackets instead of just one.

On May 12, SEAL Donald Zillgitt was leading a team of fifty-three South Vietnamese soldiers to counterattack a Viet Cong force in Vinh Binh Province. The Viet Cong had overrun the hamlet of Giang Lon, three miles northwest of Hu Vinh. Zillgitt and his men landed by helicopter south of the hamlet, but soon were under heavy Viet Cong fire and were pinned down in a rice paddy. The Viet Cong, in great force, prepared to surround and overwhelm them. Zillgitt led two attacks against the Viet Cong, and on the second he was mortally wounded. The South Vietnamese took heart and drove the Viet Cong out of the hamlet, killing seventeen of them.

Mike Platoon was having its problems with this and other losses. On May 15, while operating in Vinh Long

Province, the SEALs ran across a land mine, and the explosion wounded seven men and killed Donnie Patrick. The losses were so great that Mike Platoon had to suspend operations until the end of the month, when some of the men had recovered and some replacements had arrived.

The Viet Cong were also becoming more adept at resisting ambush than they had been earlier. On May 11 Team No. 2 set up an ambush on a guerrilla force, but the force responded with heavy fire, pinned the SEALs down and wounded the patrol leader. He called for close air support and led a stiff attack that pushed the Viet Cong back and made it possible for the helicopters to get the SEALs out of the area.

Sometimes intelligence was correct enough, but faulty in not indicating the strength of the units involved. On May 14 SEALs of Team No. 2's 8th Platoon set up an ambush of a guerrilla force that was supposed to be working along the Cambodian border. The intelligence was completely accurate, but it did not tell the SEALs that the force numbered eighty-two men, which was quite a handful for the SEALs to manage. They were also extremely well trained and well armed. Soon the Viet Cong had the SEALs pinned down in a graveyard. The SEALs moved from tombstone to tombstone for four hours, returning fire. Just as it seemed that the SEALs must be overwhelmed by superior numbers, Navy Seawolf helicopter gunships arrived and drove the enemy across the Cambodian border. In this fight twenty-four Viet Cong were killed and forty were wounded; the SEALs had no casualties.

The next day Mike Platoon was patrolling near Chau Lach, hoping to break up a Viet Cong meeting that intelligence had warned about and to capture some high-ranking Viet Cong prisoners. Suddenly an explosion rocked the landing craft, killing one man and wounding Lt. (jg) Beall, Lt. (jg) Brierton, and five other SEALs. That was the end of the operation but not the end of the casualties. Four days later PO Gordon Brown was killed leading a group of Vietnamese on patrol in Kien Giang Province. The Vietnamese had discovered a large box and were opening it, and Brown was moving up to take a look when the box exploded. It had been booby-trapped with a land mine.

At about that time replacements arrived from the United States to strengthen Mike Platoon. At that same time, early in June, Bravo Platoon was relieved by Juliet Platoon, and Golf Detachment moved its headquarters to the Naval Support Detachment at Binh Thuy. The men were assigned to bigger operations than the SEALs liked. The big change was that higher authority was now emphasizing training of Vietnamese to do some of the jobs that the SEALs had been doing, and the SEALs worked in cooperation while teaching them the ropes. The ambush was replaced as the primary SEAL operation by abductions and the destruction of supply caches. The abductions had a particularly chilling effect on the Viet Cong because they never knew when or where the SEALs would strike next. Although there were only two hundred SEALs in Vietnam, their reputation had become fearsome, and some Viet Cong opted out and became voluntary Hoi Chanh because of their fear of abduction from their homes. Sometimes the Viet Cong would be so frightened of the SEALs that they would volunteer information about arms caches after they were captured. In September SEAL Team No. 2's 3d Platoon rescued a Vietnamese intelligence agent who had been captured by the Viet Cong, killed several Viet Cong, and captured three others, and who agreed to lead them to arms caches; in the next three days he showed them five places. The SEALs captured two 60mm mortars, two rocket launchers, three machine guns, and many other weapons and ammunition supplies.

That fall the SEALs managed to convince higher authority that it was more important to secure intelligence about Viet Cong activity than to kill Viet Cong.

For their part the Viet Cong caused more casualties this year with booby traps against the SEALs. In August and September MMi Joseph Albrecht and Lt. Frederick Trani were both killed by booby traps.

More often the SEALs began to get into firefights with forces much larger than their own, as on November 26, when a squad of the 4th Platoon made a night reconnaissance near the Cambodian border. While patrolling, the SEALs saw a single armed man standing in a field and knew he must be Viet Cong. Two SEALs set out to capture him, intending to interrogate him to get information about the Viet Cong in the area. But as they approached, the Viet Cong opened fire, and they killed him. The noise alerted the base camp that was nearby and from the camp, fire began coming toward the SEALs. Mortar shells began to land around them, and they estimated that two companies of Viet Cong were after them. The main body of the squad immediately began to lay down covering fire for the two SEALs in the open. The SEALs began to move back, and the Viet Cong sent a company of men to cut them off. The SEALs called in a helicopter gunship and formed a tight perimeter to hold out until it arrived. When it came, the whole squad was airlifted out of the area.

They were convinced that this camp was still a good target for them, and on December 7 they returned to this base camp undetected and waited. They called in helicopter gunships. An hour later the helicopters came, and the SEALs also set up heavy fire with automatic weapons. The Viet Cong returned the fire, and the SEALs fell back to avoid encirclement. After they moved out, fifteen Viet Cong were found dead and twenty-nine wounded.

So 1968 came to an end. The SEALs had lost nine men from Team No. 1 killed that year and six men from Team No. 2, plus the commanding officer of UDT No. 12, and many more men of both teams and the UDT had been wounded. But the Tet offensive had been stopped, and the Viet Cong had lost many men and much equipment to the SEALs. The SEALs had also developed some new equipment, including a new boat, the Light SEAL support craft, and by the beginning of the next year a dozen of those new boats would be in Vietnam. They had also introduced a new weapon, the "Hush Puppy," a pistol with silencer that made virtually no noise when fired. All the SEALs in Vietnam now had silencers for both rifles and pistols; this was very important when stalking the Viet Cong in the depths of the jungle.

The war seemed no closer to an end than before, but that was the responsibility of the American politicians who made the policies and who had engaged to fight a war. The SEALs would be committed to continuing their counterguerrilla operations.

In 1969 the United States was becoming increasingly disaffected with the commitment of its government to a Vietnam policy that was costly in money and lives of Americans and that continued for reasons many people could not understand. President Richard Nixon seemed to understand this feeling and wanted to extricate the United States from what had turned out to be a folly. But it was not easy. The North Vietnamese, scenting victory in the disaffection of the American people, did nothing to make it easy for the American effort. Negotiations began and stopped, began and stopped, as did escalation of the bombing of North Vietnam. The pattern continued much as it had in the last days of the Johnson administration. One of the last acts of President Johnson in January was to award a Presidential Unit Citation to SEAL Team No. 1 for its work in Vietnam. The ceremony at the White House was attended by seventeen men of the team, all of whom had served in Vietnam.

In January, four-party peace talks began in Paris, but the political maneuvering of the early days of 1969 had no effect on the operations of the SEALs and the Underwater Demolition Teams in Vietnam. Their mission remained the same: to harry the Viet Cong, pave the way for amphibious operations, and collect intelligence. Both Team No. 1 from California and Team No. 2 from the Virginia coast operated in Vietnam as they had for months.

The action began with Team No. 2 on January 10, when they were patrolling along the Vam Co River as part of Operation Giant Slingshot, another attempt to prevent the Viet Cong from receiving supplies from the

North, but this one working at the end of the Ho Chi Minh trail, along which the enemy brought their supplies overland. On this day the SEALs discovered a very large arms cache, so large that it took them three hours to move it. Here was proof positive of the success of the Viet Cong in bringing large supplies of armaments overland.

Two SEALs were killed in Vietnam in January, one from Team No. 1 and one from Team No. 2. David Wilson of Team No. 1 was on a mission southeast of Vinh Long when leaving a boat. He stepped on a booby-trapped 105mm howitzer shell. SEAL Harry Mattingly was killed while leading an operation of a provincial reconnaissance unit of SEAL-trained Vietnamese who used SEAL tactics. There were many more such operations in 1969, in response to the policy of Vietnamization of the war.

The Viet Cong were bringing in more arms than ever. Alpha Platoon of SEAL Team No. 1 sent a patrol out to locate some sampans that were apparently carrying arms. They found the sampans and fired on them, killing five Viet Cong, but more important, hitting one of the sampans and causing a large secondary explosion that meant they had destroyed an arms shipment.

This winter both teams concentrated on hitting important officials of the Viet Cong and interrupting their organization. On February 5 a squad from Team No. 2 on the My Tho River captured a Viet Cong postal station and many pounds of mail and documents. Another Team No. 2 ambush, a few days later, netted five high-ranking Viet Cong officials.

Early in March, intelligence came in to indicate that an important Viet Cong intelligence team was operating on Ham Tam Island in Nha Trang Bay. From here they had infiltrated many agents into South Vietnamese organizations, where they had disrupted a number of operations. The American command and the South Vietnamese wanted to capture some of these people, but it was a very ticklish job to try to take them alive. The task was given to Lt. (jg) Joseph Kerrey and his group, who were known as Kerrey's Rangers. On March 14 Kerrey led six other SEALs to the island, with three South Vietnamese, two of whom had been Viet Cong.

Kerrey's men were not seen as they slipped ashore on the island on a moonless night. He led them about 350 feet up a rocky cliff to get at the enemy without being discovered. When they came down on the other side, they located part of their quarry. Kerrey split his force and took half of them with him. They took off their shoes, as SEALs were wont to do these days, so as not to disturb the Viet Cong. Despite the precautions, they were spotted, and the Viet Cong began firing. One of them threw a grenade that exploded at Kerrey's feet and threw him onto some sharp rocks. The lower part of his right leg was blown off, and he was bleeding very badly, but he maintained control of the team and kept giving orders. He called in the second part of the team, and they started a crossfire against the Viet Cong that caught them off balance. Seven Viet Cong were killed. The other SEALs put a tourniquet on Kerrey's leg, and he was evacuated. The raid proved every bit as valuable as had been hoped, netting many documents and a list of the Viet Cong agents in the area. For his exploit, Lieutenant Kerrey received the Medal of Honor, the first SEAL ever to do so. (He later returned to his native Nebraska, ran for office, was elected governor, and later became a U.S. senator.)

One reason the SEALs were so effective was the toughness of mind instilled in them in the BUD/S training program, which stood them in good stead all the rest of their military careers. As an example, take the behavior of Radioman 2c Robert J. Thomas in a mission on March 23, 1969. Some members of his 7th Platoon of SEAL Team No. 2 were flying on two Seawolf helicopters on a visual reconnaissance and strike mission in Kien Giang Province. They were over Da Dung Mountain when they came under enemy fire and began strafing in return. On one strafing run, Thomas's helicopter was hit and damaged and crashed in a rice paddy. He was thrown from the helicopter by the impact and injured. For a few moments he lay stunned, but then he remembered the others in the helicopter, and he saw it begin to burn. He dragged himself to the wreckage and managed to get one crewman out and put him in a safe place. All this time Thomas and the helicopter were under fire from the Viet Cong.

The other helicopter dropped a second man on the site to help Thomas, but he, too, was wounded. Still, the pair went back to the helicopter and got the pilot out. They tried to get the other two crewmen out, too, but the heat of the flames grew so intense it drove them away, and the ammunition aboard the helicopter began to explode. They took the two injured men to a safe distance from the burning helicopter. But now they had the problem of the enemy closing in on them.

Thomas was a crack shot, but he had lost both his rifle and his personal handgun in the crash. He borrowed the handgun of one of the crewmen and with that held off the Viet Cong, killing one of them and wounding several others. His fire was so accurate the Viet Cong held back in their rush. Finally an Army helicopter arrived, landed, and picked up the four men and got them out to safety. A bit later two other SEALs rappelled into the paddy from another helicopter and recovered the bodies of the two dead crewmen.

This combination of guts and skills saved many a SEAL and those around him under the most trying of circumstances, as on April 3, when two SEALs and one Vietnamese frogman took off in an Army helicopter on a mission from the compound at Ha Tien near the Cambodian border. The helicopter had mechanical problems and crashed into the Gulf of Thailand. One SEAL was thrown into the cockpit, while the other was knocked out. Both recovered and got to work. One SEAL pushed the Vietnamese frogman and a door gunner over the side of the helicopter, and the other SEAL released the other door gunner from his safety harness and swam him to the surface and then to a sampan nearby. This SEAL then went back to the sinking helicopter and he and the other SEAL dove down to the pilot's compartment, pried it open, and freed the pilot, then swam him to the surface and to safety.

But even with their skills, the SEALs' luck did not always hold. On May 18 a small SEAL team was assigned to disarm an unexploded 82mm mortar round that had fallen into the Allied compound at Rach Gia. Suddenly in the process the shell exploded. SEALs Kenneth Van Hoy and Ronald Pace were killed immediately, and a week later SEAL Lin Mahner died of his wounds.

The Underwater Demolition Teams all this time were working steadily at their assigned tasks—making the way clear for amphibious missions, and training Vietnamese to take over their tasks as part of the Vietnamization process. In this, UDT No. 13 suffered its first casualty, on April 12. A sweep-and-destroy mission was in progress on the Duong Keo River in the Mekong delta, and a whole convoy of rivercraft were involved. They ran into a Viet Cong ambush and as the last in the column, the boat ridden by UDT man Robert Worthington was at the end of the line. The Viet Cong let the others go and concentrated their fire on this craft. They fired machine guns, rifles, and rockets, and one rocket exploded in the boat, killing Worthington. The other men in the boat manned all their weapons and kept the Viet Cong off for forty-five minutes, using grenades with such accuracy that the enemy withdrew in the end. The boat was wrecked and abandoned.

Toward the end of April a combined UDT-Vietnamese force moved into the Cua Lon River from the Gulf of

Thailand for raids on the Nam Can Forest, a hive of Viet Cong activity. By the end of May they had killed 126 Viet Cong and wrecked thousands of bunkers, buildings, and various kinds of watercraft. All the while they were teaching their Vietnamese counterparts the arts of demolition so that they could take the future responsibility.

In the summer of 1969 the UDT men of Team No. 13 had begun to operate from the submarine *Grayback.* She was originally launched at Mare Island and was one of the platforms for the launch of the Regulus II missile, but when the Polaris submarines began to arrive with the fleet, the Regulus-type submarines were phased out, and the *Grayback* was refitted for swimmer operations. The hangars for missiles in her bow were converted and fitted with pressure hulls. Each bay could be flooded and lock out, launch, and recover swimmers while the submarine lay submerged. The UDTs now also used swimmer delivery vehicles, which were small craft like the Italian World War II "chariots" that resembled nothing more than big torpedoes. Frogmen sat astride the submersibles and guided them into enemy harbors to attack vessels there. In later models the frogmen guided the submersible craft from inside while breathing through Aqua-Lungs. The *Grayback* could launch and recover these craft without ever surfacing.

The *Grayback* was recommissioned in May 1969, and she moved to the underwater men's base at Subic Bay, took 12 UDT men to train, and soon was engaged in operations off the Vietnam coast.

In June 1969 President Nixon announced the first withdrawal of twenty-five thousand soldiers from Vietnam, and the pressures began to build for further withdrawals, but they did not seem to affect the SEALs and the UDTs. Operations went on as usual that summer and fall. On July 1 the men of the 5th Platoon of Team No. 2 infiltrated a Viet Cong base camp in Dinh Thuong Province. At four o'clock in the morning they heard voices north of their position; they moved north and found the camp about seventy-five yards away. They opened fire and killed four Viet Cong, then searched the camp and found much information and some guns and supplies. They searched the bodies and found that one of the Viet Cong they had killed was an engineer with a degree from a Soviet engineering university.

That summer the SEALs made innumerable raids, capturing hundreds of pounds of documents, many pieces of ordnance, and killing Viet Cong in handfuls almost every time they went out. On August 11 they captured a grenade factory, which they burned down. In a combined operation with Vietnamese on September 12 they captured a large cache of enemy arms, including several mortars, machine guns, light machine guns, and rockets as well as rifles.

The fighting with the Viet Cong was almost always desperate, for neither SEALs nor the dedicated Viet Cong were inclined to give up. On November 24 members of SEAL Team No. 2 in the Rung Sat spotted a camouflaged sampan, encountered a number of Viet Cong, and started a firefight. The SEALs were greatly outnumbered, but they continued to fight. One of their techniques was to put the machine gunner directly behind the point man, in case heavy fire was needed at the beginning of an engagement. This avoided surprise and lent firepower. On this day the tactic saved the SEALs. The machine gunner started firing and put heavy fire at the Viet Cong instantly. The gunner was wounded in the left leg but continued to fire until he was shot in both hands and his ammunition box was destroyed. After these wounds, this SEAL pulled hand grenades from his webgear and hurled them until he fell unconscious.

On this same day, Lt. (jg) John Brewton was leading his men against a superior force when he was wounded in the arm and back. He continued to call for gunship support and to direct activity. He was wounded again but continued in action until the evacuation. He died of wounds in a hospital in Saigon.

The year wound down, but there were still more casualties. Team No. 1's Mike Platoon lost a man on November 30 when chasing a reported Viet Cong finance chieftain. One helicopter landed on the roof of a hut where the man was supposed to be. The SEALs then got out and slid down the roof. But the helicopter was too heavy for the structure and broke through and crashed in the wreckage of the "hooch." SEAL Richard Wolfe was killed in the crash. The others managed to get to safety and then saw that he was missing. Coming back to the site, they found his body along with those of two Viet Cong who had been in the hut and had been killed by the crashing helicopter.

This was an operational death, but in reality it was an accident. And as many SEALs were killed by accident as by the enemy, especially if one regarded a booby trap as an accident that might be avoided. On December 27 came one of these accidents—perhaps unavoidable, but still an accident. SEAL Team No. 2 was taking a Vietnamese patrol in Long An Province, eight miles southeast of Nha Be, back in well-known country. They laid an ambush on the river and settled down, moving into positions of watchfulness. SEAL Curtis Ashton was moving into his position when one of his concussion grenades detonated accidentally and killed him.

Although antiwar sentiment in the United States was rising, when Ashton's body was taken back to his hometown of Sweetwater, Texas, all business was suspended while the townspeople paid homage to a brave man who had served his country as best he knew how.

And so 1969 came to an end, and the SEALs were still engaged in Vietnam. To paraphrase President Johnson's unit citation for SEAL Team No. 2 that year, one might say that the SEALs distinguished themselves by exceptionally meritorious and heroic service in Vietnam in the conduct of unconventional warfare although working in almost impenetrable terrain and a totally hostile environment. Their accomplishments were great in relation to their numbers. When they were wounded they fought on, and nearly always came out alive. They did not fear to conduct offensive patrols in the strongholds of the enemy, although they used caution and common sense in their operations. In all, the distinguished and heroic conduct of the SEALs under fire reflected the highest credit on them and on the U.S. Navy.

20   Vietnamization and
More Work

The Nixon administration wanted to end
U.S. military action in Vietnam. To that
end, President Nixon sent his national
security adviser, Henry Kissinger, to conduct secret talks
with the North Vietnamese. The talks began, but they did
not have visible positive results. The North Vietnamese
were playing a waiting game, now quite sure of the dis-
comfiture of the Americans and their eventual withdrawal. What the world saw was a succession of hopes
raised, dashed, and then raised again. The reality was that
the war as it was waged was virtually already lost by the
Americans, and the South Vietnamese government did
not have the stability or the public support to take over its
own fortunes. So the process of American military disengagement continued. As far as the Navy Special Forces
men were concerned, this meant more work for them, for
they were a major factor in the maintenance of security,
and the SEAL operations in the deep forests and mangrove swamps were more important than ever. In January
the ambushes were much as usual, involving a handful of
SEALs, or SEALs and Vietnamese forces. On January 15
they ambushed three sampans and killed seven Viet
Cong. A week later they killed six Viet Cong in another
ambush and captured some documents, including a number of maps.

There were more medals, one for UDT man Donel
C. Kinnard, who had several exploits. He was involved in
a sweep operation with others when he swam out and
captured a sampan single-handedly from three enemy
troops. While he did this he was observed by other Viet
Cong and was under constant fire. On another occasion

Kinnard and his team came under heavy fire; he was wounded in the arms and legs by shrapnel, and he replied with grenades. A North Vietnamese Army officer crept up behind him and attacked. Kinnard then grappled with the officer and eventually overpowered him. For these actions Kinnard received the Navy Cross.

On January 27, 1970, UDT man Guy F. Stone was involved in a bunker destruction sweep when he discovered in a graveyard eight Viet Cong who had set up an ambush for his teammates. He shouted a warning and then attacked, charging to with fifteen feet of the enemy ambush point and hurling grenades. He saw two Viet Cong trying to escape; he grabbed a weapon and shot them down. Six Viet Cong were killed in this operation but no Americans. Stone saved the team with his timely warning and his attack. He, too, received the Navy Cross.

This year the SEALs and the UDTs set up a new sort of camp deep in Viet Cong territory, at the tip of the Ca Mau Peninsula. The problem with being so deep in the swamp and jungle was security, but the men solved this by welding fourteen barges together and anchoring them in the middle of the Song Cua Lon River, near old Nam Can. Local county Vietnam forces provided security on the two banks and the SEALs lived in what was called Seafloat, or "The Pontoon Palace," where they were almost immune to attack. But "almost" was the key word for several times during the year attempts were made by the Viet Cong to attach explosives to the barges to blow them up.

The SEALs kept learning from their own operations. They found that short ambushes were more effective than long ones, and they arranged to set up their ambushes just before dawn, which they found the most effective time. They made more use of the Light SEAL support craft as ambush platforms, pulling the boats up next to the bank and concealing them.

But in March the Vietnamization process did affect

the SEALs for the first time. Bravo Detachment, which had been training, advising, and leading Vietnamese soldiers into action for several years, was closed down.

With Vietnamization the Viet Cong became more numerous and more active in the Mekong delta. Sometimes it was necessary to abandon operations in progress to go to the aid of someone else, lest the Viet Cong move in on the men in difficulty. This occurred on April 2, when a SEAL Team No. 1 unit was on a raid operation twelve miles northeast of the Seafloat base. Then they learned of the crash of a helicopter not far away. They knew that the Viet Cong would probably try to capture the crew, so they canceled their operation and moved to the crash area. Soon a larger helicopter came to lift out the damaged aircraft, but so did a number of Viet Cong. The SEALs began firing; they killed five Viet Cong and drove the others off.

Acts of heroism continued to be common. On April 9, in the Mekong delta, SEAL Barry W. Enoch was leading a combined SEAL and Vietnamese frogman patrol that was seeking a group of important Viet Cong in the Long Phu District, about twenty miles southeast of Tra Vinh. The team went in by riverboat and began to patrol toward the village that was their target. Enoch, the senior adviser, was carrying a radio and a grenade launcher. He saw six Viet Cong trying to move around the Allied force, and he charged forward and engaged them, hitting three of the six men. But the noise aroused the Viet Cong in force, and they surrounded Enoch's unit. Enoch deployed the men into a defensive perimeter and kept in touch with air support, directing it during the attacks. Helicopters came in, but they could not operate here to pull the men out. But under Enoch's direction they attacked the encircling Viet Cong in one area and cut a hole through the encirclement. Enoch led the men in a charge through the hole and to a river nearby, from which they were taken out by boat. Intelligence later indicated that eighteen Viet Cong had been killed in this action, and for his heroism SEAL Enoch received the Navy Cross.

The SEALs continued to have casualties. SEAL Douglas Hobbs was killed when his unit was caught in a Viet Cong ambush on May 16. Then on June 23 came a more extensive tragedy. Five SEALs from Golf and Echo platoons of Team No. 1 were on a simple administrative helicopter trip from Seafloat to Can Tho when for unknown reasons the helicopter crashed. SEALs Richard Solano, James Gore, John Durlin, John Donnelly, and Toby Thomas were killed.

The SEALs were involved in an attempted rescue of prisoners held by the Viet Cong on July 15. This was an important mission because two Americans were reported among the prisoners. All of Juliet Platoon was used. The Coast Guard cutter *Point Cypress* and several riverine craft were involved in this attempt. The SEALs approached the target area but ran afoul of a booby trapped grenade, and the resultant explosion alerted the enemy before the SEALs ever got to the holding point. The Viet Cong fled, taking their prisoners, and so the Americans were not rescued, although one South Vietnamese soldier was saved. In the fighting that followed the SEALs killed three Viet Cong but could not find the trail through the swamp that the others had used, so the rescue mission had to be deemed a failure. Similar missions on July 30 and 31 also failed.

On July 24 the 6th Platoon discovered a Viet Cong weapons factory eight miles southwest of Ca Mau. The power source was a big French tractor, and next to it, under camouflage, was part of a downed American airplane. The Viet Cong were using it for raw material to make rockets.

The failure of the POW rescue missions caused the SEALs concern, which was shared by the entire U.S. command because a number of American POWs had been held for several years in jungle camps under e tremely primitive conditions. The rescue problem prompted the start of a whole series of intelligence reports under the code name "Brightlight." The SEALs often launched raids based on Brightlight reports, but they never seemed to be successful in locating the camps. In October 1970 a department SEAL team proposed establishment of three or four man Brightlight teams, each to cover the three southernmost provinces of South Vietnam. The teams would be located in the provincial capitals and should thus have the best and most up-to-date intelligence available. If reports came in, the SEAL teams would lead the operations and would spend their entire energy on this problem. But with the increase of Vietnamization and the feeling that it was time for the United States to withdraw, not to expand activity, this proposal died before it was born.

The interest in freeing POWs, however, did not die down. Late in August the SEALs had intelligence about the location of a prison camp, and Lt. Louis H. Boink of SEAL Team No. 2 took the 6th Platoon of Alpha Detachment and a Vietnamese Army company into this territory by air. Meanwhile, Australian bombers plastered the area to cut off escape attempts, and U.S. Army gunships attacked as another blocking move. By the time the SEALs reached the camp, it had been vacated, but they picked up the trail, which headed south, and began to pursue the Viet Cong. They called in more air support, including gunships and naval gunfire from the destroyer *Sutherland.* For two hours the SEALs pursued through the swamp. The enemy moved as fast as they could, abandoning equipment and even weapons and clothing as they went. Just before one o'clock in the afternoon the SEALs came to a clearing and found twenty-eight POWs, whose jailers had just abandoned them in their rush to escape. The released prisoners were evacuated by helicopter.

Even at the height of Vietnamization, there was much in Vietnam for the SEALs to do. There were intelligence missions to be run, high officials to kidnap, and POWs to search for. There also were new weapons in the hands of the Viet Cong, including directional claymore mines, which could be detonated by command. On a mission to destroy a Viet Cong munitions factory, the 6th Platoon encountered one of these, which was detonated as they approached the target, and wounded the last seven members of the line of SEALs. It may have been another of these mines that killed UDT men Luco W. Palma and L. C. Williams one day in September as they were on a bunker demolition mission. Several other members of UDT No. 13 were also injured in the explosion. Still, the Viet Cong were now increasing in power in the delta and other areas of South Vietnam as the Americans pulled out. In November SEAL patrols made two significant captures of ordnance that showed how strong the Viet Cong were becoming and how successful they were in bringing arms from the north in spite of all the efforts to interdict these. The dumps contained fifteen thousand rounds of AK-47 ammunition, dozens of mines, hundreds of grenades, and many other weapons.

On November 21, 1970, U.S. Army Special Forces (Green Berets and the Air Force Special Forces men) staged a highly publicized raid on a POW camp in the North, near Hanoi. The raid was carried out with great precision. The only problem was that when they got to the camp, the prisoners were gone. This incident created a bad press in America, but quite unknown was a very successful mission the SEALs conducted the following day. SEAL Team No. 1 sent Lieutenant Couch with ten SEALs and nineteen Vietnamese to raid a suspected camp in the Mekong delta. A sentry they captured on patrol revealed the location of the camp, about eight miles east of New Nam Can. The SEALs found the camp and got into a firefight with about eighteen guards, who soon fled. The SEALs freed nineteen POWs, but they were all Vietnamese. Although many raids were to be made and much information collected, no Americans were ever discovered in the Viet Cong prison camps of the delta country.

Toward the end of the year, the firefights in which the SEALs engaged seemed to grow more desperate. On December 13, when the SEALs conducted a raid and captured one Viet Cong, he pulled a grenade in a suicide attack. He was killed, but four SEALs were wounded. On December 20 the SEALs, on a mission to Trai Cheo Canal, followed one Viet Cong until eleven more appeared. The SEALs called on them to surrender, but the Viet Cong went for their weapons instead. In the firefight eight of the Viet Cong were killed, but the others escaped. The Viet Cong seemed to be gathering strength at the end of this year. On December 20 a five-man SEAL patrol set out east of Ben Tre to break a Viet Cong trail and walked into a well-planned ambush. Were they the victims of planted intelligence? Perhaps. In any event, they were ambushed by a force three times as large as their own, with heavy weapons and firepower. Chief Frank Bomar, the patrol leader, was mortally wounded, and so was SEAL James Ritter. The radioman and the Vietnamese guide were also wounded in this first burst. SEAL Harold Baker, who was the rear security man, went into the river and struggled to save Ritter's body. On the bank he kept up a powerful fire, protecting the rest of the SEALs from being overrun. Six other SEALs came into the area to help with the evacuation of the hard-hit unit.

By this time, the effects of Vietnamization were definitely being felt in the SEAL camp in many ways. One was the greater difficulty of their missions, since the Viet Cong had more power to concentrate. Another was their own diminishing numbers as the Navy began to withdraw them and UDT units. In the next few months some SEALs would remain as advisers to the South Vietnamese, but the heyday of the Special Forces units had come to an end in Vietnam.

It was just as this was occurring that the SEALs and UDT men were coming into their own. That fall of 1970 Special Forces insignia was authorized by the Navy for the underwater men. The UDT and the SEALs had different designs. Both had an anchor at the center, housed vertically, with a trident behind the anchor running horizontally and a flintlock musket standing before the anchor. But the SEAL insignia had an additional American eagle set astride the trident. But the two insignia were too confusing, and in the early 1970s they were combined and everyone wore the SEAL insignia.

By this time, too, the SEALs had established their own reputation. Within the naval service they were not entirely popular, and some said their insignia was too large and stood out too "noisily"—just like the people who wore it. Some senior commanders felt the SEALs were undisciplined, a sort of mafia of the Navy. The underwater men were indeed a breed apart and proud of it. As the Vietnam War wore down, they were willing to stand on their reputations for accomplishment.

〜〜〜〜
〜〜〜〜
At the beginning of 1971, in spite of Vietnamization, Navy special units were still very active in Vietnam. Although they were supposed to spend most of their effort in training and helping the Vietnamese, they continued their raids on the Viet Cong, too. But in the overall picture the effort was at turning all over to the Vietnamese, and in that effort in America a SEAL Team No. 2 platoon was sent to Puerto Rico to train Vietnamese naval officers in special warfare. A new unit, Sierra Detachment, was brought into Vietnam. It was designed to train South Vietnamese frogmen, and it consisted of five small units spread through the Mekong delta. The remaining direct-action platoons had the primary mission of locating and trying to destroy POW camps.

On January 9 Victor Platoon set up an ambush and killed three Viet Cong. Three days later, other SEALs, of Whiskey Platoon, were almost caught in an ambush when destroying bunkers and barricades near Nam Can, but turned the tables on the enemy and killed two more Viet Cong. More Viet Cong were killed and captured in the Nam Can area that month. And Lt. J. E. Thames of SEAL Team No. 1 became the first casualty of the year in fighting there when the boat on which he was riding was hit by two rockets. Thames and two Vietnamese frogmen were killed, and the boat was severely banged about. Two others—one SEAL and one Vietnamese—were wounded. This action might have ended very badly had not Zulu Platoon heard of the action at the Nam Can base and rushed by helicopter to help in the evacuation of the hard-hit unit. Several SEALs jumped thirty feet from their helicopter to get down to the ground and join the fighting. The Viet Cong were pushed back, and more gunships came in to sweep the area. MEDEVAC helicopters were brought in to evacuate the dead and wounded. SEAL Harold Birky was also killed at the end of the month, on a sweep-and-destroy operation, which under the new direction of the war did not seem to have much point. During February SEALs and UDT men were still engaged in raids, ambushes, and firefights, attacking small areas and getting small results, as on February 24, when a platoon from Team No. 2 attacked a Viet Cong camp, killing eight Viet Cong and capturing a few weapons and five pounds of documents. But more often now, the results of raids were not so satisfactory. On February 28 all the members of a SEAL squad were wounded when a rocket hit their rivercraft. And the Viet Cong seemed to have more rockets and more heavy weapons these days.

But by the end of February the direct-action phase of SEAL operations was coming to an end. SEAL Team No. 2 began to pull out its direct-action platoons and leave the country, with no replacement. The work was turned over to Team No. 1's Golf Detachment, and it began operations from the Navy base at Dong Nam. But on March 4 Golf Detachment's X-ray Platoon went home. Its accomplishments reflected the times and the change in the war. The platoon had been in 58 combat missions and accounted only for 36 Viet Cong dead, 12 captured, and a quantity of arms captured, including 340 mines, which had been brought for use against American forces. They also captured 46 kilograms of Viet Cong documents, but their use then is debatable. They certainly did not change the course of the war.

Four men from the platoon had been killed and all the others wounded at least once, three of them wounded so seriously that they had to be evacuated to the United States for hospitalization.

In the earlier stages of the war, when there seemed hope for victory, SEAL operations had appeared to be useful in harrying the Viet Cong and bringing intelligence. But now there was not much use in securing the intelligence because the Vietnamese were not making proper use of it in many cases.

In March the SEALs continued their small-unit raids into the countryside, although there did not seem to be much point in such raids, such as one that was staged in the middle of a wedding, killing two Viet Cong members of the wedding party and taking three prisoners and some documents and a Viet Cong flag. But the urge to sting was still there, and as long as the SEALs would remain in Vietnam, they would continue their typical operations. Once in a while, as in a combined operation with Australians on June 6, they destroyed an important cache; that day it was twenty thousand pounds of rice. But usually a raid netted one or two killed and a handful of prisoners. The impressive results of earlier years were gone.

By August, SEAL Team No. 2 was down to two representatives. The results of the war were not always pleasant now: Two members of SEAL Team No. 1 were arrested for trying to smuggle heroin into the United States.

In November President Nixon ended the American offensive role in Vietnam with his announcement that from this point on the Americans were in a strictly defensive posture, no longer having any expectation of winning the war and no expectation that the South Vietnamese government could long survive.

The SEALs were mostly reduced to running operations with Vietnamese frogmen, and by November the SEALs who remained in the country were said to be there just in case there was a possibility of getting some American prisoners of war out of the country.

The SEALs were very unhappy about this turn of events, and some of them told a reporter for *The New York Times* that the change in the rules covering their operations had made it impossible for them to carry out missions successfully. Since the My Lai scandal, the SEALs also operated under the fear of being accused of atrocities in their ambushes and attacks.

On December 7, SEAL Team No. 1's Mike Platoon left the country, and that took out the last remaining direct-action platoon of SEALs. More UDT men were left, as part of the Seventh Fleet, but their role was also greatly diminished. Still, the war continued, and so did offensive American action in the bombing of North Vietnam, which was resumed in December, as punishment for North Vietnamese stalling of the peace talks again. In this atmosphere the role of the SEALs officially, and the one they really played in Vietnam, were not always the same. The ingrained methods of operation were difficult to change. As a result, two of the three Medals of Honor won by the SEALs during the Vietnam War were won in 1972.

By this time there were no direct-action SEAL platoons left in Vietnam, although UDT boat crews continued to run the Nasty boats for a few more months. SEAL Team No. 1 still had four members in the country, acting as advisers to Vietnamese frogmen. One of these SEALs was critically wounded on January 15 during a combat operation. The remaining Team No. 2 members left in mid-February. SEAL Team No. 1 kept one platoon for possible contingencies, mostly relating to POWs, but this platoon was on Okinawa, waiting.

With American participation at a new low and an American presidential election in the offing in the fall of 1972, the North Vietnamese stepped up their plans for a win-the-war offensive. And at the end of March they launched a full-scale invasion of South Vietnam that would be known as the Easter Offensive.

A few days after the beginning of the invasion the Americans were flying a bombing mission near the demilitarized zone in support of South Vietnam defense efforts when suddenly an American EB-66 electronic warfare jet on the escort was hit by a surface-to-air missile. One man of the crew escaped the aircraft as it went down. He was Lt. Col. Iceal Hambleton, the electric warfare officer aboard the plane. He parachuted to safety and was able to radio to a spotter plane, which pinpointed his location deep inside enemy territory along the Song Mieu Giang River. The North Vietnamese Army sent units to capture him, but U.S. Air Force planes dropped a minefield around his position, which held the North Vietnamese off. Four Army helicopters tried to rescue him, but they were attacked from the ground by the North Vietnamese with powerful antiaircraft weapons, and one helicopter was shot down and all aboard were killed. Another limped away, damaged from the fire, and crash-landed south of Quang Tri.

Now it was standoff. The U.S. Air Force prevented the North Vietnamese from getting to Hambleton, but the North Vietnamese blocked every rescue attempt with heavy fire. Two spotter planes and one rescue helicopter were shot down. All this action continued from April 2 to April 13.

At this time, Lt. Thomas Norris, a member of SEAL Team No. 2, was on duty with SEAL Team No. 1 with what remained of the U.S. advisory group in Vietnam. This was the sort of mission for which the remaining SEALs in Vietnam were equipped and prepared. On the night of April 10 Norris led a five-man team and rescued one of the spotter plane crewmen. Then he and two others tried to rescue Hambleton but were thwarted by the presence of so many North Vietnamese troops in the area.

Norris and a South Vietnamese frogman dressed in peasant clothing and took a small sampan to try again. A pickup point on the river had been designated, and Hambleton had been told to move there. He did, and the two men in the sampan found him on the night of April 12. They covered him with banana leaves and then moved slowly down the river, hugging the bank and trying to avoid attention. When they saw enemy directly in their path, Norris called for air strikes, which knocked those troops out before the sampan arrived. After three hours the men were near safety, but then they came under heavy attack. Another air strike knocked out that point of enemy activity, and the three men reached the forward operational base of the South Vietnamese and safety.

For this mission, Lieutenant Norris won the Medal of Honor, and his South Vietnamese companion, Nguyen Van Kiet, became the only Vietnamese during the war to win the Navy Cross.

The North Vietnamese Easter offensive failed. The U.S. Air Force helped immeasurably in this regard. When the offensive was over, the last two advisers to the Vietnamese in the once big base at Danang were called home, and all that remained of the SEALs in Vietnam was the special group that waited for American POW action.

The process of disengagement continued to be difficult for the Americans, and they increased their bombing efforts that spring. The Navy also made preparations for a maritime operation, using the submarine *Grayback*. The platoon of SEALs on Okinawa was to be used, but in the process of moving into action, the SEAL leader, Lt. Melvin Dry, was killed, becoming the last fatality among the SEALs in the Vietnam War.

That summer and fall the North Vietnamese stepped up their military activity, as did the Viet Cong. Around Danang rocket attacks became almost commonplace. Henry Kissinger announced that the war was about to end, but one would never have known it at Danang. Two SEALs were working deep inland, performing the same type of missions they had done before, trying to capture prisoners and gather intelligence about the enemy. With three Vietnamese, Lt. Tom Norris and SEAL Michael Thornton set out in a boat from a South Vietnamese Navy junk and landed at a beach near the Cua Viet Naval

Base, which had been captured by the North Vietnamese. It was about four-thirty in the morning, and the beach was very quiet. The men landed and went on patrol through the sand dunes. All went well until dawn. At that time they were informed by radio that they had landed too far north of the base. The area in which they were operating was all sand dunes, and they had no identifying landmarks for reference if they wanted to call in fire support. They turned back toward the beach to rework their position. When they passed through the last few dunes before hitting the beach, they were seen by two North Vietnamese soldiers, who began firing at them. The noise brought more North Vietnamese soldiers, and the frogmen set up a defensive perimeter, intending to call for fire support. From offshore they received naval gunfire, which disrupted the enemy unit, but then about fifty more soldiers were seen coming up. For the next forty-five minutes the Americans and the Vietnamese frogmen held off the enemy, who came to within twenty-five yards of the perimeter. One of the Vietnamese frogmen was hit in the leg, and SEAL Thornton was wounded by grenade fragments in both legs. They were low on ammunition but could not get out—there was no place to go except to the open beach and the ocean. Lieutenant Norris ordered the men to move out, and he and one Vietnamese stayed behind to cover the retreat. SEAL Thornton and the other two Vietnamese frogmen ran through enemy fire the last hundred yards through the dunes. When the last Vietnamese reached the final dune, he told Thornton that Lieutenant Norris had been shot and was dead. Thornton went back then to recover the body of his officer. Again running the gauntlet of gunfire as he arrived at the position where he had left Norris, he saw two North Vietnamese soldiers overrunning the site. He attacked and killed them both. Then he found Lieutenant Norris, shot in the head and unconscious but still alive. SEAL Thornton picked up Lieutenant Norris, slung him over his shoulder, and dashed back for the last dune, again through gunfire.

The North Vietnamese then began to move to surround the Americans and South Vietnamese frogmen, who headed for the sea and safety. Thornton carried Norris 250 yards across the open beach, then through the surf. He inflated both their life jackets, swam out to beyond gunshot range, gave Norris first aid, and towed him for two hours.

Shortly before noon they were picked up by the South Vietnamese junk that had dropped them off. Soon they were transferred to the USS *Newport News* for medical treatment. Lieutenant Norris survived, and after a long time in hospitals was rehabilitated and joined the FBI as a special agent. Thornton continued on with the SEALs and was awarded the Medal of Honor, the third SEAL so honored.

The end of the year 1972 saw the Americans launching Operation Linebacker II, which was another sustained aerial bombing program against the North Vietnamese. This time the bombing was effective enough to persuade the North Vietnamese to sign a cease-fire in January 1973. By mid-March the last American field command in Vietnam was closed, and all the American advisers, including the few SEALs left in the country, went back to the United States. One SEAL, however, was assigned to a mine disposal unit in and around Haiphong Harbor, to honor part of the cease-fire agreement, which called for the Americans to dispose of the mines they had sowed in North Vietnamese waters during the Linebacker bombing operations.

Even after the American military withdrawal the role of the SEALs in the Vietnam War continued. In California they began to train Cambodian frogmen, and they continued to train them at Subic Bay in the Philippines. Five SEAL officers served as naval attachés to Cambodia between 1973 and 1975, as the U.S. government contin ued its forlorn efforts, although much reduced, to control events in Southeast Asia.

Among the SEALs the attitude toward the whole Vietnam involvement varied. Some had found it a great adventure and never looked back. Some had been scarred by the carnage of the war, to which they had contributed so much violence, and wondered why, a matter most destructive to the spirit of a fighting man. Some began to believe the United States had been on the wrong side in the war, particularly when the South Vietnamese government began to collapse in its own corruption and incompetence. After the American SEALs left Vietnam, the people in whom they had invested so much time and effort, the Vietnamese frogmen, did not fare well. They, too, were affected by the inept leadership.

The whole Southeast Asian ball unraveled in the early months of 1975. The North Vietnamese launched their final offensive, and the South Vietnamese armies fell apart. The Cambodian government collapsed, and the Khmer Rouge captured the capital of Phnom Penh. During this period Naval Special Warfare Command men were still peripherally involved. UDT units and a SEAL platoon were maintained on standby in Asia. When in May the Khmer Rouge captured the USS *Mayaguez,* the UDT men were alerted, but they were not used in the effort to recapture the vessel. This action was done by the Marines. SEALs would argue that the whole operation would have been easier and more successful, with fewer casualties than the eighteen men killed and missing and many more who were wounded, if there had not been within the military hierarchy residual resistance to the idea of Special Forces operations. This same resistance had caused the disbandment of the Marine Raider battalions and amalgamation of the Marine Raider Regiment within the Marine 4th Division during World War II.

Overall, the Naval Special Warfare Command did not come out unscathed in the public's negative reaction to the Vietnam War. A major public criticism concerned the Navy's role in Operation Phoenix. This operation was the American attempt to wipe out the Viet Cong using counterinsurgency tactics, to disrupt the Viet Cong's command structure and supply system, and to collect intelligence that would permit the capture of leading Viet Cong figures. The SEALs were deeply involved in this program, particularly in the direct-action aspect, and SEALs made more than four thousand missions. Much of their effort was wasted because of incompetence at top levels, and sometimes as a result of Viet Cong infiltration of the intelligence community. By the time the authorities were ready to act on "hot" intelligence, that information was no longer news and often of no value at all. Operation Phoenix was largely successful in harrying the Viet Cong and decreasing their effectiveness, but its critics found it to be "organized assassination," which, of course, it was, plus organized kidnapping. The finger of guilt was pointed at the CIA and the people who worked with the CIA, of which the SEALs were a major part. Public reaction to the Phoenix program was so negative that it was brought to an end in the early 1970s, but because the operations had been held in such top-secret classifications, no real evidence of wrongdoing was forthcoming.

The SEALs always denied any wrongdoing in the whole of their operations in Vietnam. They were professionals, they claimed, doing a professional job, and their main function was gathering intelligence. The record does not bear this out, for the reports of SEAL operations are studded with firefights and operations in which hundreds of Viet Cong were shot down. But what were the SEALs to do, given the missions (many of which they developed themselves) they were assigned?

Since Vietnam the Naval Special Warfare Command has made a serious effort to change the public image of the SEALs, as creators of derring-do, almost supermen who take on one "mission impossible" after another and bring them off. Partially because of the backlash of Vietnam, the emphasis has settled on cooperative effort.

Perhaps the most cogent public document created by and about the SEALs and their operations in Vietnam is a novelized account of SEAL operations by Jerry J. Fletcher, a former lieutenant commander in the SEALs who also served with Underwater Demolition Teams No. 11 and No. 13 and who resigned from the Navy in 1980. This novel was characterized by Lt. Frank F. Thornton, the most decorated SEAL of the Vietnam War, as an accurate portrayal of their activity in Vietnam. The impact is to present a portrait of the SEALs as superbly competent terrorists and assassins. It is a portrait with which naval officialdom now will quarrel, but the fact is that once the United States got mired in the Vietnamese civil war, it was necessary to conform to the tactics of that war, and the principal tactic of the Viet Cong in South Vietnam was terrorism. So the Navy, the Army, the Air Force, and the CIA set out to fight terror with terror.

The Thornton account of SEAL operations is stark and terrible, bearing out the claim that the SEALs were bent on terrorism and destruction of the Viet Cong by confrontation. The SEALs portrayed, also, are not men the average American would like. They were portrayed as hard-drinking, fornicating adventurers, with a definite indication of a certain sadism on the part of some of them during their operations. But wars against terrorism, using counterterror, cannot be fought without employing the people who know how to carry out such missions. The responsibility and justification for whatever the SEALs did in Vietnam lies much higher up the military totem pole.

If the critics of the SEAL operations in Vietnam call them assassins and terrorists, they were certainly no more culpable for carrying out their specialty than the air pilots who bombed villages all over Vietnam, killing innocent civilian men, women, and children. The fact that there was a certain neutrality in air bombing that deprives a man of a sense of personal responsibility for the killing he is doing is really only a change of emphasis. As SEAL author Jerry Fletcher says a number of times in his novel, in justification of his heroes' activities: War is hell, and no more need be said. In the world of the twentieth century, where terrorism has made its place secure, he seems to be right in his assessment of the struggle in Vietnam.

SSSS
SSSS　The untidy end to the Vietnam War left
　　　　　a sense of frustration with the American
　　　　　military and a lack of confidence in the
military processes that had been followed by the United
States since 1950. The truism that it was suicidal for the
United States to involve itself in a land war on the Asian
continent without the strongest of Asian allies had twice
been proved to be accurate. The first reaction of Americans was to withdraw from military participation, but this
could not be done in Europe because of the entangle-
ment with NATO allies. Even so, the military suffered in
the 1970s from an eroded public confidence and had to
rebuild its image and some parts of its structure.

Until 1975 the SEALs continued to be involved peripherally in the Southeast Asian struggle that centered
around Vietnam, but the fall of Cambodia to the Communist regime ended that. The Underwater Demolition
Teams continued in a useful activity that had begun in the
1960s, the recovery of American spacecraft that landed in
the waters around the world, and attaching flotation gear
to the spacecraft so they would not be lost. But in the
reorganization of the Naval Special Warfare Command in
1983, the Underwater Demolition Teams as such went
out of existence. Their members became SEALs or members of SEAL delivery vehicle teams.

The SEALs continued to train for various specialized activities. Their air arm (Seawolf helicopters) was
disbanded as an operational unit in 1972, but four years
later two new helicopter groups were formed to work
with the SEALs: the Redwolves on the U.S. East Coast,
and the Blue Hawks, assigned to the Naval Special War-
are Group on the West Coast.

After a reevaluation of the role of the SEALs, and the roles of other special military forces in a world where terrorism had become commonplace by the 1970s, the Navy created SEAL Team No. 6, a supersecret organization that became part of the overall Special Warfare Command, which was placed under Army control. Team No. 6 is at the disposal of the White House and the secretary of defense for special missions, obviously counterterrorist activity, although the secret is so closely held that the existence of Team No. 6 was not officially admitted. As time went on the various special warfare units of the services became more integrated under the Joint Special Operations Command. One of the first joint operations in which Seal Team No. 6 was involved was the Grenada invasion of 1983.

The small island of Grenada in the Caribbean was known to Americans primarily as a vacation resort until 1983. Grenada became independent from Britain in 1974 under a government so corrupt that it invited a coup, and such came in the spring of 1979, when Maurice Bishop seized power for the left-oriented Provisional Revolutionary Government. That government turned to Cuba and the USSR for support. The U.S. government became unfriendly and suspicious of Bishop's motivations, and when he began construction of a new airfield with a runway long enough to handle strategic bombers, the suspicions were increased. The Bishop government's claim was that the new nine-thousand-foot-long runway was needed to enhance the tourist trade, but American military men began to think that it was really to accommodate Soviet long-range bombers. In the early 1980s Bishop came into conflict with a pro-Communist faction led by Bernard Coard, the deputy prime minister, who wanted Grenada converted to a Communist government. On October 13, 1983, Coard seized power, put Bishop under house arrest and declared the Provisional Revolutionary Army to be in control.

This change became a matter of serious American concern, first of all because of the potential expansion in the Caribbean of Communist Soviet influence, which had been held in check since the Cuban missile crisis of the 1960s. Second was the welfare and fate of some one thousand Americans on Grenada, many of them medical students at St. George's University Medical School. An emergency meeting was held at the State Department, and the next day October 14, the National Security Council ordered the Joint Chiefs of Staff to prepare for a military rescue of the Americans. The job of drafting the operation was given to Adm. Wesley McDonald, commander of the U.S. Atlantic Fleet. But a request was also made by the Joint Chiefs of Staff of the Joint Special Operations Command to draw up a plan. As it turned out, this dual request was a serious mistake, one that indicated the uncertainty of the U.S. military organization, even a decade after the disaster in Vietnam.

While this was being done, the situation in Grenada became more complicated and more risky. On October 19, Grenadian foreign minister Unison Whiteman began making speeches in the streets in an attempt to secure the release of Prime Minister Bishop. The crowd responded and decided to go to Bishop's place to secure his release. When they got there and the guards saw the large and angry crowd, they disappeared, and Bishop was released. They all returned to St. George's and to Fort Rupert, where a number of the members of Bishop's government had been held. They were released. Then three armored personnel carriers arrived, filled with soldiers of the Provisional Revolutionary Army. They opened fire on the crowd, killing fifty people and wounding as many more. The crowd fled, and Bishop and four of his ministers and three of his supporters were taken into Fort Rupert and shot.

U.S. authorities learned this from the American consul in Barbados, for the United States did not have diplomatic relations with Grenada. Soon the State Department had a report of the deteriorating situation in Grenada and a recommendation for the immediate evacuation of all U.S. citizens from Grenada.

Now a combination of circumstances prompted American action. First of these was a desire by the American military to flex its muscles, so badly deteriorated and bruised by the Vietnam experience. Second was a real concern for the safety of the Americans on the island, with Provisional Revolutionary Army soldiers patrolling the streets and shooting civilians after having murdered the duly constituted prime minister and most of his government. In addition, there was a strong desire to have an operation that was planned to succeed without any hindrance from the American media. Many in the military still blamed the media for the American defeat in the Vietnam War and for turning the American people against the military. So there could not be the slightest interference with the military plan of action, the National Security Council approved a degree of secrecy for this operation that was probably unconstitutional and certainly was unhealthy. The media were given no information and were not included in the operation. Despite requests, for the first time in many years the media were denied access. They would not be taken along on the operation as they always had been before, in a tradition that went back to the Spanish-American War. This Grenada operation was to be secret and kept secret from the American people until it was completed.

The problem with American action in Grenada was that it could arouse a storm of protest about a great power interfering with the affairs of a small Western Hemisphere government. To avoid this, the Americans decided on a diplomatic demarche as well as military action. Two State Department officials were dispatched from Barbados to report on events in Grenada. On October 23 they reported that people were being arrested and that the authorities were maintaining a shoot-on-sight curfew. Grenada was said to have some 300 soldiers in its small army, with 250 Cuban military men also on the island in connection with the building of the new airport. The State Department then conferred with members of the Organization of Eastern Caribbean States. Tom Adams, the prime minister of Barbados, reported receiving a letter from Governor General Sir Paul Scoon of Grenada, requesting the organization for outside intervention to restore the duly elected government of Grenada. Scoon was a holdover from the Britannic days, but he still held the title of governor general, which had been honored only formally in recent years. Still, that request was enough for the Organization of Eastern Caribbean States and the U.S. State Department to justify direct action.

Meanwhile, with two military entities being given the responsibility for planning an operation, the Americans disagreed about the plan to be followed for military action in Grenada. The Joint Special Operations Command, in view of the fact that the Grenadian forces were so small, wanted the whole operation to be performed by Special Forces. The Atlantic Fleet plan was conventional. The United States would send in the Marines, backed by the fleet. Two elements for this plan were immediately available. One was Task Force 124, built around the helicopter carrier *Guam,* and Amphibious Squadron 4, which was on its way to Beirut to relieve another Marine amphibious group. The other group was a battle group organized around the carrier *Independence,* which was just leaving for duty in the Mediterranean.

Each command stood stoutly by its own plan, and the meeting with the Joint Chiefs of Staff became long and acrimonious. The final decision was a compromise that resulted in confusion and overkill. The Rangers and Special Forces would attack the southern half of the island in their way. The Marines would attack the northern half of the island. The overall command would be in the hands of the Navy, and the tightest possible security would be imposed. The two naval battle groups already at sea were told to stand by, but not what for.

By October 24, the Atlantic Fleet had completed its invasion plan and had ordered the Joint Special Operations Committee to produce its plan, using the Army Delta Force and the Navy SEALs. So great was the obsession with security that there was to be no advance reconnaissance, which violated one of the rules of the Special Forces, who liked to know what they were getting into. In this operation against this little island, parts of SEAL Team No. 4 and SEAL Team No. 6, the Delta Force, the 1st and 2d Ranger battalions, the 82d Airborne Division, the 1st Special Operations Wing of the Air Force, and the 22d Marine Amphibious Unit would be used. The whole operation was to be called Operation Urgent Fury. Vice Adm. Joseph Metcalf proceeded to join the carrier *Guam* and take charge of a plan complicated enough for a major invasion.

The Special Forces were first to parachute a Delta detachment in before dawn, to secure the airfield at Port Salinas. They would clear the runway, and the Rangers would come in by aircraft. Another Delta detachment would attack the prison at Richmond Hill and free the people held there. A detachment from Seal Team No. 6 would go to the residence of Governor General Sir Paul Scoon, rescue him and his staff, and evacuate them from the island. A platoon from SEAL Team No. 4 would capture Radio Free Grenada and keep it off the air until U.S. forces could take it over. Another platoon of SEAL Team No. 4 would reconnoiter the beaches at Grenville and Pearls airport in the North to pave the way for the 22d Marine Amphibious Unit. The Marines would land with tanks and troops and secure the island.

However, the obsession with security interfered with the plans. The mission of the SEAL Team No. 4 platoon that was to reconnoiter the beaches for the Marines was changed. Instead, they were to bring in an Air Force Combat Control Team at the Port Salinas airfield to help guide the aircraft carrying the Rangers. The Marines were left high and dry. The reason was the jealousy of the Atlantic Fleet Command of its authority over every phase of the operation.

Almost immediately the complex plan, changed so many times already, began to fail. Before dawn on October 23, a team of twelve SEALs and four Air Force specialists was flown to a point forty miles northwest of Port Salinas and dropped in the Caribbean near Grenada to make contact with a Navy destroyer. The SEALs had all of their equipment and two rubber boats. The weather was fairly rough and the seas fairly high, and in the operation one rubber boat and four SEALs disappeared. So four SEALs were the first casualties of the Grenada operation.

The rest of the men and the Air Force men moved toward the shore. They saw a Grenadian patrol boat approaching, and cut the power of the outboard motor so the boat could slip past the patrol boat without detection. The cut in power resulted in the pooping of the rubber boat by its own wake and the swamping of the boat and drowning of the motor. So the overloaded single rubber boat was caught in the strong current around the island and drifted rapidly out to sea. The four SEALs and the four Air Force men were lost to the operation at this time, although they were rescued many hours later by the destroyer *Caron*.

So far the Special Forces operations had been a complete failure, as had the overcomplicated plan. A second team of SEALs was assembled by cannibalizing the force sent to take the radio station. It was sent to drop near the *Caron*, and it succeeded in this. These men, combined with the rescued men in the rubber boat, then tried to infiltrate the island. They were already about twenty-four hours behind schedule. On the final run into the beach, both rubber boats swamped and all the equipment of the airmen was lost. This new team, and part of the old one, failed completely in its mission, too, although the men were finally recovered.

These errors had cut deep into SEAL Team No. 4. The Special Forces planners had wanted to let the SEAL team assigned to the Marine landing force do the scouting for the Marine landing, but the Atlantic Fleet men had said no. Now they reversed themselves, and the Marines would have their own SEAL team in action, but without advance planning or all the information needed. They received the information Monday evening, October 24, and the reconnaissance was to be made that same night. This SEAL unit reconnoitered the beaches and made its landing undetected, arriving on the island during a heavy rainstorm. In a few minutes they were within listening distance of the Grenadians on the beach who were digging trenches for defense against a possible American invasion. The SEAL unit completed its mission and reported back to the Marines that they would have to negotiate reefs off the intended landing beaches, a difficulty no one had suspected. The only vessels that could land would be very-shallow-draft craft. Admiral Metcalf then switched plans and called for helicopter transport of two companies of troops, one at the Pearls airport and the other at nearby Grenville. So the Marine landing plan was also changed. Golf Company, which had been scheduled to go in by boat, would now be held in reserve.

Marines began to go ashore by helicopter on Tuesday, October 25, at 5:20 A.M.

The Delta Force team that was supposed to make the initial landings did so successfully, but the Americans were immediately detected by the Grenadians, who were guarding the Port Salinas airport in force, and the Delta Force unit was almost immediately pinned down and unable to clear the runways to make way for the Rangers.

SEAL Team No. 4 men had been scheduled to make

the raid on Radio Free Grenada and keep it off the air. They had intended to go in at night, but the delays in other plans delayed them, too, and they did not get in until after daylight, when the Grenadian forces were already alerted to the Delta drop and ready for action. The SEALs landed by rubber boat north of the Salinas airport and started for the radio station. But the element of surprise had been completely lost as well as the cover of night, and they came under heavy fire from the Grenadians as they came. Of the eight-man team, four were wounded.

Also by the time they were moving toward the radio station it was already in operation, broadcasting an appeal from the revolutionary government to Grenadians to resist the American invasion. So the whole objective of the mission was lost.

A group of American reporters, denied participation by the military, had chartered a boat and were coming to the island anyhow, and they heard Radio Free Grenada go on the air before six o'clock and then, about an hour later, go off the air abruptly. That was when the SEAL team finally arrived at the radio station. Hearing the station go off the air, a unit of the Grenadian Army came to investigate and attacked the SEALs, who were supposed to hold the station but who could not in the face of superior firepower and their own numbers, diminished by administrative changes and the military action on the beach. They had to destroy the transmitter and withdraw to hiding. So the transmitter would now be of no use to the American forces, as had been planned.

The superspecial SEAL Team No. 6 had been chosen for the primary SEAL mission, the rescue of Governor General Sir Paul Scoon and his staff from house arrest at Government House on the outskirts of St. George's. These SEALs, too, were delayed by the foul-up of the whole operation until it was nearly daylight, when their helicopters began approaching the landing site.

When the first helicopter came in, the Grenadians were waiting for it and opened fire. The helicopter was damaged, but it dumped out the SEALs and hurried off. The team radio had been damaged, so the men had left it behind in the helicopter. The second helicopter came under such intense fire that it was ordered away without landing by the SEAL commander on the ground. The first group of thirteen men fought their way across the lawn and into Government House. They pushed the governor general into a closet and locked it, then manned their barricades. They had clear views of all sides of the mansion. One SEAL was a sniper with a sniper's rifle, and he moved around the building, firing at the enemy. He was credited with killing a large number of them, and also with saving the men inside Government House from a concerted attack by the Grenadian forces, who called for reinforcements, including some armored personnel carriers, and waited.

So the SEALs of Team No. 6 were in difficulty. They had lost their radio, which put them out of touch with the rest of the invasion forces. The plan had been for the helicopters to stand by until the governor general and his staff could be bundled across the lawn and embarked, and then all would take off and return to the fleet and safety. But the helicopters were gone, and one of them was badly damaged. By using the local telephone system the SEALs inside the mansion were able to get word to Admiral Metcalf that they were in trouble, and he sent a pair of helicopter gunships to give air support.

The first of these Sea Cobra helicopters stopped to strafe the antiaircraft emplacements at Fort Frederick, which was the Cuban military headquarters. Fire from antiaircraft guns wounded the pilot, and he crash-landed the helicopter in a field in the middle of St. George's. The weapons controller of the helicopter dragged the pilot out of the burning aircraft, but was then shot down by the Grenadians as he was trying to signal the other helicopter. The second helicopter was shot down in the harbor when it was covering a MEDEVAC helicopter going to get the pilot of the first helicopter. So the air support mission had failed and had cost the lives of three Marines.

The Grenadian armored personnel carriers arrived outside Government House, and the Grenadian Army then began its attack on the mansion but was stopped in short order by an American gunship, which destroyed one of the personnel carriers. The gunship circled over the mansion, staying out of range of antiaircraft fire. Admiral Metcalf ordered a full air strike on the defenses of St. George's from the carrier *Independence*. The air strike knocked out most of the antiaircraft guns.

Still, the SEALs inside the governor general's mansion were besieged, and they had not rescucd the governor general and his staff. That is how the battle stood at the end of the first day.

That night Admiral Metcalf ordered the LST that was carying the Marine Golf Company to steam around the island, land at St. George's, and lift the siege on the SEALs. Meanwhile, the Marines of Fox Company crossed the island by helicopter and landed in that same area. At four o'clock in the morning the Marines of Golf Company landed and were reinforced by five tanks. The two Marine companies teamed up and moved toward the governor general's mansion. One armored personnel carrier tried to stop them, but it was knocked out by the 105mm gun of one of the tanks.

As morning came, the SEALs inside the governor general's mansion were running low on ammunition, but when the local Army commander learned that the Americans had tanks with big guns ashore, he abruptly broke off the siege and with his troops disappeared into the interior of the island. So shortly after seven in the morning the governor general was let out of his closet and the SEALs escorted him and his staff to the fleet.

This was almost the end of SEAL participation in the Grenada invasion. Actually, with the arrival of the Marines and the tanks in St. George's, it was all over but the mopping up. The number of Cubans found to be on the island was minimal, and the Provisional Revolutionary Army had disappeared into the bush. For the next few days, two fast SEAL team patrol boats worked around the island, interdicting small craft that were trying to effect the escape of the Provisional Revolutionary Army from Grenada. And so a very badly managed fleet operation came to an end. The only reasonable performance of American forces was that of the Marine ground combat force. The SEALs had been misused in the operation, and so had the members of Delta Force. The Grenada invasion could never have been anything but a victory, but the sort of victory it was did not reflect any glory on the Naval Special Warfare Command forces or on the fleet.

§§§§
§§§§
In the 1970s and early years of the 1980s, the Navy SEALs concentrated on training and perfecting their skills. The Vietnam days were over, and although the men at Coronado had their eyes open for a chance to rescue some American prisoners of war, it never came. The SEALs were not involved in the attempt to rescue the hostages at the U.S. embassy in Teheran. They trained some frogmen for other countries, and kept the operating bases in Okinawa and the Philippines.

One of their main preoccupations was the development of new weapons and new systems. During the Vietnam War their need for a powerful stopping weapon caused the Remington Arms Company to deliver its 7188 shotgun, which seemed at first to fill the bill completely. The weapon had an eight-shot magazine, a select fire capability, and a ventilated barrel shield. Fired on full automatic, the weapon could operate at 420 rounds per minute, emptying its magazine in just over a second. That meant a SEAL could put a burst of 00 buckshot out, each shell loaded with nine pellets, and effectively fire seventy-two .33-caliber bullets in a second and a half. It was the greatest firepower of any personal weapon invented. But when the gun was fired on full automatic, difficulties developed, and the "glitches" caused the Remington Arms Company to withdraw the weapon. The SEALs still wanted a weapon of that sort, however, and work began and continued to develop a fully automatic shotgun that could deliver the firepower without the problems. During the 1960s and early 1970s in Vietnam the SEAL three-man teams were armed with one eight-shot Ithaca 37 pump shotgun; one M-16 rifle with a grenade launcher attached; a Stoner Mark 23 machine gun; 150 rounds of ammunition in a belt; an assortment of grenades, knives and handguns; and a radio. But by the 1980s most of the weapons of the Vietnamese era were no longer in use. The Heckler & Koch submachine guns of three series replaced the Mark 24 submachine gun developed for the SEALs by Smith & Wesson. The Stoner machine gun, which always had parts problems because the parts were so small, went out of style and now is only used for training. The M-16 rifle and the M-14 rifle continued to be used, and the grenade launcher as well. New sniper rifles were designed, and new silencer pistols replaced the Hush Puppy. But the SEALs are constantly experimenting with new weapons, and this is one aspect of their operations that will not cease. Their search for the best weapons they can find is endless.

In the 1970s also the SEALs were experimenting with new swimmer delivery vehicles, and in 1983, when the last UDTs were taken out of commission, some of their members were transferred to the new Swimmer Delivery Vehicle Teams that were just going into service that year. These new SDV platoons had new delivery vehicles. The idea of Swimmer Delivery Vehicles goes back to the 1960s. The first SDVs used by the SEALs were of the Italian Sea Horse type, a four-man vehicle that carried two men in an open front compartment, one in front and the other in back of him, and the same in the back compartment. From this came the development by General Dynamics Corporation of the Mark VII SDV, a wet submersible powered by six sixteen-cell batteries. It could travel at 4.5 knots to depths of 200 feet and continue for 8 hours, covering 40 nautical miles. It could carry the four swimmers and 55 pounds of equipment.

By the late 1970s new types of vehicles had been developed, with Fiberglas hulls and fittings made of nonferrous materials. Instrument and electric systems were built into watertight compartments. Sliding canopies covered both cockpits, protecting the men from pressure. The pilots had a view screen for guidance.

New models of SDVs were developed during the 1970s. The Mark VIII is more sophisticated and can transport four swimmers in the rear compartment, with a crew of pilot and navigator up front, and it has a more complex steering system and better buoyancy control. This latter permits the vehicle to dive and surface without the old awkwardness. This vehicle has an on-board breathing system that allows talk between or among the crew members. It has a Doppler computerized navigation system and an obstacle avoidance system using sonar, and a radio system that can be used when the vehicle is on the surface.

The next vehicle to reach the SEALs was the Mark IX SEAL Delivery Vehicle, which was designed for two swimmers and much more weight. It was foreseen that this vehicle would carry torpedoes that SEALs could launch against enemy vessels, thus opening a whole new field of action to the SEALs. The SDV could be carried on the deck of a conventional submarine. The SEALs could use their lockout and escape procedure to get out of the submarine underwater, enter the vehicle, and cast off. But the problem with this system was that the maintenance of the SDV had to be carried out on the surface. This problem was solved when the USS *Grayback,* with its big missile hangars, was made available to the underwater men during the Vietnam War. The *Grayback* was the first amphibious transport submarine. She could carry four SEAL Delivery Vehicles. She became the pride of the underwater men and was used extensively in training and operations until she was finally decommissioned in 1984. At that point a new program was developed to carry the SEAL vehicles on the decks of nuclear submarines. The submarines used for this were the Sturgeon-class attack submarines, and six of them were expected to be con- verted to SEAL use and be in service by 1992. Meanwhile, two submarines of the Ethan Allen class were converted for SEAL use. These were the *Sam Houston* and the *John Marshall,* each of which could carry two vehicles.

In the beginning of the SDV program, assignment to a SEAL Delivery Team was regarded by new graduates of the SEALs program as a demotion, but as time went on and the activities of the SEAL Delivery Teams increased and became better known, it became a prize assignment. One reason was that it increased the technical proficiency of the SEALs involved and gave them a new set of skills that would be important to the fleet. As of 1990 eight SDV classes a year were being conducted. It was generally conceded within the SEAL organization that the use of the SEAL Delivery Vehicle was the most important development in modern SEAL history, particularly in its implications for future naval warfare. The SDV made an enormous increase in the naval capability of the SEALs in the overall fleet picture.

24 Adventure in International Politics

𝒮𝒮𝒮𝒮
𝒮𝒮𝒮𝒮 On the morning of October 7, 1985, four passengers left Cabin 82 of the Italian luxury cruise liner *Achille Lauro*, which had docked at Alexandria, Egypt, while most of the passengers aboard went off on a tour.

The four men were armed with AK-47 Soviet assault rifles, pistols, and hand grenades. They were members of the Palestine Liberation Front, and their mission was to hijack the ship and use it as a weapon to secure the freedom of fifty Palestinians held by the Israeli government.

The hijackers entered the ship's main dining room, where most of the passengers who had not gone ashore were having breakfast. The gunmen entered the dining room firing their weapons, and wounded two people. Then they set about sequestering the 80 passengers and 20 crewmen of the Italian liner. They paid particular attention to the British and American passengers, whom they placed on deck with a wall of oil drums around them, which they threatened to ignite.

Then the terrorists went to the bridge, broke into the captain's compartment, and ordered Captain Gerardo de Rosa to get the ship in motion and sail to the Syrian port of Tartus.

When word of the hijacking reached Washington, D.C., President Ronald Reagan called for action. Units of the Army Delta Force and of SEAL Team No. 6 were ordered to a base in Sicily. Since the action was taking place at sea, the SEALs were considered to be the primary action force. The Italians were also acting, ordering their own commandos of the Commando Raggruppamento Subaquaried Incurso and the Gruppi Interventi

Speciali at a British base in Cyprus to stand by. The first group was like the SEALs, a combat swimmer and commando organization. The second group was a special unit of the Italian paramilitary police set up to counter terrorists.

As the ship headed for Syria, the Italian and American governments were in touch with the Syrian foreign office. After consultation, the Syrians refused the *Achille Lauro* permission to dock at Tartus. The hijackers began to grow nervous, and they decided on a show of force to gain their ends.

Because he was a Jew, they took Leon Klinghoffer, a sixty-nine-year-old American retired businessman from New York, away from the other British and American passengers. Klinghoffer was in a wheelchair, because he had been paralyzed by a stroke, and he was traveling with his wife. She was rudely thrust aside, and they vanished on the deck with him. They then shot him dead and made two crewmen throw the body and the wheelchair overboard. The hijackers then ordered the ship to sail for Cyprus, but soon learned that the Cypriot government would not let them dock either. So they ordered the ship to sail for Port Said, which was its original destination.

As the ship moved along, the Americans sent a surveillance plane aloft, which monitored the ship's activities insofar as possible as it moved toward Port Said. Very little was known by the SEALs about the hijackers, but the SEALs prepared for action. The Italians and Americans agreed on a plan. The SEALs would take the action and the Italians would take credit for it. When darkness came, the SEALs would move; then after they had done their job they would move out silently, thus preserving what SEAL Team No. 6 prized, their anonymity.

On October 9, two days after the hijacking, the *Achille Lauro* arrived at Port Said and anchored in the harbor. The SEAL team was aboard the amphibious aault ship *Iwo Jima*. The ship was outside, some distance away from Port Said, waiting for night to fall, when the SEALs would go into action. They would approach the *Achille Lauro* in small boats with silenced engines. They would climb aboard the ship and find and eliminate the terrorists. Then they would slip overboard and the Italian teams would come aboard and take over.

But the SEALs had not made any provision in their plans for international politics to intervene. After the hijacking, Yasser Arafat, head of the Palestine Liberation Organization, sent two emissaries who declared they wanted to negotiate a peaceful settlement of the issue. One of the representatives was Abbu Abbas, who was really a leader of the Palestine Liberation Front, whose members had hijacked the *Achille Lauro*.

On Wednesday, as the SEALs waited offshore, the two Palestinians and ambassadors from Italy and West Germany went to the cruise ship. They had been given guarantees by President Hosni Mubarak of Egypt that the hijackers would receive safe passage from Egypt and transportation to a country of their choice if they would release the passengers and crew of the ship without harm. That offer was made by the Egyptians without reference to the murder of Klinghoffer, because they did not then know about it.

The terrorists, who knew they had lost and now feared the consequences of their murder, were quick to take advantage of the Egyptian offer. Before dark they were off the ship, and the Egyptians said they were taking them out of the country.

The American ambassador to Egypt, Nicholas Veliotes, went to the ship that evening and there learned of the murder of Klinghoffer. Veliotes then sent a radio message to the embassy, telling his aides to demand from the Egyptian foreign office guarantees of the prosecution of the murderers.

The Egyptian government insisted then that the terrorists had already left Egyptian territory. But that night American intelligence agents learned that this was a lie. The terrorists were still in Egypt, planning to fly to Palestine Liberation Organization headquarters in Tunisia the next day.

This information was sent to Washington, where Marine Lt. Col. Oliver North received it at the White House. He was the National Security Council representative responsible for counterterrorism. He told President Reagan that the terrorists could still be captured, and President Reagan authorized such a move.

On the morning of October 10 an Egyptian military plane left El Maza airbase near Cairo carrying the four hijackers, the PLO negotiators, and four men from the Egyptian counterterrorist unit, Force 777. When the Americans learned this, the National Security Council plan went into effect. Four American F-14 fighter planes were already in the air from the U.S. carrier *Saratoga* which was in the Aegean Sea. An American electronic surveillance plane was tracking the Egyptian plane. In response to American demands, the Egyptian plane was refused permission to land at Tunis. Next it sought permission to land at Tripoli in Libya, which was also refused after American pressure. Then the plane turned toward Athens.

The American fighters then took action. They surrounded the Egyptian plane and ordered it to fly to the NATO air base at Sigonella, in Sicily. The pilot of the Egyptian plane tried to raise Cairo on his radio, but his transmissions were jammed by the electronic surveillance plane. The pilot then gave up and allowed the plane to be escorted to Sicily, where it landed.

The American SEAL team, frustrated in its effort to kill the hijackers, had given up and was preparing to return to Gibraltar and then to the United States. Next orders came for them to prepare for a second mission. They headed for Sigonella, where they expected to encounter and deal with the terrorists. The U.S. government had not notified the Italians that the hijackers had been taken over and were coming into Sigonella, and they did not so notify until the plane entered Italian airspace. Even the air traffic controller at Sigonella did not know, and he first refused the Egyptian plane permission to land and relented only when the pilot declared a fuel emergency.

As the Egyptian plane landed it was surrounded by the SEALs, fully armed and ready to kill the terrorists, whom they expected to resist. The Italians had rushed *carabinieri* to the scene, furious with the Americans for taking action on Italian soil. The Americans surrounded the plane. The *carabinieri* surrounded the Americans. The situation was so tense that some of the SEALs expected to be fighting the Italians at any moment.

The impasse continued for a long time. But it was finally settled when Secretary of State George Shultz received assurances that the terrorists would be tried by the Italians for murder. So the Italians got the prisoners, and the Egyptians went home. The SEALs were not convinced. Earlier experience with the Italians indicated that they did not always do what they said they were going to do. So when the Italians took the prisoners to Rome, the SEALs followed in their own plane, shadowing the Italian *carabinieri*. Claiming engine trouble, they swooped in to land just behind the *carabinieri*.

But this time the Italians lived up to their word, and they did put the terrorists on trial for murder. The whole affair was regarded with some satisfaction by the U. S. government. What it proved, mostly, was that the international waters that are stirred up by terrorism run deep and the currents are tricky. The SEALs were operating in a political environment, and that is not a very comfortable place for a direct-action organization to be. But the

Achille Lauro hijacking was a sign of the times, and it shows the reason for the need for special warfare organizations that can handle big jobs and small jobs without "calling out the Marines."

25   And Then Came
Panama . . .

〜〜〜〜
〜〜〜〜   1989. The Central American Republic of
Panama had created many problems in
Washington, particularly since the days
of the Carter administration, who promised control of the
Panama Canal to the Panamanian government in 1999. In
the years since President Carter, the CIA and a succession of administrations had suffered through a love-hate
relationship with the Panamanian government that had
become seriously affected by the dictatorship of Manuel
Noriega.

Noriega, as commander of the Panama Defense
Forces, had been the ruler of Panama since 1981. As dictator he had ruled the country with an iron hand. Dissat-
isfaction with his rule had been shown conclusively in
May, when he ran for the presidency and was defeated,
whereupon he had declared the election nullified. But the
fact remained that an election had been held, and it was
certain he had been defeated. Civilian control of the
country would be inaugurated with Guillermo Endaro—if
he ever managed to take power. Noriega had seized the
ballot boxes after the election and was doing everything
he could do to retain power.

In spite of the fact that the Americans, particularly
through the CIA, had been pouring money into Noriega's
coffers for years, by the fall of 1989 Washington had become so totally disaffected with him that at the highest
level it was decided military action would be necessary to
remove him. Having taken American money for all this
time, he had recently compounded his political sins by
becoming, the Americans claimed, a kingpin in the Cen-
ral American drug traffic that was crippling America.

This was the major reason given by the Bush administration for planning military action. The other reasons were concern about the safety of the Panama Canal, violence against American military personnel, and election fraud. Noriega, said the administration, was to be deposed.

The move against Noriega was to be called Operation Just Cause, and it did have a justification. Noriega had been indicted in Florida on drug charges. In retaliation, he had begun a fright campaign against the United States in the Panamanian National People's Assembly, which he controlled, resulting in the legislature making the mistake of declaring war on the United States on December 15, 1989, and at the same time installing Noriega as maximum leader. This was the excuse the Americans needed to act, but there was more provocation. On December 16, Lt. Robert Paz of the Marines was shot and killed by Panama Defense Forces troops when he got lost while driving with some fellow officers to a restaurant. Another officer and his wife had witnessed the shooting. They were arrested and mistreated for several hours. The officer was beaten and his wife was threatened with rape. When President Bush heard of this incident, he decided to act.

The options for interference in Panama had been established during the Reagan administration. Operation Blue Spoon had been a plan for the takeover of Panama by the American military. But now the situation was somewhat different. Gen. Colin Powell, chairman of the Joint Chiefs of Staff, and Gen. Thomas Kelley, director of operations for the Joint Chiefs, changed Operation Blue Spoon to fit the current circumstances.

So Operation Just Cause was ordered to begin. It had three aims:

1. It was to neutralize or wipe out military resistance to U.S. forces. Two groups were involved: the Panama Defense Forces of fifteen thousand men and eight thou-

sand men of Noriega's private army—or Dignity Battalions, as he called them.

2. Noriega was to be captured.

3. The duly elected government of Guillermo Endaro, certified by a team of observers, would be installed in office.

Operation Just Cause was to be preceded by maximum use of U.S. Special Warfare Command forces, and in this matter the Navy SEALs were to play a major role. The first move would be to send a number of American military units, totaling forty-two hundred people, to air drop on various installations in Panama and take them over as swiftly as possible. It would be the largest airborne operation staged by the United States since World War II. Another twenty-one thousand American troops would be involved in the invasion, but the brunt of the action was to be borne by the Special Warfare forces, airborne forces, and the Marines.

The Navy SEALs had two parts of the operation. First, they were to capture the *Presidente Porras,* a sixty-five-foot patrol boat that Noriega might try to use to escape once the action had begun. It might have been an easy matter for naval vessels or aircraft to sink the *Presidente Porras,* but the Americans did not want to cause any more loss of life than necessary or create an incident. Worse to contemplate would be the killing of Noriega aboard the vessel, because the Americans wanted him alive. They did not want a martyred Noriega on their hands. So four SEALs were assigned to cripple the patrol craft. They would go out in rubber boats with four members of a special Navy boat unit, a medic, a coxswain for each of the two boats, and a mission commander. The boats would take the SEALs in close and pick them up when the mission was finished.

The SEALs were wearing black spandex wet suits and were equipped with closed-circuit Aqua-Lung breathing devices that would let them stay under water for as long as four hours. There would be no telltale bubbles, because these systems recirculated and reoxygenated the diver's air. Each two-man SEAL team carried a bag containing a time bomb made of twenty pounds of C-4 plastic explosives with a waterproof clock to set it off, a safety and arming device, and a detonator. Each swam with a compass board that had a compass, watch, and depth gauge attached. Each swimmer had a short-range radio to use when he emerged from the water. And each carried a sheath knife strapped to his leg.

At eleven o'clock that night the swimmers left on their assignments, slipping silently away from the dock. An hour and forty-five minutes later, Operation Just Cause was to begin. This represented a change, because the original plan set H-hour at 1:00 A.M. The SEALs had not received word of the change until just a few minutes before their mission, not in time to reset the timers on their bombs.

The raiding group headed first out to sea, so they would cross the channel as far away as they could from the *Presidente Porras*. Their boats were powered by thirty-five-horsepower outboard motors, but they were running them at low speed so as not to make any unnecessary noise or to leave a foamy wake. Two U.S. Navy patrol boats carrying other SEALs would move to midchannel and stay there, prepared to assist the swimmers, particularly to rescue them if they were discovered and the Panamanians began shooting.

The attack boats crossed the channel together and headed along the mangrove shoreline. Half an hour after leaving the pier, the first boat was within 150 yards of the quay where the *Presidente Porras* lay with all her lights on. The first two divers slipped over the side of their boat and began their swim in. Following standard SEAL procedure, the swimmers estimated the number of kicks with their fins it would take to reach the shore. The second team was delayed. The engine of their boat had failed, and they were stalled some way back. The first boat now went back for the second and towed it closer to the shore to make up for the lost time. The second team of swimmers now had to adjust their swimming time because they were starting from a different point and the number of kicks would be fewer. Like the first team, before they went down, the divers took a compass reading on the *Presidente Porras,* and below they followed their compasses.

Once underwater, one swimmer went down to twenty feet and then began swimming for the shore, using his compass board. His buddy grasped his arm, counted the number of kicks, and watched for trouble.

Before midnight the two swimmer teams met under the long pier and then went down again and swam to the *Presidente Porras.* They surfaced and confirmed the identity of the vessel. Then one team hung their time bomb from one of the patrol boat's twin propeller shafts. The second team swam under the patrol boat, attached its bomb, and then linked the two bombs with a cord fuse. Thus when one bomb went off it would detonate the other.

As the divers finished their job, they were surprised to hear the engines of the *Presidente Porras* start to move. They swam for the pier. There they heard gunshots, H-hour had come, and Operation Just Cause had begun. The crew of the *Presidente Porras,* hearing the gunshots, had gone into action. They began throwing grenades over the railings of the ship. The SEALs took refuge behind the pilings of the pier. The explosions set off shock waves, but they were not too close. The swimmers moved under the pier and waited. More explosions of grenades were felt. Just at 1:00 A.M. came a loud explosion from the *Presidente Porras.* The bombs had gone off.

The SEALs swam out into the channel to make the rendezvous with the rubber boats. But the boats were not there. The first boat had towed the second back to the naval base to have the bad motor replaced.

The swimmers were now in the channel. All around the harbor the engines of boats were starting up as the Panamanians became nervous about swimmers. Then a large ship moved into the channel almost on top of the swimmers. They went down hastily, to forty-five feet, and stayed there for ten minutes while the ship passed. They came back up to twenty feet then and moved out to the point, twelve piers away, where they were to be picked up.

The boats arrived at the rendezvous point, but they found no swimmers. Ten minutes later there were still no swimmers. If there were no swimmers, they were supposed to receive radio transmissions, but there were none. The pickup crew now took refuge from gunfire. Firefights had broken out in various places. The crews then began to check other piers, but they found no swimmers.

Finally, at 2:00 A.M., the first swimming team bobbed up, and five minutes later the second team came up. They were late because of the passing ships and the many motorboats churning up the harbor. The boat engines had blocked their radio transmissions. But now they were safe, and the job on the *Presidente Porras* had been done. Whatever else, Noriega would not escape from Panama aboard that patrol vessel.

Other SEALs involved in the Panama operation were not so successful. They were to capture Paitilla airfield in southern Panama City, where Noriega was known to keep a Learjet, to prevent his escape by air. Two platoons from SEAL Team No. 4 were given the job of capturing the airfield. They were taken by air over the Pacific Ocean west of Panama City and dropped with their rubber boats and equipment. From this point on, they would approach by sea. They headed for the beaches along the edge of Paitilla airfield. They had their plan worked out because they had done it all before. Since the U.S. Air Force had a strong presence at Paitilla airfield normally, the SEALs had been able to scout the field and plan their assault on the ground a few weeks before the operation began. They expected to slip onto the airfield, disable the aircraft that Noriega might possibly use, and then slip back out to sea without being seen.

But there was some careless planning by the logistics experts of Operation Just Cause. For twenty-four hours before the operation began, the experts had taken advantage of the normal flow of traffic to and from Panama to step up the size of the airlift to bring in people and equipment for the operations. The Panamanians immediately sensed that something unusual was afoot. The logistics flights alerted Noriega and his men to the coming invasion almost a full day before it happened.

Because of their confidence in the success of the plan, the SEALs saw no need for heavy weapons, expecting all to be accomplished by stealth. But when they arrived at Paitilla airfield, they found the field full of Noriega's troops with heavy weapons and armored vehicles. The SEALs came in and were greeted by gunfire. They responded, and a firefight began. In the end the SEALs captured the airfield, but it cost them eleven casualties, including four killed in action.

A third group of SEALs had more success with an operation at the docks of Balboa where the Panamanians stored some high-speed patrol boats. The Americans were afraid that Noriega might try to use one of these to escape, so they assigned the SEALs to disable them. This operation went very smoothly, the SEALs coming in from the sea, doing the job quickly and efficiently, and then getting out again, using the methods of the old Underwater Demolition Teams.

Operation Just Cause had its anxious moments, most of them caused by the logistical error of alerting Noriega and his men to coming events. He managed to elude the

Americans, his troops fought for him, and the operation was extended for a number of days while Noriega was hunted down. In all, twenty-three Americans were killed, but Operation Just Cause was successful in all its aims, to give the country back to the people, protect Americans and American interests, eliminate Noriega from power, and whisk him back to the United States to stand trial on drug charges. After the failure that succeeded at Grenada, the Panama operation was much more efficient, but still the efficiency of the operating teams was marred by bad planning and execution at the top level. One fact was certainly being learned about Special Warfare: Much depended on surprise and planning as well as swift and efficient operation. If the planning was faulty and the surprise factor was lost, then the chances of success of the operation were greatly diminished, and there was nothing that the Special Warfare units could do about it.

26 Operation Desert Storm

By 1990 the SEALs and the U.S. Naval Special Warfare Command were a comfortable part of the Special Operations Command in Tampa, Florida, with virtual autonomy at their headquarters in Coronado, California, and at the Naval Amphibious Base and the satellite operation at Little Creek, Virginia, which served the Atlantic Fleet.

The SEALs expected plenty of action in the next few years, because as their command brochure put it, "Rising nationalism, religious fundamentalism, rapid population growth, poor health care, and socioeconomic decline will continue to foster terrorism, insurgency, and instability for the next ten to fifteen years." If that was a bleak prospect for the political world, it was in any event the assessment of the Naval Special Warfare Command of its immediate future.

Granted that the danger of global war by 1991 had nearly vanished in the smoke of burned Communist Party membership cards, from the U.S. Navy point of view, the threat to American interests in a changing Third World remained very high. And the world continued to be a dangerous place, full of ethnic strife, such socioeconomic decline as the breakup of the Soviet Union and the resulting possible political instability for a whole group of new republics, and narcotics traffic and arms proliferation, all of which were serious threats.

The Special Operations Command Forces were confident of the future because of their low cost factor, an important aspect. Only 1 percent of the Department of Defense budget was being spent on all these forces, and they demanded only 1.1 percent of the total military personnel. In times of trouble the Special Forces were politically acceptable when conventional forces were not. Calling out the Marines was no longer the answer worldwide.

Most important about the Special Forces was their "surgical strike" capability and their ability—more than that, their insistence on—keeping a low profile and not talking about operations, no matter how successful. In that way, in the pattern of the SEALs in the *Achille Lauro* hijacking—when they were prepared to do all the work and turn over all the credit to the Italians—the special forces would not be an embarrassment to any government.

Already the Special Forces had been active in eighteen of America's military involvements since 1975, most of them very secret at the time, and still very secret. Since the days of the Combat Demolition Units in the early times of World War II they had come a long, long way.

Each of the Special Forces had its own expertise and its own area of operations staked out. The Navy's realm —that of the SEALs—was to operate with the fleet either afloat or from forward bases, to be prepared for air drops into the sea, and operations on and involving helicopters to be as at home in the sea in their scuba gear as a por poise, and to employ many weapons, all designed to get the specific job done with minimal difficulty. They were prepared to take direct action, as they had for so long in Vietnam; to do strategic reconnaissance, as they had in various places; to carry out unconventional warfare, as they had last done in Panama; to assist other countries with internal defense; and to move anywhere in the world against terrorism.

They could go in by submarine, they could play advisory roles to government and other forces, they could carry out underwater demolition, limpet attacks on vessels, they could give naval gunfire support with their boats, they could find targets with lasers, and they could go into an area by parachute or by boat. They were familiar with shoreline operations against guerrilla enemies.

The SEALs were prepared to work in any environment and had—in the surf zone, along the shore and in the rivers, in the desert, in the tropical rain forest, in the dry forest, and in the Arctic.

All of the capabilities had been tested, and they would be tested further in the next few months, because one Middle Eastern dictator set out to conquer his neighbors and establish hegemony over the oil-rich Middle East. When Saddam Hussein of Iraq decided to attack his virtually defenseless neighbor of Kuwait and take over its oil empire, he set in motion a chain of events that propelled the Navy SEALs and the other American Special Warfare Forces into action.

By midsummer the more than half a million American troops who would eventually arrive in the Middle East had begun to move into Saudi Arabia to defend that country against further incursions by Saddam, who had his troops poised on the border and appeared ready to use them. The SEALs were there early, engaged in close air support training of the Saudis, and training a force of royal Saudi SEALs and Marines and helping build the Saudi Navy. The SEALs were also involved in strategic reconnaissance of the Kuwaiti border, watching for Iraqi moves. They made night harbor security patrols in Jubail, they effected hull searches of incoming ships to check against timed mines, and they made hydrographic reconnaissance of the Kuwaiti beaches on which the Marines might land an amphibious force. They boarded and searched many vessels looking for contraband. By January 15, the day that President George Bush had warned Saddam Hussein would be the deadline for his withdrawal of Iraqi forces from Kuwait to forestall Allied attack, the SEALs had a small but complete organization in the Middle East: They had a headquarters unit, four SEAL platoons, one FAV detachment, one high-speedboat detachment, and one joint communications support element, and with them were a Kuwaiti Navy unit with three fighting craft and a Kuwaiti Marine organization.

When the air war began on January 17, the SEALs were ready. In the few short weeks of war they conducted many operations that helped assure the success of Operation Desert Storm and helped make it look easy. They carried out 13 harbor patrol missions; 92 mining and countermining missions with helicopter; 118 combat search and rescue sorties during the preplanned air strikes; seized an oil platform, a ship, and the island of Qaruh; and effected 3 missions to recover enemy prisoners of war.

Their high-speed boats conducted patrols along the vicinity of Rasal Mishab to prevent infiltration and attack by Iraqi boats. Every morning and every night they made mine patrols, and in the process they destroyed 25 floating mines that otherwise might have damaged Allied ships. When they were involved in search-and-rescue operations they were often diverted for mine destruction or aerial reconnaissance missions, all of which they carried out.

The Iraqis had occupied seven oil platforms in the Durrah oil field in the northern Persian Gulf, and when two helicopters from the USS *Nicholas* were fired upon from four of these platforms, the Allies began to act. The *Nicholas* and the Kuwaiti ship *Istiqlal* engaged the platforms, and so did gunships.

After this initial assault, Iraqi soldiers were seen on the platforms, so the SEALs went in and boarded, searched, secured the platforms and captured all the enemy forces and their equipment. Five Iraqis were killed and twenty-three captured in these actions. There were no American casualties. The SEALs, then, were the first to have face-to-face contact with the Iraqi enemy and the first to capture Iraqi prisoners of war. A few days later an American A-6 aircraft damaged an enemy vessel in an air strike. The USS *Curts* launched a motor whaleboat with a team of SEALs aboard to capture the enemy prisoners of war from the vessel. They found the vessel dead in the water and boarded it. They found that two men had been killed in action in the air strike; fifty-one Iraqis became prisoners of war and were taken back aboard the *Curts*.

A few days later, helicopters from the *Curts* on patrol were fired on by Iraqi soldiers on Qaruh, a Kuwaiti island in the gulf, close offshore, that had been occupied by the Iraqis. The helicopters returned the fire, whereupon the Iraqi soldiers raised white flags of surrender. SEALs were then detailed to go in and capture the enemy soldiers and their equipment. When they got to the island, they took twenty-nine Iraqi prisoners of war, many weapons, and some explosives.

One day, an American plane reported seeing a life raft in the water offshore, and the report was transmitted to the SEALs for action. They launched a boat and sped to the scene, went into the water, and rescued from the life raft twenty Iraqis, whom they took back to the *Curts*.

Then a plane reported enemy soldiers occupying an oil terminal, and the SEALs in helicopters were sent in to take them prisoner. Their approaches were covered by two helicopters and one fighter plane. The SEALs winched down to the platform from their helicopters, recovered sixteen prisoners, and destroyed their weapons. On another occasion the SEALs had a report of an F-16 pilot down in the water two miles off the Kuwaiti coast, and they were called to make the rescue. Thirty-five minutes later they had the pilot safe and sound aboard a boat. They also conducted special reconnaissance missions along the southern Kuwaiti border with Saudi Arabia, and strategic reconnaissance of the Kuwaiti coastline on eleven different missions.

But in the annals of Operation Desert Storm, the SEALs' most spectacular missions were two: their "faking out" of the Iraqi Army, and their wild ride into Kuwait

City in their fifty-thousand-dollar fast attack vehicle, which could zoom over the sand berms and hit speeds of more than sixty miles an hour.

The first mission occurred on February 23, the day before the Allies were to launch the ground phase of Operation Desert Storm. Off the coast of Kuwait stood án armada of U.S. ships, carrying seventeen thousand Marines, ready to make an amphibious invasion of the coast. Just about everyone in America expected the sort of amphibious operation for which the Marines were famous. The SEALs had already paved the way for that with their reconnaissance of the beaches. But the Allies preferred not to launch an amphibious invasion. For one reason, as the SEALs had discovered in their reconnaissance missions along these beaches, they were heavily mined and heavily defended by Iraqi troops in fortified positions. Besides, the Allies preferred to come at the Iraqis frontally on the ground, which the tanks and Marine infantry were all in position to do. The hope was that they could pull some of the Iraqi troops away from their defenses inland. That is where the SEALs came into play.

As darkness began to fall, Lt. Tom Dietz of the SEALs, with five swimmer scouts, left their coastal base at Ras al Mishab in two speedboats powered by one-thousand-horsepower engines. They moved at forty miles per hour up the Kuwaiti coast, bouncing as high as five feet over the waves, through mine-infested water. They moved blindly, only hoping they did not hit anything.

At 10:00 P.M. Dietz's speedboat stopped fifteen miles off the Kuwaiti coast. His team untied the rubber boats lashed to the bow of the speedboat. It was familiar territory—the SEALs had swum here many times before—but this night the water was a chill fifty degrees Fahrenheit. It was not going to be comfortable. The SEALs got into the two motorized rubber boats and moved slowly to the shore, stopping frequently and stopping the motors, to look and listen.

A little over a quarter of a mile from the beach the boatmen killed the engines, and the SEALs slipped over the side of the boats. Each man carried buoys, which were strung out as they swam to the beach. Each man also carried a haversack packed with twenty pounds of C-4 explosive.

The buoys were to create lanes, which the Iraqis would think were to be used as markers for incoming waves of Marine landing craft. The haversacks were really mines, with twin timers, one to back up the other, set to go off two hours after being set.

If this plan was to work, the explosions had to occur at one o'clock on the morning of Sunday, February 24, just about three hours from this time that the SEALs were working in to the coast.

The SEALs swam two men abreast, each carrying a Heckler & Koch submachine gun on his back and a pistol at his side. Every hundred yards the team stopped and looked. Dietz used a night-vision scope wrapped in a cellophane bag to scan the beach for enemy activity. It was hard to see in the darkness of night, the murk compounded by the acrid oil smoke that hung over them. This was the smoke from the wildfires that Saddam Hussein had ordered in his fury and his contempt for his enemies, emotions doubled by his frustration at having been stopped in his drive for conquest.

Lieutenant Dietz saw nothing. The white sand of the beaches was undisturbed by fires or any activity. The SEALs went on.

As they came to the shoreline, they reached out and unloaded the haversacks in a foot of water. The timers were set, and then the SEALs slid back into the ocean and moved back to their rubber boats. As a diversion, the speedboats moved in then to make a racket, firing wildly at the shore with .50-caliber machine guns. This diversion was to wake up the Iraqis so they would be aware that something was happening offshore. Every five minutes two-pound explosive charges were dropped off the speedboats and blown up. The noise continued, and then came the magic moment: 1:00 A.M. The haversacks blew up to light the beach brightly. The impression was of underwater demolition men making way for an amphibious invasion. Now it was all up to the Iraqis. Dietz radioed back that the mission was completed.

Eight hours later, the SEALs sat waiting in a debriefing room back at the headquarters, and finally a message came in from Commo. Ray Smith, the SEAL commander in the Persian Gulf.

"Your mission was a success," said the message. "Elements of two separate Iraqi divisions moved to the beach immediately after your operation. Pass it on to your men. Job well done."

So half a dozen SEALs had saved seventeen thousand Marines from having to conduct amphibious operations that could not have helped but produce casualties from the beach defenses alone. This was the way to fight a war.

ACKNOWLEDGMENTS

I am indebted to Lt. Dane LaJoye of the Naval Public Information Office in the Pentagon for getting me started on the SEALs research. As always, the archivists at the Navy Classified Archives in the Navy Yard were very helpful. I am grateful to Bernard Cavalcante, Mrs. Kathy Lloyd, and Dale Andrade there particularly. Librarians in the Navy Library helped me with books.

When I visited the Naval Special Warfare Command Center at Coronado, California, Lt. Comdr. Robert Pritchard was extremely helpful in briefing me on the SEALs and their training program. I met a large number of SEALs there and had the chance to talk to them, but nearly everything they do, and much that they know, is so classified that they are reluctant to discuss any operations and never like to be quoted. So I have respected their desire for privacy and will not mention names, except for that of Frank Thornton, now retired, who holds the distinction of being the most highly decorated SEAL of the Vietnam War. He now lives in Coronado, where he conducts a worldwide security business dealing with corporations and governments.

I happened to be in the BUD/S compound when Hell Week was going on, and observed with a great deal of sympathy the pressures and tensions under which the trainees and candidates operate. For example, I was watching the trainees assembled with their big rubber boats. At a command they assumed position on the edge of the boats, legs stiff, and began doing push-ups. I watched particularly sympathetically three men, all who were left of a boat team in midweek, because the others had opted out of the program. These three young men were trying valiantly but unsuccessfully to lift a 250-pound rubber boat above their heads, to carry it out of the compound, and to join the others. There was no way they could do it, but they did manage to lift the boat off the ground and get it out of the compound. I assume that their instructors, who had been watching this performance with interest, managed somehow to give them relief from an impossible situation.

I am indebted to E. J. McCarthy, my editor at Dell, for providing the original inspiration for this book, and to Diana Hoyt for rescuing from the computer three chapters of the book that I had lost in transit from Washington, D.C., to Coronado. I must thank Hiroko Hattori for editing and Alice Norris for typing. Above all, I am indebted to Olga G. Hoyt, my longtime partner, for her editing and editorial management of the entire enterprise.

BIBLIOGRAPHY

U.S. Government and Other Documents

Atlantic Fleet, Amphibious Training Command. *U.S. Naval Administration in World War II*, Vol. II.

U.S. Army Office of Chief of Public Affairs, Print Media Branch Command Information Division. *Soldiers in Panama: Operation Just Cause.*

U.S. Naval Special Warfare Center. *Officer Guide to Naval Special Warfare: The Navy SEAL.*

U.S. Naval Special Warfare Command. *A Guide to Naval Special Warfare: The Navy SEAL.*

U.S. Naval Special Warfare Command. *Summary Report.* 1991.

U.S. Naval Special Warfare Task Group Central. *Summary of Operations, Desert Storm.* 1991.

U.S. Navy Department. *Navy Divers, SEAL Fleet Diver.*

U.S. Navy Operational Archives. *Biography of Rear Adm. Draper L. Kauffman.*

The following unit histories were consulted in the Navy Operational Archives, Washington, D.C., or in the Naval Special Warfare Command Archives in Coronado: *History of Commander Underwater Demolition Teams and Underwater Demolition Flotilla, Amphibious Forces, Pacific Fleet.*

Action Reports, Underwater Demolition Teams

Marshalls
Marianas
Leyte
Lingayen Gulf
Iwo Jima
Okinawa
Japan
Balikpapan

History of Underwater Demolition Teams, Command History, 1946–58

History of Underwater Demolition Team No. 1

History of Underwater Demolition Team No. 2

History of Underwater Demolition Team No. 3

History of Underwater Demolition Team No. 4

History of Underwater Demolition Team No. 5

History of Underwater Demolition Team No. 6

History of Underwater Demolition Team No. 7

History of Underwater Demolition Team No. 8

History of Underwater Demolition Team No. 9

History of Underwater Demolition Team No. 10

History of Underwater Demolition Team No. 12

History of Underwater Demolition Team No. 13

History of Underwater Demolition Team No. 14

History of Underwater Demolition Team No. 15

History of Underwater Demolition Team No. 16

History of Underwater Demolition Team No. 17

History of Underwater Demolition Team No. 18

History of Underwater Demolition Team No. 19

History of Underwater Demolition Team No. 20

History of Underwater Demolition Team No. 21

History of Underwater Demolition Team No. 23

History of Underwater Demolition Team No. 25

History of Underwater Demolition Team No. 27

History of Underwater Demolition Team No. 30

History of SEAL Team No. 1

History of SEAL Team No. 2

U.S. Naval Special Forces Command, Public Information Section. *SEAL History.*

Magazine Articles

Andrade, Dale. "Swamp Warrior." *Vietnam* (April 1990).

Barnette, Robin. "SEALs in Action Around the World." *All Hands* (December 1987).

Brown, F. E. *SEAL Team Operations. Military Journal* (September–October 1977).

Coffey, Tom. "Desert Storm Tests Total Force." *Full Mission Profile, the Professional Bulletin of Naval Special Warfare* (Spring 1991).

"Desert Storm." *Soldier of Fortune* (July 1991).

Green, L. Steve, "U.S. Navy Special Warfare from Frogmen to SEALs." *Special Warfare* (Spring 1989).

"Secret Warriors." *Newsweek* (June 17, 1991).

"The Seals." All Hands (December 1987).

Sundberg, Peter D. "The Navy SEAL: The Ultimate Warrior." *All Hands* (April 1985).

Books and Other Publications

Blassingham, Wyatt, *Underwater Warriors*. New York: Random House, 1964.
Bosiljevac, T. L. *SEALs, UDT/SEAL Operations in Vietnam*. Boulder, Colo.: Paladin Press, 1990.
Brown, Dale, ed. *Special Forces and Missions: The New Face of War*. Alexandria, Va.: Time Life Books, 1990.
Dockery, Kevin. *SEALs in Action*. New York: Avon Books, 1991.
Fane, Francis, and Don Moore. *The Naked Warriors*. New York: Appleton-Century-Crofts, 1956.
Fletcher, Jerry J. *Devils with Green Faces: Navy SEALs in Vietnam*. San Diego: Shann Press, 1989.
Forbes, John, and Robert Williams. *Riverine Force*. New York: Bantam Books, 1987.
Morison, Samuel Eliot. *United States Naval Operations in World War II*, 13 vols. Boston: Atlantic Little Brown, 1950–1960.
Padden, Ian. *U.S. Navy SEALs: From Boot Camp to the Battle Zones*. New York: Bantam Books, 1985.
Schnepf, Edwin, ed. *Navy SEALs USN/USMC Series*. Canoga Park, Calif.: Challenge Publications, 1991.
Young, Darryl. *The Element of Surprise: Navy SEALs in Vietnam*. New York: Ivy Books, 1990.

NOTES

Introduction

Whereas the Europeans, and particularly the Italians, had recognized the importance of underwater swimmers to a naval war effort long before the outbreak of World War II, the Americans had given this matter no concern, and did not until impelled by necessity. Even then they treated underwater demolition as an engineering matter, to be accomplished from the surface by men skilled in the use of explosives, but with no regard for swimmers as self-contained warriors. The concept was many months in developing. I have dealt in this Introduction with the matter of training of the SEALs because it is the same basic program that the underwater men have followed since the middle of the 1940s, when UDT training began. Like the UDT men before them, the SEALs never forget their training program, which is one of the biggest morale factors in their organization.

Chapter One

The origin of the underwater warfare unit is cloudy because the same idea came at about the same time to meet needs in the European and Pacific wars. The American invasions in the Solomons Islands on New Georgia and Rendova had been conducted without any examination of the beaches, or any apparent feeling that this was needed. But when the casualties were so heavy at Tarawa and it was realized that the cost might have been alleviated by exploration of the landing beaches before the operation and with demolition of obstacles, the Pacific command decided on the establishment of underwater demolition organizations. Concurrently the same decisions were being made in Europe, even before the North Africa landings. But in those days, as Dale Andrade explained to me, the Atlantic and Pacific theaters were scarcely in touch with one another. On the Atlantic side, the Navy established the school at Fort Pierce, Florida. Independently, in the Pacific, the Navy established its school on Maui Island. This chapter depended largely on the study of Rear Admiral Kauffman's career and that of Capt. Phillip Bucklew. Fane's book was extremely valuable for my study of this chapter, as was Padden's. The story of the adventure of Lieutenant Starkweather is from Padden.

Chapter Two

The background material in this chapter comes from Morison's volume on the Aleutians, Gilberts, and Marshalls and from my own studies made for a book on Carlson's Raiders. The material about Lieutenant Commander Draper comes from his biography in the Navy files and from Fane. The story of the UDTs in Europe is from several sources, notably Padden. The story of the Stingrays in the Marshalls is from the UDT histories and from Fane. The story of the invasion of the Marshalls is from Morison and Fane. The story of Eniwetok is from Fane and from a long interview with Adm. Harry Hill in 1968.

Chapter Three
This chapter depended heavily on Fane and Padden. I also used Dockery here and Morison for the general material about the invasion of France. The Fane account is much the most detailed here.

Chapter Four
The histories of UDT Teams No. 1 and No. 2 were important to this chapter, as was Morison for general detail. I also used the histories of Teams No. 3 and No. 4 and the very detailed history of Team No. 5, which was Commander Kauffman's team. The Kauffman biography was useful. George Dyer's *The Amphibians Came to Conquer,* the biography of Adm. Richmond Kelly Turner, published by the U.S. Navy, was useful in helping to establish Turner's interest in development of the Underwater Demolition Teams. The Team No. 5 history has the complete story of the Saipan operation from the UDT men's point of view. Commander Kauffman's personal story is from the UDT Team No. 5 history.

Chapter Five
This chapter depended on the histories of the teams involved at Tinian in the Marianas, Team No. 5, and Team No. 7. Morison was used as the source for the background.

Chapter Six
The story of the UDT men in the Guam invasion is the story of Team No. 3 and Team No. 4 from their official histories.

Chapter Seven
The story of the employment of the Stingrays again in Europe is from Padden. The background is from Morison.

Chapter Eight
The story of the UDTs at Palau is from the history of Team No. 10; from Padden; and from Morison, who gives the details of the invasion of Peleliu and of Angaur. Some of the material comes from my earlier researches in connection with books on the Battle of Leyte Gulf and MacArthur's return to the Philippines. The roles of the UDT men are described in connection with Leyte by Morison and in the team histories.

Chapter Nine

The history of Team No. 5 was important to this chapter, as was the history of Team No. 8. Also, the history of Team No. 15 was vital to the Lingayen Gulf story.

Chapter Ten

At Iwo Jima a number of Underwater Demolition Teams was employed: Team No. 12, Team No. 13, Team No. 14, and Team No. 15. Team No. 8 was supposed to be employed, but the invasion command discovered that they had too many UDT men, so Team No. 8 headed for Guam, where the men occupied their time by building a camp for UDT men. The bombing of the USS *Blessman* was thoroughly described by Morison and in the UDT histories.

Chapter Eleven

In a sense, the invasion of Okinawa marked the end of UDT operations in World War II, although UDTs would go on to other activities, and make a combat mission at Balikpapan in connection with the Australian recapture of that island. Team No. 12, Team No. 16, Team No. 17, and Team No. 21 went to Okinawa. Team No. 18 went to Balikpapan.

Chapter Twelve

At the end of the war, the UDTs were used in many ways. They were alerted to work the Japanese beaches, but to their surprise the Japanese beaches were clear. Obviously the Japanese military had never really accepted the concept that an invasion of the homeland would come until the last, and then all the planning was in the hands of the Army, who never seemed to give any thought to the beaches. The UDTs then spent the first weeks after the war doing demolition work, blowing up Japanese two-man suicide submarines, and destroying suicide power boats by the hundreds. In the last months of 1945 most of the UDTs were decommissioned, and a change occurred, into what the Americans thought would be a peacetime Navy. But very soon came the Korean War.

Almost immediately after the beginning of the Korean War, the UDTs changed in nature. Their responsibility for intelligence and covert operations increased enormously. Soon they were training South Koreans in guerrilla operations. The story of Lieutenant Atcheson is in a way the story of the metamorphosis that began in 1950. It would change the Underwater Demolition Teams into SEALs before it was finished and revolutionize the American concept of special warfare.

Chapter Thirteen

The Korean War experience expanded the role of the UDTs to include guerrilla warfare, something hitherto unknown for them. The sources for this chapter are the team histories and Dockery and Bosiljevac. The concept of the SEALs was not far away, with the rapid development of this new world, in which terrorism and sudden actions by small nations assumed new significance.

Chapter Fourteen
President John F. Kennedy was the father of the Navy SEALs. Looking at the world around him in 1961, he had the feeling that the U.S. military establishment was ill prepared to face the brush wars and incidents that would be coming in the 1960s, and he ordered the upgrading of special warfare units in all forces.

Chapter Fifteen
The Bucklew report recommendation for the further involvement of the SEALs in Vietnam was the most important development in the SEAL history of the 1960s, and the implementation of it meant SEAL involvement in Vietnam on nearly every level. Their most effective use, however, was as counterterrorists, with their kidnapping and direct-action raids against the Viet Cong. How much effect these had in changing the war, is debatable and probably not great, but they did keep the Viet Cong off balance and may have prevented them from becoming a greater threat to communications than they were.

Chapter Sixteen
This chapter depended on Bosiljevac, Dockery, and the SEAL histories. Ambush-to-kill soon gave way to ambush-for-intelligence, which was much more to the SEALs' liking, since they could not expect to kill all the Viet Cong in South Vietnam. In a way the UDT team operations in the riverine war were more important than the SEAL operations. The UDT man were needed by the Marines to stage their amphibious operations, and they did a great deal of work in stopping movement of Viet Cong supplies on the waterways.

Chapter Seventeen
The continued escalation of the Vietnam War in 1967 meant more buildup for the SEALs and the UDT, as the histories show. Again, the team histories as well as Bosiljevac and Dockery were the basic source for the discussion of events, plus the official naval studies of riverine warfare in the period. The improvement in techniques, such as the use of the destroyer to support SEAL operations, was an indication of the greater reliance the Navy had begun to make on unconventional warfare.

Chapter Eighteen

The year 1968, during which Tet offensive was staged, was a major milestone in SEAL involvement in Vietnam. It was also the year in which the American public began to get a distorted and negative view of the SEALs as professional killers. The whole of the American commitment to unconventional warfare became very unpopular with the advocates of immediate withdrawal from Vietnam. The SEALs began to spend more time training and working with the South Vietnamese in this period, too. All this is reflected in accounts collected by Dockery and Bosiljevac and in the team histories, which were their basic source as well as my own.

The best look at how it was to be a SEAL in Vietnam in the late 1960s and early 1970s is given by Jerry J. Fletcher in his thinly disguised autobiographical study *Devils with Green Faces,* which is cast as a novel.

Chapter Nineteen

It seems apparent that the modern SEAL preoccupation with professionalism and a matter-of-fact approach to their life of high adventure is a product of the American public reaction to the Vietnam War. In that period, as is quite apparent from my discussions with a number of SEAL team veterans, there were a number of men who thoroughly enjoyed the concept of war as high adventure. It is also certain that there still are such people in the SEAL organization, but in the 1990s the official Navy policy regarding the SEALs is that organization and teamwork are the hallmarks, and individual effort, except when it contributes to the team, is not acceptable.

This chapter contains three stories of heroism and high adventure that resulted in three SEALs receiving the Medal of Honor during the Vietnam War. Three Medals of Honor out of a total number awarded during that war of 238 does not seem a high figure, unless one realizes that at the high point the American military had 550,000 men in Vietnam, and at no time were there 100 SEALs serving there. The ratio of 238 to 550,000 means that about 1 man in 2,311 received the Medal of Honor. The ratio for the SEALs, then, had to be on the same basis, 1 man in 33. The medals awarded to SEALs Kerrey, Norris, and Thornton, as noted in the presidential citations, were all given for heroic action above self, in the interests of the group.

Chapter Twenty

As is apparent from the record, when Vietnamization came to the war in Vietnam, it did not make much difference in the initial operation of the SEALs, who continued in their own way, with their main aim being the disruption of the Viet Cong way of making war. In view of the degree to which they were outnumbered by the Viet Cong, by the thousands, one has to say that the SEALs were inordinately successful, although in the end the SEAL contribution did not shorten the war. Beginning in 1969, the SEALs worked more with others than before, and had the assistance of more gunships and more support. In this year also there was more concentration on rescuing POWs from the Viet Cong.

Chapter Twenty-one
At the end of 1971, SEAL involvement in Vietnam had decreased significantly, although they still carried out typical SEAL operations. They were much more involved in trying to pass along their techniques to the South Vietnamese. Also in this period Michael Thornton won his Medal of Honor.

Chapter Twenty-two
The story of the Grenada invasion comes from several sources, but the best one is Dockery. What is remarkable about the Grenada operation is how badly it was managed by the Navy, starting at the Atlantic Fleet level and working down. The field troops performed as best they could bedeviled by time changes and high-level switches that imperiled the whole invasion.

Chapter Twenty-three
It is apparent from the record again that after Grenada the SEAL organization was again tightened and worked to become more effective with even a less bold exposure to public scrutiny.

Chapter Twenty-four
The *Achille Lauro* adventure was clouded by international politics. Through restraint an explosive situation was brought to a more or less successful conclusion, and the SEALs escaped from the affair without damage to their reputation.

Chapter Twenty-five
The Panama invasion was far better planned and executed than any operation the joint operating group of Special Forces had undertaken before, showing a certain maturity that had not previously existed. The SEAL role is well told in the Time Life book, and Dockery also has material on the subject.

Chapter Twenty-six
The account of the SEALs' role in Operation Desert Storm comes largely from materials supplied by the Naval Special Warfare Command in Coronado, but some also comes from the *Newsweek* article mentioned in the Bibliography.